• REALISTIC PRAGMATISM •

SUNY series in Philosophy
George R. Lucas, Jr., Editor

# • REALISTIC PRAGMATISM •

## An Introduction to Pragmatic Philosophy

NICHOLAS RESCHER

State University of New York Press

Published by
State University of New York Press, Albany



Printed in the United States of America



For information, address State University of New York Press, State University Plaza, Albany, N.Y., 12246

Production by Diane Ganeles
Marketing by Anne Valentine

Library of Congress Cataloging-in-Publication Data

Rescher, Nicholas.
Realistic pragmatism : an introduction to pragmatic philosophy / Nicholas Rescher.
p. cm. -- (SUNY series in philosophy)
Includes bibliographical references and index.
ISBN 0-7914-4407-4 (hardcover : alk. paper). -- ISBN 0-7914-4408-2 (pbk. : alk. paper)
1. Pragmatism. I. Title. II. Series.
B832.R42 2000
144,.3-dc21 99-15030
CIP

10 9 8 7 6 5 4 3 2 1

# *Contents*

# *Preface*

Along with process philosophy, pragmatism represents a predominantly American contribution to systematic philosophy. It is a philosophical doctrine that has long interested me and to which I have dedicated a steady stream of publications since the 1960s.[1] Over the years, I have become increasingly dismayed at the tendency in recent times to misconstrue pragmatism as a freewheeling form of relativism designed to *abrogate* rational standards instead of a normatively rigorous doctrine designed to substantiate them. And it is this dismay that has motivated me in writing the present book.

1. "Pragmatic Justification: A Cautionary Tale," *Philosophy*, vol. 39 (1964), pp. 346–348; "Peirce and the Economy of Research," *Philosophy of Science*, vol. 43 (1976), pp. 71–98; "Scientific Truth and the Arbitrament of Praxis," *Nous*, vol. 15 (1980), pp. 59–74; "The Epistemology of Pragmatic Beliefs: Some Observations on the Rationale of Pascal's Wager," *Proceedings of the American Catholic Philosophical Association*, vol. 58 (1984), pp. 173–187; "Counterfactuals in Pragmatic Perspective," *The Review of Metaphysics*, vol. 50 (1996), pp. 35–61; "Perspectives on Pragmatism" in Kenneth R. Westphal (ed.), *Pragmatism, Reason, and Norms: A Realistic Assessment* (New York: Fordham University Press, 1998), pp. 1–13; "Pragmatism in Crisis" in P. Weingartner et al. (eds.), *The Role of Pragmatics in Contemporary Philosophy* (Vienna: Hölder-Pichler-Tempsky, 1998).

The book is, in a way, a companion volume to my *Process Metaphysics: An Introduction to Process Philosophy* (Albany: State University of New York Press, 1996). That book, as its subtitle indicates, was designed to provide an introduction to process philosophy, but it nevertheless provides a defense of the doctrine that presents it as a plausible and attractive position in philosophy. Exactly the same sort of thing is the dual aim of the present book in relation to pragmatic philosophy. Between the two, these books thus survey both the two main spheres of originative contribution of American thought to systematic philosophy.

The book was written in Pittsburgh during 1996–98 and polished in Oxford over the summer of that second year. I am indebted both to Richard Gale and to the publisher's referees for constructive comment. And I am grateful to Estelle Burris for deploying her word-processing skills to prepare a copy of the book suitable for the printer's needs.

Pittsburgh PA
October 1998

# *Introduction*

Once the centerpiece of American philosophy, pragmatism has to all appearances recently become transfigured into a mode of antiphilosophical nihilism. It nowadays has the sort of friends that render enemies dispensable. For example, Richard Rorty explains:

> Pragmatism suggests that we do not ask questions about the nature of truth and goodness. . . . They [pragmatists] would simply like to change the subject. . . . Secularists doubt that the vocabulary of theology is one we ought to be using. Similarly, pragmatists keep trying to find ways of making antiphilos-ophical points in unphilosophical language.[1]

On such a view, pragmatism is not so much a philosophical doctrine as a position that urges the abandonment of philosophy and recommends finding something else to do instead.

The aim of this book is to defend the pragmatic tradition against this sort of deconstruction into philosophical

1. Richard Rorty, *Consequences of Pragmatism* (Minneapolis: University of Minnesota Press, 1982), p. xiv.

vacuity. It argues that we simply cannot escape the concerns and problems of traditional philosophy by some sort of vocabulary shift and reaffirms pragmatism as a viable basis for rational procedure in philosophy. For even if we were to join Rorty in not bringing "truth" or "goodness" into the pragmatic tradition, the quintessentially philosophical question of what sorts of considerations can substantiate our beliefs or legitimate our choices cannot be avoided altogether by thoughtful people.

The aim of the pragmatic enterprise as originally conceived was not to abandon ideas like true and right but to clarify them and to elucidate the rationale of adequacy and appropriateness on whose basis our beliefs, evaluations, and actions can receive suitable guidance. It is this traditional pragmatic concern for sensible standards and rationally defensible judgments that will stand in the foreground throughout the present book. After all, classical pragmatism was not a mode of scepticism or issue-dissolution, but an approach to the rational resolution of the theoretical issues regarding our cognitive and practical affairs.

For Rorty and his congeners, however, "[pragmatism] is simply anti-essentialism applied to notions like 'truth', 'knowledge', 'language', 'morality', and similar objects of philosophical theorizing. . . . "[2] And this actually puts it mildly, since what this deconstructionist sort of pragmatism actually opposes is not just the essentialistic approach to such concepts but their very viability. A pragmatically minded scepticism about essences may well be all to the good if indeed it is the case that these in and of themselves "will not enlighten us about why truths are good to believe or whether our present view of the world is, roughly, the one that we should hold."[3] But what a postmodernly nihilistic approach fails to acknowledge is that pragmatism's moti-

2. Ibid., p. 162.
3. Ibid., p. 162.

vating insight is *not* simply a negative response to essentialism but a positive doctrine that goes on to offer a complex and cogently articulated theory of language, cognition, and action that resolutely addresses the substantive issues of traditional philosophy.

As the traditional objectivistic pragmatists saw it, there are impersonally cogent principles that root in the primacy of practice and the inherent teleology of human endeavor. Precisely because of its gearing to considerations of purposive efficacy, traditionalistic pragmatism is not an invitation to freewheeling, but a doctrine that nails its flag to the mast of reality's rulings with regard to the efficacy of our contrivings. It does not abandon our familiar thought instrumentalities—and not even those ideas and theories that are at work in philosophical discussions—but proposes a rational means for putting them to the test.

It is a pragmatism of this substantive sort that the present book will endeavor to expound and defend. Such a pragmatism—which is what C. S. Peirce actually had in view—by its very nature manifests an impetus that is "objective" and "realistic." It does not turn its back on standards, but upholds a standard of adequacy that is a matter of efficacy, effectiveness, and efficiency in purpose attainment. And this is always something objective, something that rests not with ourselves but with the actual arrangements of the world. For even where we ourselves propose the ends and select the means to their attainment, the issue of *the efficacy of those particular means for those particular ends* is beyond our control because it lies not with us but with "the nature of things." And on this basis a recourse to pragmatism can provide a "reality principle"—an objective monitor whose operations lie above and beyond the reach of our own arbitrary contrivings.

The book accordingly seeks to give a compact but nevertheless comprehensive overview of pragmatism that seeks to do justice to this doctrine's original realistic and objectivistic purport. The object of the enterprise is to set out an historically faithful version of a pragmatist position that is at once grounded in the root inspirations of the doctrine and able to overcome the sorts of objections that have often been advanced against it over the years—with very uneven degrees of justification. What these deliberations will thus endeavor to present is a version of pragmatism that is able to take a constructive rather than deconstructive line in its relation to the traditional range of philosophical issues.

# CHAPTER ONE

# *Setting the Stage*

*Synopsis*

*(1) It is instructive to begin with a brief tour of pragmatism's long and checkered history, which extends back to classical antiquity. (2) As such an historical survey indicates, pragmatism is not a specific doctrine but a diversified and many-sided approach to philosophical issues. Its characteristically practicalistic perspective has been applied to the theory of language, to epistemological truth criteriology, to ontological issues in the metaphysics of truth and reality, as well as to moral and political issues. (3) Pragmatism's prismatically many-sided nature means that the real question for philosophical deliberation is not "Is pragmatism plausible?" but rather "Can really plausible versions of pragmatism be articulated?"*

## 1. The Historical Background

Bertrand Russell once suggested that Karl Marx should be regarded as a prime exponent of pragmatism, remarking on "its close similarity to . . . [the doctrine] of Karl Marx as stated in his *Theses on Feuerbach* (1845) and afterwards embodied in the theory of dialectical materialism."[1] Russell then quoted Marx's famous passage ending with "The truth, i.e., the reality and power, of thought must be demonstrated in practice. Philosophers have only *interpreted* the world in various ways, but the real task is to *alter* it." And he went on to observe that "Allowing for a certain difference of phraseology this doctrine is essentially indistinguishable from [pragmatist] instrumentalism" (p. 144). However, this view is based on a serious misunderstanding. With Marx, theorizing as such does not matter, the only thing that counts is productive action; in effect he wants to *replace* theorizing with action. But sensible pragmatists do not want to dispense with theory and substitute action in its place. Rather, they propose to retain theorizing and merely *evaluate* it in terms of its effectiveness in the guidance of action. Such an approach does not so much glorify action as prioritize it as a standard of appraisal.

The characteristic tactic of the philosophical movement that has come to be designated as pragmatism was to pivot legitimation on success by adopting efficacy in application and implementation as the salient criterion of adequacy. And a thoroughgoing pragmatic philosophy will take this stance all across the board, alike in intellectual as in practical contexts, in matters of logic and language (theory of communication) of ontology (theory of the real), of episte-

---

1. Bertrand Russell, "Dewey's New Logic," in *The Philosophy of John Dewey*, ed. P. Schilpp (New York: Jordan Publishing Co., 1939), pp. 143–56; see p. 144.

mology (theory of knowledge), of axiology (value theory), and even ethics and politics (the theory of right conduct of individuals and groups).

In exploring this terrain of ideas, it is useful to begin with a preliminary look at the historical background.

### *Ancient Skepticism and Empiricism*

The original pragmatists were its pioneers among the Academic Sceptics in classical antiquity. To be sure, they did not use the term itself, but this doesn't mean much; people spoke grammatically long before the idea of grammar as such was ever thought of, and the same sort of thing is true of philosophers who thought pragmatically. Viewing all claims to knowledge with distrust, the ancient sceptics fervently opposed self-authenticating evident certainties—the "cataleptic perceptions" (*kataleptikê phantasia*) of the Stoics. They rejected any possibility of achieving authentic knowledge (*epistêmê*) regarding the real truth of things, and taught that we must make do with plausible beliefs (*to pithanon*) in its place, acceptances that forego claims to unqualified correctness but are merely adequate to the needs of practice. Thus, according to Arcesilaus, the *reasonable* beliefs (*to eulogon*) that we achieve through testing our experiential impressions and natural belief inclinations against each other in a systemic way constitute our only available basis for reliable information, and suffice to provide a basis for rational action. And this sort of plausibility geared to the guidance of effective action—affording practical adequacy rather than theoretical certitude—is as much as we can actually manage to realize in this world. The illusion of theoretically adequate knowledge must accordingly be subordinated to the realities of mere practical adequacy. Theory must yield pride of place to practice as regards the standards of belief. So reasoned the proto-pragmatists among the Academic Sceptics.[2]

In particular, the Empiricist wing of the sceptical school taught that our cognitive life affords a realm of appearances (*phainomena*) that provide no secure basis for making judgment about the actualities (*hypokeimena*) of things. These phenomena suffice to guide action—what appears to be honey generally tastes and nourishes like honey. And this practical adequacy amply accounts for their prominent role in our life and thought. But they do not and cannot inform us not about the actual condition of things, seeing that they only convey the "affection" their impressions have upon us—their effects on our sensory and cognitive apparatus. We thus learn about the world only on the basis of an experience whose instruction suffices to provide "a guide to life." Whatever deeper reality does (or may) in actual fact underlie those appearances is something regarding which we can form no reliable judgment. We have to settle for the practicalities of ordinary life.

In this way, the ancient sceptics made the initial move towards a theory of knowledge geared to the standard of practical adequacy. And in doing this, they launched pragmatism on its way.

## *G. W. Leibniz (1646–1717)*

How are we human inquirers, lacking any sort of direct, intuitive insight into the real and actual nature of things, to come into the possession of general truths regarding matters of fact? In addressing this issue, Leibniz characterized the proper approach here as "the conjectural

2. For details regarding the cognitive theory of the sceptics see Myles Burnyeat ed., *The Skeptical Tradition* (Berkeley-Los Angeles-London: University of California Press, 1983).

method *a priori*" which "proceeds by hypotheses, assuming certain causes, perhaps without proof [i.e., *direct* evidence], and then showing that the things which actually happen would follow from these assumptions."[3] It is conjectural because it reaches beyond the evidence rather than being confined to it. But it is certainly not arbitrary, since it is subject to a rational quality control—in particular that of practical adequacy.

The fact that this method relies crucially on conjectures whose full assertoric content lies beyond the reach of available experience means that it affords no entry into the domain of the *metaphysically* certain. But the method can indeed attain the "moral" or "practical" certainty that suffices for the guidance of affairs in everyday life:

> Some hypotheses can satisfy so many phenomena, and so easily, that they can be taken for certain. Among other hypotheses, those are to be chosen which are the simpler; these are to be presented, in the interim, in place of the true causes. The conjectural method a priori proceeds by hypotheses, assuming certain causes, perhaps without proof, and showing that the things which this kind is like the key to a cryptograph, and the simpler it is, and the greater the number of events that can be explained by it, the more probable it is. But just as it is possible to write a letter intentionally so that it can be understood by means of several different keys, of which only one is the true one, so the same effect can have several causes. Hence no firm demonstration can be made from the success of hypotheses. Yet I shall not deny that the number of phenomena which are happily explained by a given hypothesis may be so great that it must be taken as morally certain. Indeed, hypotheses of these kind are sufficient for everyday use. Yet it is also useful to apply less perfect hypotheses as substitutes for truth until a better one occurs, that is, one which explains the same phenomena more happily or

3. *G. W. Leibniz: Philosophical Papers and Letters*, ed. Leroy E. Loemker (Dordrecht: Reidel, 1956), p. 283.

> more phenomena with equal felicity. There is no danger in this if we carefully distinguish the certain from the probable.[4]

The knowledge that our well-tested hypotheses affords does not lie on the categorical realm of the metaphysically certain but on the practical side of moral certainty.

The degree of probability that is attained through the conjectural method will hinge on the nature of the conjectural hypotheses at which the method arrives:

> Yet it must be admitted that a hypothesis becomes the more probable as it is simpler to understand and wider in force and power, that is, the greater the number of phenomena that can be explained by it, and the fewer the further assumptions. It may even turn out that a certain hypothesis can be accepted as certain for nature [*pro physice certa*] if, namely, it completely satisfies all the phenomena which occur, as does the key to a cryptograph. Those hypotheses deserve the highest ranking (next to truth), however, by those aid predictions can be made, even about phenomena or observations, which have not been tested before, for a hypothesis of this kind can be applied, in practice, in place of truth.[5]

As Leibniz saw it, such effective certainty is tantamount to a probability of the very highest grade.

Leibniz' exposition of inquiry as based on a "conjectural method *a priori*" makes it clear that what is at issue here is in essence what subsequently became known as the hypothetico-deductive method of scientific method. And his account of this method and its modus operandi shows that *he sees its justifactory rationale as pragmatic and as preemi-*

---

4. Ibid., p. 283.
5. G. W. Leibniz, *Philosophische Schriften*, ed. C. I. Gerhardt, vol. I (Berlin: Wiedemann, 1875), pp. 195–196; Loemker, *Philosophical Papers and Letters*, p. 188.

*nently validated in the order of practical reason*. The test of hypotheses is a matter of "satisfying the phenomena" by way of descriptive coordination as regards the past and effective prediction as regards the future. The crux here lies in the principle "by their fruits shall ye know them." The successful guidance of experience provides us with a practical, working equivalent of the actual truth of things. And so, at any rate, in these matters relating to the operative criteriology of the contingent generalizations of empirical science, Leibniz was also a pragmatist before the days of pragmatism as such.[6]

### *Utilitarianism*

The utilitarianism of Jeremy Bentham (1748–1832) and John Stuart Mill (1806–1873) proposed an ethic which appraises human projects and processes by the standard of "the greatest good of the greatest number." Even as "the proof of the pudding is in the eating," so the utilitarian test of the appropriateness of actions lies in seeing how their consequences impact upon the happiness of people-in-general. In this way, utilitarianism based its moral and social philosophy upon an altogether pragmatic approach.[7] And from early on, clearheaded students of philosophy recognized in pragmatism the epistemological counterpart of ethical utilitarianism. For where J. S. Mill saw ethical principles as properly validated through social utility in fostering the affective condition of people-in-general (the greatest good of the greatest number), there C. S. Peirce and his congeners came to regard

---

6. For Leibniz's theory of scientific investigation see Nicholas Rescher, *The Philosophy of Leibniz* (Englewood Cliffs, N.J.: Prentice-Hall, 1967).
7. See J. C. C. Smart and B. A. O. Williams, *Utilitarianism: For and Against* (Cambridge: Cambridge University Press, 1973).

their pragmatic efficacy (i.e., utility) in the service of our purposes as validating our principles for securing trustworthy information about the world.[8] And so, as Émile Durkheim already maintained, pragmatism is closely akin to an epistemic utilitarianism: utilitarians classed as *right* that which proves beneficial to the community ("the greatest good of the greatest number"), pragmatists classed as *true* that which proves useful to the individual (i.e., useful through being effectively conducive to the realizations of his ends).[9]

## *Charles Sanders Peirce (1839–1914)*

The ruling idea of pragmatism is that decision, choice, and action have priority over thought, ideation, and belief in human affairs—that practice (*praxis*) here takes primacy over theory (*theoria*). Anticipated by the Academic Sceptics in antiquity, and reaffirmed by Renaissance thinkers like Francis Bacon, this idea reemerged into prominence in Cambridge, Mass. in the 1870s with a group of young Turk thinkers of whom C. S. Peirce proved to be the most profound. Peirce was inspired to call his position *pragmatism* by Kant's use of the term *pragmatisch* for "expressing a relation to some definite human purpose."[10] But Peirce had a very particular purpose primarily in view, namely, cognition.

---

8. With William James, "it was but a step from utilitarian empiricism to pragmatism" according to Antonio Aliota, *The Idealistic Reaction Against Science* (London: Methuen, 1914), p. 165. (The book originally appeared in Rome in 1912 as *La reazione idealistica contra la scienza*.) Hans Vaihinger characterized pragmatism as "epistemological utilitarianism" (erkenntnistheoretischer Utilitarianismus), *Philosophie des Als ob* (Leipzig: F. Meiner, 1924; original ed. 1911).
9. Émile Durkheim, *Pragmatism and Sociology* (Cambridge: Cambridge University Press, 1983), p. 54. Translated from the original French, *Pragmatisme et sociologie* (Paris: Alcan, 1955).
10. Charles S. Peirce, *Collected Papers*, eds. C. Hartshorne and P. Weiss, vol. V (Cambridge, Mass: Harvard University Press, 1934), sect. 5.412.

In the hands of this founding father, pragmatism had two principal components; one as regards meaning and one as regards truth. Peirce's meaning pragmatism encompasses a pragmatic view of the meaning of concepts and ideas. Take the concept of an "apple," for example. When we characterize something as such, we commit ourselves to treating it in a certain way—to handle it, store it, use it, discuss it, and so forth in the particular way appropriate to apples. And this is what it means to be an apple. It is all a matter of practical ramifications: To be what we call an "*X*" is to be treated *X*ly by us. The crux, so Peirce maintained, lay in the "pragmatic maxim": "To ascertain the meaning of an intellectual conception one should consider what practical consequences might conceivably result from the truth of that conception; and the sum of these consequences will constitute the entire meaning of the conception."[11] Meaning, in sum is, as meaning does. As Peirce put it in his classic essay on "How to Make our Ideas Clear" (1878): "there is no distinction of meaning so fine as to consist in anything but a possible difference of practice."[12] Peirce insisted that the prime function of our beliefs regarding the world is to commit us to rules for action—to furnish guidance to our behavior in point of what to think, say and do—above all, to canalize our expectations in matters of observation and experiment in scientific contexts.[13]

11. Ibid., sect. 5.9. Note that Peirce here says "from the truth of that conception"—that is, from that conception's: actually being true—and not "from *believing* the truth of that conception." This difference is one point that separates him from William James.
12. Ibid., vol. V: 248–71; see sect. 5.400.
13. In this essay, Peirce prescribed that clarity in the apprehension of ideas is to be determined by the "pragmatic maxim": "Consider what effects, that might conceivably have practical bearing, we conceive the object of our conception to have. Then, our conception of these efforts in the whole of our conception of the object" (*Collected Papers*, vol. V: sect. 5.402). As his subsequent discussion of the matter makes clear with increasing emphasis, Peirce means by "effects" the sci-

And much the same sort of story here told with respect to meaning holds also with respect to truth. Those theses are true whose implementation in practice "work out" by way of yielding success in matters of prediction and application. And, as Peirce saw it, the best route to this distinction is the scientific method whose rivals—evidence ignoring tenacity, pious adherence to authority, a priori speculation, and such like—simply cannot compare with it in point of producing trustworthy results.[14] True factual beliefs, ipso facto, are those that achieve efficacy through in guiding our expectations, beliefs, and actions in satisfying ways—where specifically cognitive satisfactions are at issue. And they must achieve this on a systemic basis.

With Peirce, what matters primarily for the substantiation of an inductively based claim is not simply that a successfully predicted fact issues from it, but rather that this fact could qualify as typical—that is, would be seen as representing "a haphazard specimen of all the predictions which might be based on the hypothesis and which constitutes its pivotal truth."[15] It is the objective realities of statistical sampling theory that are pivotal for the rational validation at issue here. The role of chance, of probability theory and statistics—was prominent throughout Peirce's theory of knowledge and of nature (as evidenced in his "tychism"). On the side of nature, he envisioned the historical emergence of increasingly stable laws and forms. On that of

entifically determinable consequences, and by "practical bearing" then implications for the scientific understanding and explanation of things—that is, for *scientific praxis*. He recoiled with aversion from William James' tendency to take "effects" and "practical bearing" to relate to matters of psychology, religion, and the management of our ordinary life affairs. The issue is vividly and helpfully presented in H. O. Maunce, *The Two Pragmatisms* (London: Routledge and Kegan Paul, 1977); see especially chapter 3, "Peirce: Pragmatism and William James."

14. Peirce, *Collected Papers*, vol. V: sect. 5.377–87.
15. Ibid., vol. VI: sect. 6.527.

knowledge, he envisioned the historical emergence of increasingly adequate knowledge within the ongoing communal process of scientific inquiry. (For Peirce even physical reality was subject to the Darwinian process of the evolutionary emergence of processes that contribute to nature's increasing assumption of enduring, self-perpetuating structures.)

Immanuel Kant had put on philosophy's agenda the question: How can the mind come into secure possession of an authentic truth about a reality that is altogether independent of its own activities? Accepting a negative answer here—it can't—Kant's followers in the school of German idealism held that some great cosmic force leads the mind towards a truth that is at once universal and of the mind's own contriving. But after Darwin scientifically minded philosophers—Peirce included—substituted for this mysterious cosmic force a process of natural development that at once produced and coordinated the operations of the human mind. Biological evolution provides the missing link between natural reality and human thought, seeing that humans—together with their thinking facilities—are surely the natural products of this evolutionary process. Our cognitive processes find their justification in the consideration that their evolutionary emergence is bound to proceed in a manner that reflects their efficacy.

Peirce's pragmatic view of truth is thus comprehensively coordinated to effective implementation. But this must be understood against the background of certain preliminary explanations. For a "pragmatic theory of truth" is nowadays usually construed with reference to a criterion that assesses the claims to truth of a factual contention in terms of the *success* engendered by its acceptance (its conduciveness to the realization of some sort of "utility"). However, this construction takes an overly restricted view of the matter, for it interprets the pragmatic theory in its later, specifically Jamesean version, slighting the fact that other pragmatists—and most significantly Peirce—have approached the matter quite differently. Peirce's criterion for assessing the truth of a factual thesis is not simply and immediately the factor of its applicative *success*, but the extent to which it manages to secure the ongoing *long run allegiance of a community committed to the methods that successfully implement the goals of science*. Truth, as Peirce saw it, consists in those contentions that are "fated to be ultimately agreed to by all who investigate [scientifically]."[16] It is what the community of rational inquirers is destined to arrive at in the end—the ultimate consensus of informed opinion among investigators committed to the principles of science. And Peirce's position here is not simply a matter of epistemological optimism, of a Pollyanna-ish confidence that things are bound to come right in the end. Rather, what is at issue is an idealization of sorts. For by "the course of inquiry" Peirce came to understand not the actual, concrete, historical course of things (in the manner of the Hegelian thesis that *die Weltgeschichte ist das Weltgericht*), but the hypothetical course of procedure in an idealized community of *fully rational* inquirers. To his mind, it is not mere inquiring as such but *properly conducted* inquiring that must eventually get at the truth of things. The crux is something conditional, namely, that there is an established methodology of investigation—the scientific method—which if persistently used in an ongoing community of rational inquirers must ultimately yield truth. And this circumstance is not without its metaphysical ramifications, since for Peirce the methodological resources of language, logic, and scientific inquiry served as an entryway into the domain of metaphysics.

Since the time of Peirce, pragmatism has taken three principal forms:

16. Peirce, *Collected Papers*, vol. V: sect. 5.407.

- *semantical* pragmatism: the meaning of terms consists on their use.
- *epistemic* pragmatism: the successful implementation of beliefs (especially in matters of prediction and control over nature) is the proper criterion for their truth. (Sometimes construed as the contention that truth simply is (nothing else but) successful implementability.)
- *ontological* (or *metaphysical*) pragmatism: in the human realm, *praxis* (doing) has primacy over *theoria* (understanding) because all understanding must itself be the product of a doing: whatever we know (understand) is the product of inquiry, an activity of ours.

Peirce himself in effect espoused all three of these doctrines conjointly, but the last one proved particularly portentous for him. For since every human activity can always be refined, improved, extended, this means that our knowledge of the truth is always tentative and imperfect. And this line of thought led Peirce to a fallibilism that sees human knowledge as inevitably falling short of a secure grasp on the definitive truth of things. Only in the idealized long run can our pragmatically validated knowledge be equated with the truth as such.

In his attempt to de-mystify truth and bring it down to earth, Peirce was eager to connect the truth with what people (and, in particular, intelligently inquiring people—the community of scientific investigators—actually think about the matter). But, of course, he was not so heedless as to think that the truth is what the scientific community thinks, here and now. Realizing that the scientists of the day may have it all wrong, he proposed (in 1878) to shift the matter to the indefinitely remote future—the theoretical long run.

The more Peirce thought about this definition of truth as the revelations of the long run the more dissatisfied he became—and ultimately (around 1897) he gave up on this whole approach. The problem is that the natural course of observation—no matter how far extended—never extends into "the long run." *The long run lies outside our cognitive reach*, and the law of large numbers of the calculus of probability—in which Peirce initially invested great hope—really does not help us sufficiently since it only comes into play with repeatable events in countable occurrence spaces. There is, to be sure, the prospect of a shift from the actual future to the theoretical realm of possibility, for what does happen when we keep going to what would happen if we kept going "long enough." But this takes us into the speculative region of a transobservationally suppositional reality with which Peirce—scientist and empiricist that he was—could not manage to be fully content. Modern theorists have, to be sure, suggested that truth should be construed as an idealization.[17] However, such a shift inevitably leads outside the secure observational / empirical region where earlier pragmatists felt themselves constrained to operate.

But such complexities aside, the fact remains that in matters of inquiry—of resolving issues of meaning and truth—Peirce hitched his wagon to the star of science. To be sure, this focus on science emphatically does not mean that he was a materialist or positivist of some descriptions, someone drawn to a "scientism" that rejects metaphysics and has no use for philosophical speculation. For Peirce unlike, say, John Dewey in some of his positivistic moods, science represented a methodology of inquiry and not an ideology of some sort. As Pierce saw it, it is the scientific method—not the scientific doctrine of the day—that is crucial for rational inquiry. And he rejected an ideology of the look-to-science-for-all-the-answers sort for the same reason

17. Hilary Putnam, *Representation and Reality* (Cambridge MA: MIT Press, 1988), p. 115. Putnam offers "idealized rational acceptability" as a characterization of truth. And the present author defends a view of "Truth as Ideal Coherence," *The Review of Metaphysics*, vol. 38 [1985]:795–806.

that he rejected dogmatism of any sort, because it is itself ultimately unscientific.

And for similar reasons, traditional metaphysics as such was viewed with equal scepticism by Peirce, who held that "almost every proposition of [traditional] ontological metaphysics is either meaningless gibberish . . . or else absurd.")[18] However, Peircean pragmatism is not logical positivism: the test of pragmatic success is not just success in predicting observations. The success of principles in the organization of experience must also count. Highly abstract principles—of the conservation of energy, for example—can have pragmatic success not by way of producing new and unexpected observations but by way of "second-order" success, providing indispensably useful instruments for the *systematization* of our experiential-determined observations.

### *William James (1842–1910)*

William James maintained that philosophy and science must go hand in hand, seeing that philosophy aims at "the completest knowledge of the universe, [and so] must include the results of all the sciences," and moreover "it must . . . complete the sciences, and must encorporate their methods."[19] Success in squaring with experience—the standard of acceptability in science—will do service for philosophy as well. But while this was James' preaching, his practice was quite different. (Consistency was never one of James' strong points.) In particular, he aimed, not at a philosophy that completed science, but at one that transcended it so as to move off in rather different directions of its own. For science

18. Peirce, *Collected Papers*, vol. V: sect. 5.423.
19. William James, *Some Problems of Philosophy* (New York and London: Longmans Green, 1912), pp. 25–27.

seeks a uniformity of opinion, while philosophy, so James thought, must embrace diversity.

James therefore adopted an approach distinctly different from that of Peirce. For, as he saw it, pragmatism's characteristic tactic is to construe truth in terms of a potentially diversified utility in whose light there is nothing fixed or monolithic about truth:

> *The* Truth: what a perfect idol of the rationalistic mind! I read in an old letter—from a gifted friend who died too young—these words: "In everything, in science, art, morals, and religion, there *must* be one system that is right and *every* other wrong." How characteristic of the enthusiasm of a certain stage of young! At twenty-one we rise to such a challenge and expect to find the system. It never occurs to most of us even later that the question "What is *the* Truth?" is no real question (being irrelevant to all conditions) and that the whole notion of *the* truth is an abstraction from the fact of truths in the plural.[20]

On this basis, James held that " 'The true' is only the expedient in our way of thinking, just as the right is only the expedient in our way of behaving."[21] He sought to replace "the truth" by a diversified plurality of truths.

For James, pragmatism was to be an instrument of change designed to revolutionalize traditionally entrenched conceptions. It seeks to reject the construction of "highfallutin" monolistic philosophical conceptions like truth, beauty, and justice, and to put utility, serviceability, efficiency, and effectiveness in their place. And pragmatic "success" is seen as a matter of getting things done in the setting of our everyday life affairs. As James put it, "ideas become true just insofar as they help us to get into satisfac-

20. William James, *Pragmatism* (Cambridge MA: Harvard University Press), p. 115.
21. James, *Pragmatism*, p. 106.

tory relation with other parts of our experience,"[22] where those "other parts" reach beyond the range of theorizing, of inquiry and question-resolution. Turning away from matters of rational inquiry as such, James rejected the idea that there is a "pure," disinterestedly neutral and wholly impersonal realm of meaningful cognition. To his mind, concepts like "knowledge," "belief," "truth," "meaning," and the entire panoply of epistemological conceptions are factors operating in a human practice of opinion formation that serve the interests of not just of rational inquiry but of life in general. Factors standardly adjudged as nonepistemic therefore have a key role in belief validation for James.

James' turning opened the way to fragmenting truth into a plurality of contextualizations, seeing that any instrumental resource—be it theoretical of practical—may prove more effective in one sphere of application than in another. Bertrand Russell's charge that "It follows that [for James] truth is geographical"[23] is not wholly off the mark. After all, "pragmatic success" is bound to come down to efficacy in serving the purposes of this or that particular individuals operating within some limited functional range. And it thus becomes tempting for a success-oriented pragmatism to take a personalistic turning. With Peirce, the objectivity of rational inquiry was paramount; in science our results are robust since what works out for one person works out for another, because nature plays no favorites. With James, however, what counts is a matter of potentially

---

22. James, *Pragmatism*, p. 34. A first approximation to a plausibly acceptable reformulation would make certain crucial additions, namely, ideas GENERALLY COME TO BE RECOGNIZED AS true just insofar as they are seen to stand in a harmonious relationship with other parts of our COGNITIVE experience. What such a recasting does is to make explicit the epistemic aspect of the situation, recognizing that truth as such is something rather different from its *recognition* as such.
23. Bertrand Russell, "William James' Conception of Truth," *Philosophical Essays* (London: Longmans Green, 1910), pp. 147–48.

idiosyncratic personal satisfactions. In his hands, pragmatism took on a personalistic and psychologistic orientation towards matters of affective and subjective satisfaction,[24] disassembling into a virtually endless proliferation of purposive contextualizations.

Continuing to adopt pragmatism's idea of truth as pivoting on the successful guidance of experience, he construed success not in terms of specifically epistemic efficiency in scientific matters of prediction and control but rather in terms of psychological satisfactions. The utility, efficiency, and success of ideas that interested him primarily lay rather in the range of everyday life and of religious beliefs than in the realm of scientific matters of fact. With James, the issue of personal aims and reactions becomes pivotal even for the constitution of "objective" knowledge: "the popular notion that 'Science' is forced on the mind *ab extra*, and that our interests have nothing to do with its construction, as ultimately absurd." After all, "Truth for us is simply a collective name for verification-processes. . . . Truth is *made*, just as health, wealth, and strength are made, in the course of experience."[25] And at times James came perilously close to a "wishful thinking" view of truth that conflated the narrower *evidential* reasons for the substance of a belief with the broader *prudential* reasons why its adoption could prove advantageous.

---

24. Often but not always with certain factual statements what matters is, James suggests, "extraordinary fertility in consequences verifiable by sense"—that is successful prediction. James, *Pragmatism*, p. 91. The problem is that James is simply inconsistent on this point—for him "expediency is sometimes scientific success and sometimes personal satisfaction. On James' cavalier attitude towards consistency, see Richard M. Gale, *The Philosophy of William James* (Cambridge: Cambridge University Press, 1998).
25. James, *Pragmatism*, p. 104.

And so while Peirce construed those pragmatically pivotal "practical consequences" as being consequences that are observationally and experimentally determinable in a uniform way by any community of scientific investigators, James took them to relate to the bearing of beliefs on the affective condition of individuals. He had a theory of truth all right, but it was one that saw this as a matter of personalized satisfaction in a way that led to a diversified proliferation of many truths. The long and short of it is that James had to ride roughshod over traditional principles of evidence and logic—the law of bivalence included.

James therefore construed pragmatism very differently from Peirce, not as a doctrine that provides a fixed standard of adequacy, but as an invitation to pluralism—to a relativistic diversity of views that allowed not only for differences among individuals, but even differences within individuals as an embodiment of many selves with natural inclinations operating in diverse circumstances. Peirce's pragmatism was indeed success-oriented—but the success it envisioned was that of the communally impersonal objectives of science, and emphatically not as with James, a matter of serving the personal needs of differently constituted human individuals in their varying subjective reactions to objective conditions.[26] Where Peirce looked to science as a venture in quest for impersonal uniformity, James looked to human life in its multiplex and variegated diversity.[27] Truth, for James, is not something a claim or thesis exhibits indifferently but something acquired in the context of a process of belief formation that itself pivots on desire satisfaction. (The

---

26. James, *The Meaning of Truth*, p. 97. Thus, James complains that a critic is "taking the word 'true' irrelatively, whereas the pragmatist always means 'true for him who experiences the working.' "
27. When he saw James writing things like "On pragmatic principles, if the hypothesis of God works satisfactorily in the widest sense of the word, it is 'true,'" Peirce was horrified. He then proposed to rename his own position "pragmaticism" to set it apart from this sort of thing.

question of "Whose desire for what?" is one that we had best not press all that closely with James.)

From the first, critics such as Bertrand Russell and Arthur Lovejoy complained that pragmatism's "success" in implementation and "working" in application can involve very different sorts of things—namely, either *epistemic* success in the guidance of thought or *affective* success in the conduct of life. Thus, (to give Russell's example) religious beliefs—such as the coming of the Messiah or the reality of an afterlife—may well "work" in engendering individual self-confidence and social cohesion among the faithful, but yet fail to work as factual predictions.[28] And even early on, different pragmatists took different lines here. Now for Peirce, "success" and "working out" arose in cognitive and above all in *scientific* contexts and related to effective experiential prediction and control in *observational* matters. James, by contrast, understood "working" in the very different sense that the effects of believing something are good in relation to affective, emotional, and psychological issues.[29] This Jamesean line, of course, represents an approach very different from what Peirce initially had in view—and one whose bearing on the matter of actual truth is, if anything, rather tenuous. In fact even James himself ultimately came to recognize this—better late than never!—when he acknowledged that he had hitherto confused "consequences that ideas have per se and consequences of ideas *qua believed by us*."[30] After all, providing

28. Bertrand Russell, "William James' Conception of Truth," *Philosophical Essays* (London: Longmans Green, 1910), p. 143. Moreover, Russell observed, "It is far easier . . . to settle the plain question of fact: Have the Popes always been infallible? than to settle the question of whether thinking them to be infallible is on the whole good" (p. 135).
29. James, *Pragmatism*, pp. 127–49.
30. Ralph Barton Perry, *The Thought and Character of William James*, 2 vols. (Boston: Little Brown, 1935), p. 481. This objection goes back at least to A. O. Lovejoy's "The Thirteen Pragmatisms," *The Journal of Philosophy, Sociology, and Scientific Methods* (1908):1–39.

personal contentment or group welfare is one sort of thing, and facilitating to successful prediction of or effective intervention in the course of events is something else quite different. But as Russell and most readers saw it, James hopelessly straddled the fence here. And there is much justice to this complaint.

While the core of James' pragmatism lay in its prioritizing of efficacy, its concern for what actually works out in practice—as with pragmatism in general—the shortcoming of James' general approach was that he was carried away by fascination with the affective sector of life. "On pragmatic principles," he wrote in a burst of exuberant enthusiasm, "we cannot reject any hypothesis if consequences useful to life follow from it."[31] Truth could still be a matter of "correspondence with reality," but now a "correspondence" mediated not by observation but by broadly construed "satisfaction." And so, while it may well be a merit in James's position to insist that the range of human purpose is broader than the limited realm of inquiry and knowledge, its flaw lay in a willingness to have the pragmatics of those other domains exert an influence within the cognitive project itself. For as James saw it, truth is not a matter of evidential adequation between claim and reality but one of negotiation of comfort between the knower and this world: "The knower is an actor and coefficient of truth on one side, while on the other, he registers the truth which he helps to create."[32] The more realistic circumstance that knowers project a conceptualization which, once made, leaves all the rest up to the nature of reality—like it or lump it—does not fit the format of a Jamesean negotiation. For James, reality lies substantially in the eyes of the beholder: "Each

31. James, *Pragmatism*, p. 131.
32. James, "Spencer's Definition of Mind as Correspondence," p. 21. And again, "Truth is *made* just as health, wealth, and strength are made, in the course of experience" (James, *Pragmatism*, p. 104).

thinker, however, has dominant habits of attention; and these practically elect from among the various [thought] worlds someone to be for him the world of ultimate realities."[33] Walt Whitman's—"I am multitudes"—was an idea that appealed to James.

James' construal of truth in terms of utility thus seemed to many of his readers to skate dangerously close to Friedrich Nietzsche's analogous dismissal of truth in favor of what is life-enhancing or survival conducive. Nietzsche's position was more radical than James', however. Nietzsche wrote: "The falsity of a judgment is to us not necessarily an objection to it. And here perhaps our [i.e., Nietzsche's own] new way of talking sounds strangest. The real question is to what extent it (i.e., the judgment in question] is life-enhancing, life-preserving, species-preserving, perhaps even more species-proliferating; and our basic inclination is to assert that the falsest judgments . . . are the most indispensable to us."[34] Such an "evolutionary" view of knowledge is not far removed from James' position on the matter—except, of course, that Nietzsche is quite indifferent to truth, whereas James merely wishes to replace it with utility. While Nietzsche wanted to move beyond values like true and good and evil, James wanted merely to restructure the way in which we conceive of them. Unlike Nietzsche or postmodern "pragmatists" like Rorty, James was no deconstructionist, but a theorist who sought to pursue traditional philosophical projects by novel means.

James' energetic exposition and vivid writing gained for pragmatism a far-ranging if not always favorable recep-

---

33. William James, *The Principles of Psychology* (Cambridge MA: Harvard University Press, 1983), p. 923.
34. Friedrich Nietzsche, *Beyond Good and Evil*, tr. R. J. Hollingdale (Harmondsworth: Penguin Books, 1973), pp. 17–28. (I have slightly emended the translation.)

tion. The 1907 publication of his lectures on *Pragmatism*[35] was succeeded by their publication in Germany the very next year,[36] and other European languages soon followed. Debate about pragmatism was one of the central issues of the 1908 World Philosophical Congress in Heidelberg. In fact, the frenetic reception of James pushed Peirce entirely off the stage. Few members of the international philosophical community ever bothered to look into his writing and, as one recent historian puts it: "Various spellings of the name Peirce (essentially Pierce, though also Peirce) are to be encountered in articles at this time, suggesting that the critics lacked any firsthand knowledge of his essays."[37]

In recent years, Hilary Putnam has been eager to defend James against the charges of psychologistic relativism that have often been made.[38] Putnam's methodology here is to cite passages where James flatly denies or at least comes close to contradicting what his critics affirm he says. The problem with this proceeding is its neglect of the fact that James is one of philosophy's few real opportunists—that is, someone who rejects the need to worry about consistency when it conflicts with the desiderata of the moment. He views consistency as a bugaboo of small minds that intellects of larger vision need not worry about. Thus, we find James repeatedly maintaining diametrically opposite things with jaunty insouciance at different places in his prolific writings (and indeed sometimes even in the same book!). It is therefore quite wrong to think that James does not say (or even mean) those somewhat wildly relativistic claims he states from time to time simply

35. James, *Pragmatism*, originally published in New York by Longman's Green in 1907.
36. In a translation by Wilhelm Jerusalem.
37. Hans Joas, *Pragmatism and Social Theory* (Chicago: University of Chicago Press, 1993), p. 96.
38. See especially Hilary Putnam, *Pragmatism: An Open Question* (Oxford UK and Cambridge MA: Blackwell, 1995).

because he qualifies or denies them in other places. Such "inconsistencies" may worry some of his readers, but they did not faze William James himself. It was not for nothing that he saw the idea of an objective and fixed truth as a specter that must give way to expediency.

*John Dewey (1859–1952)*

With John Dewey a yet different approach to pragmatism emerged—one that was not grounded in science (à la Peirce) or in personalistic psychology (à la James), but in social ethics. For Dewey regarded the scope of practicable intellectual effort as confined to determinations of utility for us humans as beings coexisting in organized societies. For he insisted that humans can only flourish in collectively harmonious contexts in which healthily self-developed individuals can thrive. To be a human individual is to be member of a community. In its gearing not to personal purposive aims but to wider social objectives such a position clearly goes well beyond the personalistic pragmatism of James.

Let us begin with the views of the early John Dewey. In his three 1911 Harrison lectures at the University of Pennsylvania on "The Problem of Truth," Dewey reaffirmed William James' lines of thought on the matter. Hard-and-fast capital-T Truth as idealistic-minded philosophers have traditionally conceived of it is simply an illusion. Ideas and beliefs are nothing but artificial thought-instruments, mere conveyers of man-made meanings, shaped by social processes and procedures. Dewey joins with the other pragmatists in emphasizing the primacy of experience and experiment over the indications of speculation and over the urgings of experience-abstractive theorizing. As he saw it, theoretical logic is a direly insufficient basis of knowledge, because "such logic only abstracts some aspect of the existing course of events in order to reduplicate it as a petrified eternal principle by which to explain the very change of which it is the [static] formalization."[39] Truth is not a matter of logically static fixity; instead, it is that which gets endorsed and accepted in the community. Its sole validation is the sanction of social approbation and custom, and when those "truths" no longer satisfy social needs others are found to replace them. Truth resides in agreement: social consensus does not merely *evidentiate* truth, but is its *creator*.[40] The stability, feasibility, and lifestyle supportiveness of social customs, rules, and practices now became the pivotal assessment factor, with social viability and stability serving as the test standard for successful practice.

Dewey agreed with Peirce and James in seeing pragmatism as future-oriented. After all, the purpose of action of any sort is to influence what the future will or might be. And Dewey preferred to characterize his version of pragmatism as "instrumentalism." As he saw it, the usual machinery of thought—beliefs, ideas, suppositions, and so forth—are all intellectual instruments—tools by which we humans as belief-guided agents make our way in the world. Even as our organs are physical instrumentalities, developed under the pressures of need satisfaction, so our cognitive processes are also governed by the harsh impersonal realities of evolutionary selection. Our cognitive resources are not chosen on the

39. John Dewey, "Darwin's Influence upon Philosophy," *The Popular Science Monthly* 75 (1909):90.88.
40. The later Dewey backed away from this position. Thus, in his reply to Arthur Murphy in *The Philosophy of John Dewey*, ed. Paul Schilpp, 2nd ed. (La Salle IL: Open Court, 1951), Dewey endorses the stronger classical doctrine. Discussing his earlier theories that "Scientific conceptions are not a revelation of prior and independent reality" in *The Quest for Certainty* (New York: Minton Balch, 1929, p. 165), Dewey now indicates that the negative emphasis belongs on "revelation" and *not* on "prior and independent reality" (560–565).

basis of their intrinsic attractions but developed on the basis of their situational requiredness.

As was the case with Peirce, Dewey's pragmatism focused upon inquiry viewed as an instrumentality for removing doubt, that uneasy state of an organism which leads to irritation and a loss of equilibrium. To avoid this unhappy condition, there must be a settlement of thought that engenders an internal stability. And this requires the achievement of consilence and consensus with others. But at this point Peirce and Dewey parted ways. For where Peirce saw a consensus of opinion in the community of rational inquirers to emerge under the inexorable pressure of the world's realities—its objective states and processes—Dewey viewed the impetus to consensus as rooted in sociopolitical conditions. For him, the cardinal aim of inquiry and of education, is to engender individual self-development in the context of a free, harmonious, and cooperative society. His characterization of *truth* as "warranted assertability" embodied an ominous ambiguity between *epistemic* and *social* warrant—and Dewey manifested an irrepressible impetus towards the latter alternative. Accordingly, for Dewey it is not so much the world's impersonal realities as the requisites of effective social learning that make for consensus.

Dewey himself espoused a science-informed realism that contrasted with and was designed to countervail against the more subjectivistic and voluntaristic pragmatism of James and Schiller. But the "success" of theories and ideas is not (as with Peirce) a matter of their efficacy in realizing the impartial goals of science (effective explanation, prediction, and control). Rather it is a matter of contributing to the excellence, stability, and durability of a community of agents interacting in fruitful personal and cooperative ventures. Effective individual participation in a harmonious communal living is the key.

In this way, Dewey in due course turned pragmatism into a more decidedly social direction. To be sure, Peirce, too, had looked to a community; but this was only the abstraction of an idealized long-run community of scientific inquirers. Dewey's community, however, was the concrete society as it actually functions about us here and now. His enterprise was the improvement of that society, specifically its movement in the direction of a more perfect democracy.[41] As he saw it, only in a healthy democracy will personal development achieve its best prospects and only enlightened individuals will operate a thriving democracy. And so he saw education—the training of an intelligent electorate—as a key requisite for a workable democracy. The natural Darwinism of cultural selection militates alike for social, cultural, and individual progress. Dewey viewed the human condition in terms of an ongoing process of communally beneficial self-development.

Progress was therefore a central theme of Dewey's thought. As he saw it, even logic is progressive—it is not a collection of realized principles but a progressively developed methodology of inquiry that becomes increasingly more adequate in the course of its own collaboration. Human knowledge is not a funded asset but a process of ongoing refinement through an increase "warranted assertability."

Thus, Dewey occupied a position intermediate between that of Peirce and of James, standing between them in much the same way as the interpersonal stand between the impersonal and the subjectively personalized. His pragmatism is in effect, neither objectivistic nor subjectivistic: it was, in essence, a *social* pragmatism that saw truth as a matter of communally authorized assertability. To be sure, Dewey here envisioned a community that sensibly acknowledges the findings of science. But this proved no problem for

41. His concern was for action toward "positive and constructive changes in social arrangements." See John Dewey, "Philosophers of Freedom," in H. M. Kallen ed., *Freedom in the Modern World* (New York: Coward-McCann, 1928), pp. 236–71; see p. 250.

him because he saw the good society, the *rational* society, as more or less automatically geared to a commitment to scientific endeavors and principles. For Dewey as a fervent opponent of dualism—of separations, divisions, and disconnections—it was a crucial merit of pragmatism that it was committed to overcoming the traditional gap between theory and practice. For him, thought and action were of one interrelated and interconnected whole, as were knowledge and evaluation, and man and nature. Dewey distrusted sharp contrasts and saw himself in the Hegelian style as a mediative reconciler of opposites.

In the specifically American context, pragmatism was impelled under Dewey's influence towards becoming a program in social philosophy—indeed in the socialization of philosophy as an instrumentality of enlightenment for reorienting thought along more scientifically rational and communally productive lines. While Peirce's pragmatism is strictly cognitive and oriented to natural science, and James's is personalistic and psychological, Dewey's is communalistic and society-oriented. While James looked to issues of personal character formation and religion, Dewey looks to the requisites for a viable democratic society—and, in particular, to the educational formation of the intelligent electorate needed to make a democratic mass society function in modern conditions.

Nevertheless, in the hands of some of Dewey's sociologically inclined followers, pragmatism took an increasingly spineless and flexible form. As they saw it, the "success" at issue with pragmatic efficacy pivots on the matter of a social modus operandi, the pivotal factor now being not the contentment of individuals (as with James) but the quality of life of the social community. For in following Dewey, social pragmatists have proposed to make much of the fact that customs and practices that succeed in making for a good quality of life, for example, say, in Japan, might not succeed comparably in Sweden. Once again pragmatic efficacy becomes something fragmented and relativized, albeit now not to individual preferences but to the goals and behaviors of groups. Communal benefit as construed in somewhere rather than universal terms now became the hallmark of pragmatism—unfortunately in a way that tended to relativize and fragment Deweyan pragmatism.

It must be acknowledged, moreover, that a vexing lack of clarity often infects Dewey's frequently turgid mode of exposition. For example, he characterized pragmatism as "the doctrine that reality possesses a practical character and that this character is most efficaciously expressed in the function of intelligence."[42] But just what are we to make of this? Does it mean that reality contains intelligent beings whose repertoire includes modes of practice? (Little news there!) Does it mean that the universe as a whole is a somehow intelligent being with practices that manifest a purpose of its own. (An unpromising but certainly possible construction of the formula.) Dewey struggles to explicate the matter in terms of our humanity's condition as a product of nature that is endowed by it with a nature of its own. And part of this nature is the urge to know, to comprehend the what and how and why of things. But here we can only go so far—we cannot see beyond the horizon, the limits determined for us by our mode of emplacement in nature's scheme of things. And yet why this must be so—why the mind's eye cannot look beyond its locality much as our physical eye can look beyond the earth—even devising instrumentalities (telescopes) that extend its reach into the remote heavens—in the end is left obscure, for all of Dewey's elaborations of the issue.[43]

42. John Dewey, "Does Reality Possess Practical Character?" in *Essays, Philosophical and Psychological in Honor of William James* by Columbia University Professors (New York: Longmans, Green and Co., 1908), pp. 53–80; see p. 57.
43. John Dewey, *Experience and Nature* (La Salle, IL: Open Court, 1925).

### *George Herbert Mead (1863–1931)*

George Herbert Mead was an ally of John Dewey in the development of a socially oriented pragmatism that envisions its redirection from a Jamesean atomistic, localized concern with "what works for me" to a larger, socialized concern with "what works for us." Mead's social ethic was not geared to people's standard of living, but to the *health* of a society in terms of its capacity to thrive and survive—to meet its challenges and resolve its problems. For Mead, effective human action is neither a matter of the fulfillment of individual drives (need satisfaction) nor of the achievement of individual desires (want satisfaction), but the realization of condition for fruitful, productive, and satisfying social interactions—for what he calls "creative sociality." It is, for Mead, the tenor of social relations at large as manifested in the staying power, the evolutionary survivability, of its practices and institutions that provides the crux of the "efficacy" through which a viable pragmatism must be implemented.

### *F. C. S. Schiller (1864–1937)*

Ferdinand C. S. Schiller, by contrast, espoused a personalistic pragmatism close to and appreciative of that of William James, though he claimed to have arrived there independently. And in fact Schiller's position was even more radical than James'. For while James saw knowledge as a personal reflection of objective, circumstances and conditions, Schiller regarded all knowledge—and indeed all so-called facts—as subjective through and through. Schiller characterized his own position as a "humanism" or "personalism," because of this stress upon the radically subjective and individualized. Rejecting altogether the absolutistic and monistic rationalism of radical idealism, he reemphasized the Protagorean dictum that man is (not just the measurer, but) the measure of all things. For him all "reality" and "truth" are no more than personal reflections of human intention and actions—the world as we have it is man-made artifact, the product of a vastly differentiated human creativity that is in large measure unfettered and free. This radically personalistic and subjectivistic cast of his pragmatism made Schiller's formulation of the doctrine a particularly inviting (and easy!) target for such early critics of pragmatism as Schiller's countryman Bertrand Russell.[44] He propounded such a one-sidedly extreme version of personalistic pragmatism as to engender more opposition than support for the doctrine.

### *C. I. Lewis (1883–1964)*

Clarence I. Lewis and Rudolf Carnap were pragmatists of a stripe rather different from their predecessors. For in their hands, pragmatism came to focus not on issues of effectiveness in factual inquiry—let alone on satisfactions in the conduct of life—but rather on the acceptability of claims in formal systems of logic or mathematics. Not the experiential knowledge of everyday life or of natural science, but the abstract truths of the formal sciences were the subject of their pragmatism. With Lewis, the fundamental fact that pragmatism had to address was the proliferation of different mathematical systems (different geometries, for example) and of different logical system (such as classical, modal, and many-valued logic). As Lewis saw it, this meant that there is no one single right system among competitive rivals. For when pragmatic utility is our guide, here the question is not

44. See, in particular, Bertrand Russell, "Pragmatism" in *Philosophical Essays*, pp. 87–126.

which system is correct but which system is optimal for the purposes at hand.

The framework of Lewis' reflections was already well formed before his 1929 magnum opus *Mind and the World Order*,[45] in which he proposed to project pragmatism into the domain of logic. A logical system, so he maintained, is a purely formal structure—abstract and detached from sensory experience so that impersonal facts are irrelevant to its contents. Therefore, contentions of the format "the thesis *T* obtains in the formalized logical system *L*" will be true analytically. But this, of course, pivots the issue of *T*'s actual acceptability upon that of *L*. And here Lewis took a pragmatic line, holding that we have to appraise the acceptability of entire systems on the pragmatic grounds of their efficacy with respect to the range of correlative purposes. As Lewis saw it, considerations of the format "The particular logical system *L* is the appropriate instrumentability with respect to a certain range of application" (e.g., "Intuitionistic logic is the proper instrument for developing arithmetic") provide the pivot on which the acceptability of the theses at issue in such systems depends. Only on the basis of experience—by trying and seeing—can one validate such judgments. Pragmatic success is once again our standard, but now the experiential data at issue are not sensory facts but cognitive facts about abstract relationships not success in accommodating observations but success in meeting the needs of efficient reasoning. And it is thus formal (inferential) rather than physical (experiential) practice that is at issue. "The thought which both rationalism and empiricism have missed is that there are principles, representing the initiations of mind, which impose upon experience no limitations whatsoever, but that such conceptions are still subject to alteration on

45. C. I. Lewis, *Mind and the World Order* (reprint, New York: Dover Publications, 1956). But see also C. I. Lewis, "A Pragmatic Conception of the A Priori," *The Journal of Philosophy* 20 (1923):169–77.

pragmatic grounds when the expanding boundaries of experience revealed their infelicity as intellectual instruments."[46]

Lewis extended this line of thought from a pragmatic validation of the a priori propositions of logic and mathematics to articulate also a neo-Kantian pragmatic account of the conceptual categories that afford the terms of reference for our thought about the world. He held that while it is indeed necessary to use a priori categories for the descriptive and explanatory characterization of experience, nevertheless these categories are not absolute and fixed but variable and capable of alteration or replacement in the light of our experience regarding what is useful and effective for these purposes.[47] The categories are thus a priori with respect to any particular inquiry or group thereof—but *not* with absolutely, respect to our inquiries-in-general. On this basis, Lewis contended, the pragmatic approach represents the proper way to assess both the acceptability of logical and mathematical systems and that of the fundamental presuppositions and principles of empirical inquiry.

However, in refusing to follow James and Dewey into an enlarged pragmatism of success with lived experiences at large, Lewis returned to the Peircean idea of a strictly epistemic pragmatism geared to efficacy with respect to our specifically cognitive operations.

### *Rudolf Carnap (1891–1970)*

Lewis was followed in his focus on logico-mathematical issues by Rudolf Carnap, who explicitly acknowledged this indebtedness.[48] Carnap maintained that the appropriateness (acceptability) of a formal system—say, classical *vs.* intuition-

---

46. C. I. Lewis, "A Pragmatic Conception of the *A Priori*," p. 176.
47. Ibid., pp. 169–77.
48. See Carnap's statement in P. A. Schilpp ed., *The Philosophy of Rudolf Carnap* (La Salle IL: Open Court, 1963), p. 861.

istic mathematics—lies in how effectively we can operate with the system at issue in the relevant functional context (calculation or mathematical demonstration, for example). Applicative utility is once again the key consideration here.

In much the same spirit as that of Lewis, Carnap maintained that two sorts of issues arise in communicative contexts: *system-external* questions about the existence of the entities that are supposedly available as objects of discussion, and *system-internal* questions about the substantive features that are being attributed to such objects. Internal issues have factual answers that can be substantiated through the rules and procedures of the given language-framework; external issues relate to the initial choice of that framework itself. As Carnap saw it, those external issues relating to the adoption of a particular linguistic framework are subject to his so-called Principle of Tolerance: "We have in every respect complete liberty with regard to the forms of language. Everyone, that is, is free to choose the rules of his language, and thereby his logic, in any way he wishes."[49] Or at least this is so insofar as considerations of theoretical general principles go, for such a decision is not actually a "cognitive" or "factual" but rather is a *practical* decision that can (and should) be motivated by functional consideration of purposive efficacy such as simplicity, efficiency, and fruitfulness. To this extent, then, Carnap moved in the direction of pragmatism. But then he came to a sticking point.

For while Carnap saw the choice among alternative frameworks as subject to constraints of rationality and was prepared to accept the finding of one framework's being more efficient and effective than another relative to certain purposes, he was unwilling to move from classing choices in the spectrum better / worse to classing them as correct / incorrect—and not even in the contextualized mode of "correct

49. Rudolf Carnap, *The Logical System of Language* (London: Kegan Paul Trench, 1937), p. xv.

for *this* particular application." For Carnap, applicative efficacy was not evidence of appropriateness but was the decisive factor in its own right. By thus totally disassociating the issues of utility and correctness, Carnap emptied pragmatic considerations of any evidential bearing upon matters in science or everyday life. Thus, for him, the superior utility of, for example, a framework of discussion based on the centrality of substantial things would not—even if established—support a claim that things / substances exist, and would not authorize truth-attribution for any claims to reality here.[50]

Carnap thus remained a strict conventionalist: his pragmatism is one of warranting the use of procedures on the basis of their utility while refusing to credit such consideration of purposive efficacy with any evidential bearing. He did not operate a pragmatic epistemology but set the epistemic and the pragmatic dimensions into a diametrically opposed contrast with one another. Carnap's pragmatism only warrants choice in matters of procedure and never provides for the substantiation of factual contentions, which, on his approach, one can never maintain as true but only as more or less probable. Pragmatic considerations here became a substitute rather than a basis for claims to matters of truth or existential fact. With Carnap a pragmatically oriented probability is all-predominant and matters of truth are consigned to oblivion.

### *Nelson Goodman (1906– )*

Nelson Goodman is yet another link in the chain of Harvard pragmatists.[51] His concern is for the epistemic

50. Rudolf Carnap, *Introduction to Symbolic Logic and its Applications* (New York: Dover Publications, 1958), p. 208.

51. The publication principally at issue in Goodman's pragmatics are *Fact, Fiction and Forecast* (Cambridge: Harvard University Press, 1954), *Ways of Worldmaking* (Indianapolis: Hackett, 1978), and with C. Z. Elgin, *Reconceptions* (Indianapolis: Hackett, 1988).

region of the domain. Rejecting foundationalism in all its forms, Goodman rejects certainly along with it and denies any prospect of tenable claims to truth. Epistemic worth—does not inhere in evidence or experience—empirical materials can always yield alternative credible systems. We humans make different belief-manifolds, different "worlds" for ourselves. To be sure, there are standards in operation here. However, the rationale of our beliefs—and of our belief-validity practices such as—induction—is entirely pragmatic. Thus, epistemic worth rests on utility, and since purposes are manifold there can be discordant results: beliefs useful in one context can be counterproductive in another. "We draw the line wherever we like, and change it as often as suits our purposes."[52]

The difficulty with Goodman's James-reminiscent cognitive pluralism is that it rests cognitive diversity or the diversity of purposes in a way that overlooks the holistic unity of human purposes—their systemic coherence under the aegis of generic human needs. For Goodman, practices and purposes are created equal. They are gift horses unto whose mouth we must not look. And this seems unrealistic. Consider a single analogy: a person needs nourishment and also rest. Obviously there is a potential tension here. But no less obviously this conflict is ultimately resolved by a higher level controlling purpose on the order of "leading a satisfying life"—one that is healthy and generally contentment-engendering. Analogously, the systemic impetus of cognition—the fact that we want not just answers to our questions but answers that make maximal sense overall—is bound to make for a cohesiveness awards a multitude of potentially divergent purposes. Goodman's pragmatism is still based on the radically disintegrative separateness of the isolated Cartesian knower. The systemic and communitarian strains of thought introduced by Hegel and emphati-

52. Goodman, *Ways of Worldmaking*, p. 114.

cally represented within the pragmatic tradition by John Dewey is entirely absent in Goodman. His fragmented Jamesean empiricism lacks the stabilizing force of a Peircean concern for a scientific community proceeding under standards validated by efficacy in the common pursuit of shared objectives. The fact is that "purposive efficacy" or "interest serving" afford a reasonable standard only when we are prepared to look into the validity of those purposes and interests in terms of their capacity to be productive rather than counterproductive in that critical matter of serving hence needs.

### *W. V. Quine (1908– )*

Quine's pragmatism took a line that was, in a way, even more radical than Carnap's. For with Quine the cognitive status of human language-formulated cognition as a whole—rather than that of some particular system or concept-framework—becomes the pivot upon which pragmatic considerations are to be hinged. To his mind, the issue of validation is uncompromisingly holistic.

Rejecting Carnap's probabilism, Quine returned to the earlier evolution-influenced standpoint of Dewey. And he followed Dewey in his commitment to a pragmatic approach to language as an instrumentality of human communicative practice. As he himself put it:

> Philosophically I am bound to Dewey by the rationalism that dominated his last three decades. With Dewey I hold that knowledge, mind, and meaning are part of the same world that they have to do with and that they are to be studied in the same empirical spirit that actuates natural science. There is no place for *a priori* philosophy.[53]

53. W. V. Quine, *Ontological Rationalilty and Other Essays* (New York: Columbia University Press, 1969), p. 26.

Like Dewey before him, Quine rejected the idea of a somehow absolute foundation for knowledge. For him, the authorizing basis of any such theory must lie in its broader role in our cognition, and specifically in its contribution to our scientific view of the world's modus operandi, recognizing the impracticability of claiming any absolutistic correspondence between a concept framework and the independent reality it purportedly depicts.

Quine is first and foremost a "naturalist" in regarding science as a court of final appeal. As he sees it, natural science constitutes an inquiry into reality which, while fallible and corrigible, is not answerable to any suprascientific tribunal, and needs no further justification. Observation and the hypothetico-deductive method provide for all that we need within science and all that we need for validating our claims about science as well.[54] And to this scientific naturalism Quine adds a Peirce-reminiscent touch of evolutionism in that for him scientific realism—the position that, as best we can possibly tell it, things really are as science depicts them to be—is simply part and parcel of our evolutionary imprinted cognitive endowment. "The very notion of an object at all, concrete or abstract, is a human contribution, a feature of our inherited approaches for organizing the amorphous matter of neural input."[55] But, of course, *how* we configure that "notion of an object" depends on the substantive state of things in the science of the day—a variable situation that turns on the comparative success of competing scientific theories. And so a deeply pragmatic perspective—one that encompasses explanatory utility, fallibility, success in prediction and control, and the like—enters into Quine's thought via his commitment to the primacy of scientific method. Quine therefore shares

---

54. W. V. Quine, *Theories and Things* (Cambridge MA: Harvard University Press, 1981), p. 72.
55. W. V. Quine, "Structure and Nature," *The Journal of Philosophy* 89 (1992):5–9; see p. 6.

the approach of C. I. Lewis in his pragmatic conception that our fundamental categories of thought, while indeed a priori in the local context of our particular investigations, are a posteriori in the wider setting of our experience-guided inquiry-at-large, and can always be challenged and changed under the pressure of enlarged experience.[56] For at the holistic macrolevel pragmatic considerations are determinative.

### *Donald Davidson (1917– )*

Donald Davidson represents a linkage between the logico-linguistic theories of W. V. Quine and the pragmatic tradition. Reacting against Quine's sense-experience foundationalism, Davidson rejects the idea that the acceptability of factual claims rests on their evidential grounding in our experience regarding reality's eventuations. According to Davidson: "We must give up the idea that meaning or knowledge is grounded in something [*viz.* sensory experience] that counts as an ultimate source of evidence. No doubt, meaning and knowledge depended on experience, and experience ultimately on sensation. But this is the 'depend' of causality, not of evidence or justification."[57] On this basis, Davidson sees it necessary to move in a different—essentially pragmatic—direction in matters of truth-validation, with success in the use of concept and belief as the crux and coherence as the key to success. And here, as

---

56. See C. I. Lewis, "A Pragmatic Conception of the A Priori," pp. 169–77. Quine acknowledges Lewis' influence in *Perspectives in Quine*, eds. R. B. Barrett and R. F. Gibson (Oxford: Basil Blackwell, 1990), p. 292. For a fuller account of Quine's pragmatism see Leemon B. McHenry, "Quine's Pragmatic Ontology," *The Journal of Speculative Philosophy* 9 (1995):147–58.
57. Donald Davidson, "A Coherence Theory of Truth and Knowledge," in *Truth and Interpretation: Perspectives on the Philosophy of Donald Davidson*, ed. Ernest La Pore (Oxford: Blackwell, 1986), pp. 313–14.

Davidson sees it, the proof of a coherence theory lies in its "claim that nothing can and as a reason for holding a belief except another belief."[58] The meaning of a belief lies in the issue of *how*, and its truth in the issue of *that* it conduces to systemic coherence within its wider belief environment.

From a pragmatist viewpoint, however, the problem of Davidson's approach lies in its half-heartedness. As James insisted and Dewey reemphasized, pragmatists want to abolish rigid dualisms, however well-entrenched they may be in philosophical deliberations. For pragmatists, rigid dualisms are generally anathema: with Peirce they question that between fact and belief (since fact just is what the community of inquirers will come to believe), with Quine that between the analytic and the synthetic, and with Davidson himself that between concept-schemes and substantive beliefs. And so it is somewhat ironic that Davidson's own position is predicated on subscription to what is simply just another rigid dualism, namely, that between causality on the one hand and evidence or justification on the other—between productive causes and cognitive reasons, concepts which the medievals fused in their generalized conception of *causa* but which the moderns since the time of Descartes have generally insisted on separating sharply.

It must surely be acknowledged that in the case of rational beings, these two factors of causality and justification come together in a conjoint coordination. For it is exactly here—in explaining the actions and reactions of a rational being—that these two must not be separated. A person's "experience of having a cat perception (of a suitably vivid sort)"—exactly because it is a cognitively significant experience—at once and concurrently constitutes the *cause* of *X*'s claiming that "The cat is on the mat" and affords *X* a reason for making this claim. In the cognitive experience of intelligent beings there are not separable regions of causes

58. Ibid., p. 310.

and of reasons: one and the same of experience does double duty in providing for both the ground and the reason of a belief. As William James maintained, a perception is actually "thought [with its reasons] and sensation [with its causes] *fused*."[59] The selfsame psychophysical state of things which, from the affected agent's own first-person internal perspective functions (i.e., is experienced) as reason-constituting also functions (i.e., is observed) from the observer's third-person external perspective as causally operative. Where human behavior is concerned, the cause / reason distinction is simply perspectival in representing different aspects of the same experiential transaction, the difference at issue being that between an insiders and an outsiders perspective. This sort of radical empiricism was a salient aspect of James' pragmatism and its absence signalizes a flaw in the inherent coherence of Davidson's position.

### *Hilary Putnam (1926– )*

Hilary Putnam exemplifies the continuity of Harvard's pragmatist tradition.[60] As Putnam sees it, pragmatism's salient idea is something that he (together with Wittgenstein, Rorty, and philosophical modernists generally) is prepared to endorse—namely, that it makes no sense to try to get at "the actual truth" of things if this is taken to involve anything like the Kantian contrast between "how things are in themselves" and "how things appear to us humans." Putnam has it that if *this* is what is at stake in the philosophical quest for truth, then the whole project must be abandoned

59. See the discussion in Hilary Putnam, *Pragmatism an Open Question*, (Oxford: Blackwell, 1995). p. 67.
60. Putnam's principal discussion of the subject is in *Pragmatism: An Open Question*. He also discusses James in several essays in Hilary Putnam, *Realism with a Human Face* (Cambridge, Mass.: Harvard University Press) 1990.

because the very idea of such a deeper truth is nonsense upon stilts (to use Jeremy Bentham's vivid expression), seeing that it is truth from our human standpoint that is the only thing that could possibly be of concern for us.[61] All this is decidedly reminiscent of Putnam's philosophical hero William James.

Moreover, Putnam's approach to pragmatism also returns to the wider perspective of James, Mead, and Dewey rather than to the narrower focus on logic, language, and mathematics favored by C. I. Lewis and Rudolf Carnap. He construes pragmatism as insisting upon the decisive role for normative appraisal of the quality of life as its inhabiters experience it. He quotes with approval Dewey's thesis:

> [Philosophy's] progress is criticism of beliefs, constitutions, customs, policies with regard to their bearing upon good. This does not mean their bearing upon *the* good, itself as something formulated and attained within philosophy. . . . For . . . philosophy . . . has no private access to good. As it accepts knowledge of facts and principles from those competent in science and inquiry, it accepts the goods that are diffused in human experience.[62]

Thus for Putnam, as for James and Dewey, pragmatism advances philosophy's project of enlightenment as an organon for criticism of accepted ideas of all sorts on the basis of practical considerations.

Putnam is highly effective at presenting Jamesian views in the contemporary idioms of philosophical discus-

---

61. The fundamental point is one that Putnam credits to Kant: "It does seem to me that Kant made a decisive advance over all process philosophers in giving up the idea that any description of the world can simply be a copy of the world" (p. 30). However, the credit for this particular insight actually belongs to Leibniz with his theory of well-founded phenomena.
62. Putnam, *Pragmatism an Open Question*, p. 51. The Dewey quote is from *Experience and Nature*, pp. 407–408.

sion. He is outstanding among contemporary expositions in his ability to describe James' thought in a way that at once renders it relevant to issues of contemporary debate and to highlight its philosophical creativity. Consider an example. In expounding his formula that truth is a matter of expediency—of success in application James is shockingly indecisive as to what exactly constitutes this sort of success—is it evidential adequacy, predictive efficacy, psychological congeniality, contextual fit and coherence, or what? To the frustration of his adherents and to the vexation of his interpreters, James will sometimes take the one line and sometimes the other. But here Putnam offers an ingenious resolution. A sensible pragmatism, he suggests, would not see this vacillation as a matter of inconsistency. It would, rather, exploit the idea that what is at issue is not an indecisive disjunction but a complex conjunction, and that true success "is a matter of satisfying these [multiple] desiderata simultaneously," so that the issue becomes "a matter of trade-offs rather than final rules."[63]

To his credit, Putnam seeks to free pragmatism from the anarchic relativism of the postmoderns. He writes:

> From the earliest of Peirce's Pragmatist writings, Pragmatism has been characterized by antiscepticism . . . [even while conceding] that there are no metaphysical guarantees to be had that even our most firmly held beliefs will never need revision. That one can be both fallibilistic *and* antisceptical is perhaps *the* basic insight in American Pragmatism. (*Pragmatism*, pp. 20–21)

But while Putnam is emphatic in his desire *that* our cognitive theorizing should move away from scepticism to objectivistic realism under the aegis of a pragmatism of the life-enhancing sort that he favors, he is by no means as

63. Putnam, *Pragmatism: An Open Question*, p. 10.

clear and detailed as one might wish on the questions of just *how* it will manage to do so.

*Richard Rorty (1931– )*

Richard Rorty's "pragmatism" is decidedly postmodern in its tendency to subjectivistic relativism. For as Rorty sees it, questions of truth and validity should not concern the philosopher at all: pragmatism insists "that one can be a philosopher precisely by being anti-Philosophical."[64] And despite his avowed attachment to Dewey (whom he deems one of the twentieth century's three most important philosophers, along with Martin Heidegger and Ludwig Wittgenstein), the threads of pragmatic thought that Rorty weaves together into his own so-called neopragmatism are substantially nihilistic in tenor and tendency. For Rorty, in effect, picture pragmatism as an essentially negative and deconstructionist position. According to him, pragmatism "says that truth is not the sort of thing one should expect to have a philosophically interesting theory about" (p. xiii). The pragmatist therefore advocates the "post-Philosophical culture [of] the philosopher who has abandoned pretensions to [traditionalistic] Philosophy" (p. xl). Such a pragmatism abandons any idea of rational quality controls on the processes of inquirers and question-resolving deliberations. As Rorty himself puts it:

> Let me sum up by offering a . . . characterization of pragmatism: it is the doctrine that there are no constraints on inquiry save conversational ones—no wholesale constraints derived from the nature of the objects, or of the mind, or of language, but only those retail constraints provided by the remarks of our fellow inquirers. . . . The

64. Richard Rorty, *Consequences of Pragmatism*, p. xiii.

> pragmatist tells us that it is useless to hope that objects will constrain us to believe the truth about them, if only they are approached with an unclouded mental eye, or a rigorous method, or a perspicuous language. . . . The only sense in which we are constrained to truth is that . . . we can make no sense of the notion that the view which can survive all objections might be false. But objections—conversational constraints—cannot be anticipated. There is no method for knowing *when* one has reached the truth, or when one is closer to it than before.[65]

It is curious, however, to see how readily a doctrine that rejects "wholesale constraints" is willing to offer wholesale generalizations. For Rorty has it that "truth, on this view I am advocating, is the normal result of normal discourse,"[66] while ignoring that discourse, normal or otherwise, takes us no further—even at best and most—than to what its participants happen to *purport* to be true. Yet between purported truth and actual truth there is a chasm fixed—certainly in theory and frequently in practice Truth as such is, after all, only too often something very different from what people say—and even what they agree upon. It is not the product of *actual* discourse, nor yet of *normal* discourse, but only (at best) of *ideal* discourse: discourse developed on appropriate principles under optimal conditions. To say that there are no rational constraints on the products in inquiry apart from those imposed by the conventions and practices of the inquirers is giving them unrealistically inflated credit. The community may agree by convention what words like "cat" and "mat"—or "just" and "unjust"—mean and what the accepted criteria for relating such terms to one another are to be. But once these matters of convention are settled, the issue of whether a cat is actually on the mat or whether

65. Rorty, *Consequences of Pragmatism*, pp. 165–66.
66. Richard Rorty, *Philosophy and the Mirror of Nature* (Princeton: Princeton University Press, 1978).

self-serving deceit is unjust hinges on other matters—matters that relate to the world's realities. To think that the former is the whole story whereas the latter is a negotiable irrelevancy is to take a stance that is, to put it mildly, highly problematic.

Rorty explains:

> If we give up this hope [for getting at the truth of things in contexts of inquiry regarding nature's ways] we shall lose what Nietzsche called "metaphysical comfort," but we may gain a renewed sense of community. Our identification with our community—. . . our intellectual heritage—is heightened when we see this community as *ours* rather than *nature's*, *shaped* rather than *found*, one among many which men have made. In the end, the pragmatists tell us, what matters is our loyalty to other human beings clinging together in the dark, not our hope of getting things right. James, in arguing . . . that "the trail of the human serpent is over all" was reminding us that our glory is our participation in fallible and transitory human projects, not in our obedience to personal nonhuman constraints.[67]

It is clear that this sort of pragmatism rests on a scepticism which—exactly in the manner of the ancient Sophists—proposes to abandon objectivity and impersonally rational standards and to rely on communal consensus alone, subordinating science to the social policy of shared opinion. And such a position is very questionable. Surely an inquirer who has no way of knowing that the truth has been reached with regard to a question like "Can people talk meaningfully with regard to fact-contravening hypotheses?" would be in an unhappy predicament. There are many constraints to maintaining the thesis "It is wrong to inflict needless pain on others," but the conventions governing of polite (or "conventional") conversation is scarcely one of them.

---

67. Rorty, *Consequences of Pragmatism*, p. 166.

When William James wrote that "Human arbitrariness has done away with the divine necessity of scientific logic,"[68] he half regretted this supposed fact. But Rorty rejoices in it. For him, the desirable stance in that of the "ironists"—those "never quite able to take themselves seriously," because of a recognition of the limited and imperfect nature of their own cognitive positions. For Peirce's fallibilism notwithstanding, commitment to doing the very best that we can manage in the circumstances makes good rational sense. Rorty's dismissive "ironism" embraces the insouciant indifference of the standpoint that "hundred years hence it all won't matter anyhow." One recent defender of his position declares: "To many contemporary pragmatists, Rorty's disinterest in the practical consequences of intellectual discourse—his valuing of a discourse that makes no difference—disqualifies his membership [in the pragmatic movement]."[69] This concession is pretty much on target.

## 2. The Diversity of Pragmatisms

As the preceding survey shows, pragmatism has not managed to achieve a uniform stability but has come to be construed very differently by different philosophers. Nor has pragmatism's practice always lived up to its own teachings. Already Peirce himself became uneasy about the label when he witnessed the deformations of his brainchild at the hands of William James. The fact is that pragmatism has been many things to many people and this characterization

68. James, *Pragmatism*, p. 57.
69. Lenore Langsdorf and Andrew R. Smith in the introduction of their anthology, *Recovering Pragmatism's Voice: The Classical Tradition, Rorty, and the Philosophy of Communication* (Albany: State University of New York Press, 1995), p. 7.

has been applied over the years to a considerable variety of different theses, theories, and teachings—positions of a diversified and sometimes even doctrinally conflicting tendency. But the terrain at issue here, though diverse, is philosophically instructive and interesting. It well deserves closer examination.

### *Ordinary Discourse*

In everyday usage, "pragmatic" contrasts with "principled." Pragmatic individuals or policies are concerned for *expediency* instead of *principles*—they prioritize the achievement of desired results, without much scrupulous care about the ways and means of their realization. "The ends justify the means" is their motto. In particular, pragmatism in its political sense turns on the illustrative contrast between the "principled" statesman who pursues changeless aims through acting on fixed rules and stable goals, and the "pragmatic" politician whose position is flexible and whose opinions and actions bend with the wind of shifting conditions and circumstances. Pragmatic, in this sense, involves to what is practical, down-to-earth, and opportunistic, as opposed to that which is idealistic and scrupulous about long-term consequences and larger causes. It is—or should be—clear that this sort of thing is not at issue with philosophical pragmatism.

However, "pragmatism" in the everyday-usage sense of the term and in its philosophical sense agree in one important respect. Philosophical pragmatism also accepts that absolute perfection—the idealized very best—is generally unrealizable. And it therefore insists that we must be prepared to accept that the best that we can achieve in practice has to be acknowledged as good enough: that it makes no sense—be it in matters of knowledge or planning or action or evaluation—to regard the best that can be had as just not good enough. For example, consider the sceptic who says that even the best "knowledge" we can achieve still does not qualify as genuine—as altogether certain and absolute "Get real!" replies the pragmatist: "Neither with theoretical knowledge nor with anything else does it make sense to ask for something that simply cannot be had." Against more idealistic tendencies of thought, pragmatism thus takes the realistic position that we have no sensible alternative but to make do with the best we can get.

The tenor of the term's ordinary usage therefore does carry over to philosophical pragmatism to some extent. For, on the one hand, we have a positive and cognitivistic (Peircean) pragmatism based on the *primacy* of practice over principles—through taking the systematic realization of successful results to provide the adequacy standard for the validation of principles themselves. And, on the other hand, there is also a negativistic (Jamesean) pragmatism that in effect dismisses general principles and sees the issue of successful practice as self-sufficient in and of itself. The one validates principles through subordination, the other simply dismisses them. There are thus two very different versions of pragmatism, the objectivist (via justification through systematic impersonal success in effective task-fulfillment) and the subjectivistic (via de-legitimation of stable principles through the relativistic idea that different measures meet the objectives of different individuals or groups). Curiously, then, pragmatism manifests a tension between two totally opposed versions—a theory of legitimation (validation) on the one hand and a theory of de-legitimation (deconstruction) on the other. Throughout the subject's recent history, the two have been emplaced in an unhappy but enduring union. (The next chapter will return to this issue.)

## *Semantical Pragmatism: Pragmatic Theory of Meaning*

Another mode of pragmatic reflection arises in the theory of language. Semantical pragmatism is a doctrine in the theory of language which has it that the meaning of natural-language words resides not in a formulaic definition that can be established explicitly but in their functional mode of operation—specifically in how their use influences, shapes, and canalizes behavior. Words are seen as instruments for the guidance and direction of human action (communicative action included), and what a word means is encapsulated in the way in which it functions in this regard. Meaning, that is to say, is a matter of the ways and means of language employment. At bottom, it resides in how the use of words impacts upon people's behavior rather than how words interrelate with one another in the abstract. The fixation of meaning is thus an applicative (practical / operational) rather than purely informative (theoretical / intellectual) issue—it is ultimately a matter not so much of what people *think* as of what people *do*.

And this approach to the semantics of *words* also carries over to a pragmatic construal of *statements*. To specify the meaning of a statement does not require giving further purely verbal reformulations, but rather calls for indicating what difference its acceptance makes for people's behavior. To grasp a statement's meaning is accordingly to understand how its endorsement does or would affect human action—the difference its acceptance makes for our behavioral and communicative practice. At the level of both words and statements, semantical pragmatism therefore takes action rather than conceptualization as such to be the crux of the matter. In sum, for the semantical pragmatist, the meaning of linguistic items lies in what we do with them in actual use.

In line with this approach, meaning-pragmatism sees language as an instrument for the guidance of human action and interaction. It represents a functional or instrumental approach to language geared to apprehending the role of language-use within the wider context of human action within which our communicative practices function.

## *Epistemic Pragmatism: The Pragmatic Criteriology of Truth*

The so-called pragmatic theory of truth is predicated on the idea that there is an intimate and integral connection between the applicative success of acting on a belief and its truth. It is often said—principally by opponents of pragmatism—that this connection is supposed to be one of *meaning identity*: that pragmatists stand committed to the thesis that characterizing a proposition as "true" or as "engendering applicative success" comes to the same thing. And this—so pragmatism's opponents charge—is, of course, absurd on the face of it, because it flies in the face of the all too evident circumstance that false beliefs can and do underwrite successful action in many particular circumstances and situations. (Moreover, it conflicts blatantly with pragmatism's characteristic rejection of such formulaic equivalences.) But, of course, the use of pragmatic success *as a test-criterion for truth* is something else again, something very different from a doctrine of meaning determination, since semantical meaning-equivalency is one thing and an evidential coordination another. And exactly this evidential-criteriological approach is what a reasonable truth pragmatism would propose to take—seeing in the consideration of truth and applicative success not a thesis regarding the meaning of truth but a specification of how a practical approach to truth-determination can proceed. An evidential approach to pragmatism therefore takes the line that successful guidance of implementation in action provides a useful and effective test-criterion (or standard) of propositional truth. (Even Peirce, who saw the relationship between truth and applicative success as tighter than merely evidential, was able to implement this approach only because he proposed closing the gap between evidence and meaning by looking to success only in the idealized long run.)

It can plausibly be argued that much of the controversy between pragmatists and their opponents could have been averted by paying closer heed to the crucial distinction between a definition of truth (or an explanation of *what truth is*) and a criterion of truth (or a means for determining *what is to be counted as true*). To the detriment of their cause, pragmatism's critics all too often mistook its concern for the second as one for the first.

### *Fallibilism and Scepticism*

Pragmatist thinkers of a postmodern orientation are drawn to a version of this approach that represents not so much an innovative view about truth-determination as an invitation to the all-out rejection and abandonment of the traditional idea of truth. Following some moves in this direction by William James, this line was espoused, no less enthusiastically, by Schiller and Rorty. Within the pragmatic movement, there has developed an inclination to think that the fact of fallibilism—that is, science and ordinary life are all too often wrong in our views of what is true—should be taken to indicate that the idea that inquiry is the pursuit of truth should be abandoned. After all, if the truth is somewhere between hard and impossible to come by, then there is little we can do with it.

But this, of course, is treason to the motivating root idea of Peircean pragmatism. And when he saw James espousing this truth-negativism in the name of his doctrine, Peirce was so horrified that he set about changing its designation from *pragmatism* to *pragmaticism* in order to distance himself from this sort of nihilistic view. For what he himself strove to establish was—all too clearly—not an abandonment of truth claims but a process for their plausible, rationally cogent validation. The fact is that fallibilism does not constrain scepticism. The circumstance that our hold on the truth is insecure no more indicates that truth should be consigned to limbo than the fact that our hold on life is insecure indicates that we should commit suicide.

### *Moral and Political Pragmatism*

Already William James projected pragmatism beyond its Peircean focus on matters of meaning and truth into the range of a personalistic concern for the conduct of life. And with Dewey and Mead this projection was extended yet further into the broader social and political sphere. Pragmatism's traditional focus upon success in matters of the application and implementation of beliefs was now extended to the evaluation of social and political programs, processes, and arrangements in terms of their capacity to enhance the quality of life of people-in-general. Pragmatism's orientation was thus shifted from cognitive to practical concerns. It now became a tool not for evaluating statements or personal beliefs but for assessing public policies and practices. A substantially different range of issues thus came to the forefront, and pragmatism became transmuted into an instrumentality of social reform.

All in all, then, there can be no question that in the course of its development, pragmatically oriented thought has worked itself out in a considerable variety of doctrinal directions.

## 3. The Meaning of Pragmatism's Variations

Recognition of the inherent diversity and variation of pragmatism goes back to Arthur O. Lovejoy's classic 1908 paper on "The Thirteen Pragmatisms."[70] Lovejoy's thirteen pragmatisms are as follows:

1. and 2. A semiotic pragmatism holding that the *meaning* of propositions pivots on future consequences. This divides into two parts: (1) consequences to be anticipated if the proposition is true, and (2) consequences to be anticipated if people accept the proposition.
3. An epistemic pragmatism holding that the *verification* or substantiation of a proposition pivots on the realization of the future expectations that they authorize.
4. The semantical thesis that propositions are not true or false timelessly but eventually acquire truth or falsity according to their inherent predictions in due course "work out" in the sense of being realized or disconfined.
5. The cognate semantical thesis that results when "working out" is construed, not predictively as being borne out by events, but rather as proving useful (productive) in applicative practice.
6. The metaphysical doctrine that the future is "open" in the sense that the truth or falsity of claims about it is not, as yet, determined in a definite way. (Proportions about the future thus are, or can be, devoid of a truth status.)
7. The psychological thesis that people's acceptance of the truth of propositions pivots on their providing "the maximal combination of satisfactions."
8. The epistemic doctrine that the truth of a proposition is to be assessed in terms of its "satisfyingness" in a way that transcends the specifically cognitive satisfactions to conclude any sort of satisfaction elsewhere.
9. This is tantamount to Number 8 with the "satisfyingness" at issue taken to include the specifically *cognitive* satisfactions (in ways that transcend the purely predictive concerns of Number 3).

70. Arthur O. Lovejoy, "The Thirteen Pragmatisms," *The Journal of Philosophy and Scientific Methods* 5 (1908):5–39; reprinted in his *The Thirteen Pragmatisms and Other Essays* (1983; reprint, Baltimore: Johns Hopkins Press, 1963).

10. This is the thesis that "axioms are postulates"—that truth can be *made* (rather than discovered) and that this making can be validated as practical need—that is, the satisfaction of our human requirements.
11. The psychological doctrine that our human mental faculties and processes have so evolved that assent to certain propositions—such as "pain is bad"—is (not merely useful but) effectively unavoidable for us.
12. The stance of maintaining the legitimacy (and indeed coequal legitimacy) of assenting to those propositions which are needed (1) to make intelligible sense of our experience, (2) to facilitate our moral commitments, and (3) to satisfy our emotional needs and esthetic inclinations.
13. The meaning-as-function idea of the semiotic primacy of purpose inherent in the circumstance that every concept, idea, belief, or proposition comes to be what it is because of the purpose it serves—that is, through its relation to our ends and plans of action.

Upon surveying this ground, Lovejoy proceeded to classify his thirteen pragmatisms into four groups, essentially as follows:

I. Semiotic (Meaning-Determinative) Pragmatism: Pragmatic theories of meaning
—Numbers 1, 2, 13

II. Semantical (Truth-Determinative) Pragmatism: A pragmatic theory about the nature (or definition) of truth
—Number 3

III. Epistemological Pragmatism: Pragmatic theories about the criteriology of truth (or tests of the validity of judgment)
—Numbers 4, 5, 7, 8, 9, 10, 11, 12

IV. Metaphysical Pragmatism: Pragmatism as an ontological theory about the nature of reality
—Number 6

Lovejoy therefore saw pragmatism as a mélange of different (and in some instances rival) contentions.[71] And he regarded this state of affairs as virtually fatal to pragmatism's claims as a meaningful philosophical position.

But this view of the matter is very questionable. The consideration that pragmatism overall is a theoretical stance of a general orientation rather than a single definite doctrine which can be developed along rather different lines—does not really constitute a valid objection to it. It is simply an indication that, like other philosophical positions (idealism, empiricism, materialism), pragmatism can be elaborated in different directions. Pragmatism's prismatically many-sided nature means that the prime question for philosophical deliberation is not "Is pragmatism plausible?" but rather "Can really plausible versions of pragmatism be articulated?"

It would accordingly be a grave error to interpret this sort of diversification as constituting a valid criticism—let alone refutation—of pragmatism. The lesson is simply that here, as elsewhere, a philosopher should be specific about the views he intends to propose or discuss. And the sensible question will therefore not take the form "Is pragmatism plausible?" but rather "Can a plausible version of pragmatism be articulated and substantiated as such?" The ultimate test of a many-sided and internally diversified doctrine like pragmatism is surely not that of the question "Is there some version of pragmatism that is in some way deficit and unacceptable?" but rather that of the opposite question "Is there some version of pragmatism that is in its own way adequate and acceptable?" And it is this approach to the issue that will constitute the guiding principle of the present book.

---

71. The subsequent emergence of social pragmatism made matters still worse in this regard.

# CHAPTER TWO

# *Pragmatism in Crisis*

## *Synopsis*

*(1) C. S. Peirce, the founder of pragmatism, saw in the pragmatic approach a means to objectivity by providing a reality principle for testing of the adequacy of man-made ideas. (2) With other pragmatists like James, however, the doctrine became personalized and subjectivized. (3) And this objectivity-undermining tendency was present in a different form with those who, like Dewey, gave pragmatism a social and culturally relativistic construction. (4) In the hands of F. C. S.. Schiller and R. Rorty this relativistic, objectivity-negating pragmatism reached an acme of negativism in its deconstruction of concepts like truth and validity and its rejection of impersonal standards of objective cogency. (5) There is, however, no good reason why a Peircean, objectivistic construction of pragmatism should be abandoned. On the contrary: such an approach can meet many of the objections traditionally made to pragmatism. (6) In fact, the most promising version of pragmatism is one that focuses upon general methods and standards, hinging the issue of specific results upon the outcome of using those pragmatically validated instrumentalities (rather than themselves being directly secured by pragmatic means). Such a second-level pragmatism*

*can at once be true to Peirce's root objective insights and overcome the sorts of objections that hav traditionally been made against the pragmatic approach.*

## 1. The Guiding Idea of the Pragmatic Program

A noteworthy—and distinctly curious—aspect of contemporary American philosophy relates to the fate of pragmatism, which has undergone a remarkable deformation from its original conception. Many—indeed most—philosophers nowadays think of pragmatism as something radically different from what was originally at issue with this conception. And, oddly enough, this latter-day sort of pragmatism is not a "new, improved version" but a markedly inferior product.

In following up this idea, let us begin at the beginning.

Classical pragmatism as envisioned by Charles Sanders Peirce was designed to provide a standard of objectivity, a test of the appropriateness of our factual beliefs. Its motivating rationale lay in the question: How are we to tell that our beliefs about the world—and our scientific claims above all—are objectively *true* and indeed (and even more fundamentally) that they are actually *meaningful* in characterizing reality in the way that we intend? Truth as traditionally conceived is a matter of agreement with reality (*adaequatio ad rem*), but, of course, we cannot tell what is really so *independently* of our beliefs, so as to be able to test these beliefs in terms of their agreement with this otherwise predetermined truth. However, as Peirce saw it, what we can do—and all that we can do—is to act on our beliefs and take note of the results. We can implement them in application to real-world conditions in the setting of ordinary life experience or, better yet, of scientific observation and experimentation, and *then* proceed to see if this provides for successful prediction of and effective control over the observed course of events. The obvious standard for the validation of our beliefs with respect to their claims to meaningfulness and truth lies in their capacity over the long run to convince rational inquirers of their cogency. And applicative efficacy is the best available means for doing this. Sensible believing is as such believing does, so to speak. So, in effect, reasoned C. S. Peirce.

The founding father of this quintessentially American tendency of thought therefore held that pragmatism affords a cogent *standard* for assessing the merit of our cognitive productions (ideas, theories, methods, procedures)—a standard whose basis of validity reaches outside the realm of pure theory into the domain of real-world actuality by way of the successful practical applications and implementations of such thought-instruments upon issues that concern the scientific community of rational inquirers. The guiding idea of pragmatism—in relation to knowledge, at any rate—is that propositional knowledge that not only enjoys no priority over operational how-to knowledge but even stands subordinate to it. The crux of our knowledge of things does lie in their descriptive characterization; rather it is a matter of knowing what to do with them—how they can function in the setting of our own doings and dealings. Even theoretical knowledge itself is something that has to be discovered, formulated, confirmed, systematized—and all this stands subject to processes of the how-to-do-it sort. In Peirce's hands, pragmatism certainly did not endorse the abandonment of principles; on the contrary, its task was to provide a high road to the experientially mandated confirmation and consolidation of principles on the basis of the effectiveness of their applicability in practice.

Pragmatism was thus intended in the mind of its originator as a doctrine for the rational substantiation of knowledge claims—in the realm of empirical knowledge above all. The root idea was that (1) the meaning of term or conception is constituted by the use that we make of it in the course of our communicative operations and other activities; and (2) it is appropriate and warranted to class a proposition involving such conceptions as true insofar as and to the extent that such applications are successful and effective in enabling us to realize the correlative aims and purposes. Alike by training and disposition, Peirce was a natural scientist. For him the pragmatically pivotal factors of "successful application" and "purposive efficiency" were geared to physical operations in the natural world, with the activity of a scientific laboratory seen as the principal model. For Peirce, then, what mattered was exactly the sort of pragmatic "success" at issue with the applicative efficacy at stake in science—success at prediction and control. Practice (*praxis*) is to serve as the arbiter of theory (*theoria*). Not personal satisfaction but objective efficacy is what matters for fixing opinion in a community of rational inquirers.

And so, as it originally took shape in Peirce's thought, pragmatism was certainly not designed to be at odds with general principles. Rather, it took the ingenious line of using applicative efficacy—functional effectiveness, if you will—as the adequacy standard for our cognitive resources. The leading idea was that those principles, which prove to be most successful in the course of utilization and application, are (for that very reason) to be taken to be optimal. Practice, in sum, is to monitor theory: theory is to be evidentiated through its capacity to provide for successful product. We are not to abandon principles for the sake of expediency in the manner of a so-called pragmatic politician, but rather to insist on principles—albeit on exactly those expedient principles of process that prove themselves to be systematically effective in application. This, roughly speaking, is how pragmatism stood in the thought of C. S. Peirce.[1]

1. One contemporary philosopher who acknowledges and prizes this harder, more rigoristically and "tough-minded" Peircean sort of pragmatism is Susan Haak, whose articles on the subject go back to 1976. See her papers: "The Pragmatists Theory of Truth," *The British Journal for the Philosophy of Science* 27 (1976):231–49; "Pragmatism and

## 2. The Jamesean Transformation and Its Aftermath

Other pragmatists, however, generally saw the matter in a very different light. They envisioned subjective satisfactions rather than objectively determinable functional efficacy as being the aim of the enterprise. It is instructive to examine how this deconstructive transformation of pragmatism has come about and to consider its implications and ramifications—as well as the prospects for its avoidance.

William James in particular had an agenda very different from that of Peirce. He was concerned less with the modus operandi of nature than with the psychology of humans, and his interests focused upon matters of affectivity and religion rather than upon the physical machinations of the natural world. In his characteristically jaunty way he explained:

> Any idea that will carry us prosperously from any part of our experience to any other part, linking things satisfactorily, working securely, simplifying, saving labor, is true for just so much.[2]

What James cared about in articulating his pragmatism was "success" in living—leading a satisfying life in terms of personal happiness and contentment. And James gave this idea a distinctly subjectivistic construction: what makes

---

Ontology: Peirce and James," *Revue Internationale de Philosophy* 31 (1977):377–400; "Can James's Theory of Truth be Made More Satisfactory?" *Transactions of the Charles S. Peirce Society* 20 (1984): 269–78;"Pragmatism," in Nicholas Bunnin and E. P. Tsui-James eds., *The Blackwell Companion to Philosophy* (Oxford: Basil Blackwell, 1996), pp. 643–61; "Concern for Truth: What it Means, Why it Matters," *Annals of the New York Academy of Sciences* 775 (1996):57–63; "The First Rule of Reason," in Jacqueline Brunning and Paul Forster eds., *The Rule of Reason: The Philosophy of Charles Sanders Peirce* (Toronto: University of Toronto Press, 1997), pp. 241–60; "'We Pragmatists . . .': Peirce and Rorty in Conversation," *Partisan Review* 64 (1997):91–107.

2. James, *Pragmatism*, p. 34.

you happy might well be something quite different from what makes me happy. For James, pragmatism was therefore a way of loosening things up. Where Peirce focused on the established goals of a communal project of natural sciences—rational inquiry into objective facts—James, by contrast, took a personalistic approach geared to individual psychological satisfaction.

Still, when G. E. Moore mocked William James' contention that "true ideas pay,"[3] he was so focused on what people might ordinarily mean by saying this sort of thing that he did not concern himself sufficiently with what James actually *did* mean, ignoring altogether the cautions and qualification that James attaches to assertions of this tendency. The sort of satisfactions that mattered to James were not typified by the crass euphoria that accompanied the conclusion of a profitable business deal. James was decidedly reluctant to say the sorts of things with which Moore and his friend Russell charged him. And, of course, Peirce was even further removed from this sort of position. For pragmatists in the tradition of Peirce, the truth-indicative success of proposition is certainly not a matter of economic affluence or social acclaim or public popularity.

After all, how pragmatic considerations should be brought to bear is something that very much depends on the circumstances. For it itself is a pragmatic issue where considerations of effectiveness are paramount. Clearly if the question at hand relates to the conduct of a happy life, then matters of life-satisfaction can and should be brought into it. But if the question at hand is one of the truth of historical claims then the matter stands differently. It might be eminently distressing to discover that grandfather was a horsethief but this is not a consideration that bears on the truth of this contention.

3. Moore, "William James' Conception of Truth," pp. 123–46.

Still, whereas Peirce's pragmatism looked to applicative efficacy as an acid test of impersonal adequacy—an individual-transcending reality principle able to offset the vagaries of personal reactions—various later pragmatists followed William James' lead in turning their backs on this pursuit of universalized objectivity. For Peircean pragmatism's generalized concern with "what works out *for anyone* (for humans in general) by impersonal standards," they substituted a subjectivistic egocentrism of "what works out *for us*"—those of some limited in-group—in our own subjective assessment. In their hands, the defining objective that gave the pragmatic tradition its initiating impetus—the search for objective and impersonal standards—now shattered into a fragmentation of communities in the parochial setting of limited concerns. There are no person indifferently true statements about the world; the adequacy of any way of construing it is relative to an individual's particular makeup and subjective aims.

In this way, so Peirce himself already believed, James hijacked and—as Peirce thought—corrupted pragmatism.[4] Its founder to the contrary not withstanding, pragmatism assumed a life of its own. As James already exemplified, pragmatism was to be well beyond its inaugurating ideas and interests to develop in very different, and decidedly less objectivistic directions. Nor did this process stop with William James.

In recent years, pragmatism has been further transmogrified by theorists who have quite other axes to grind. In their hands, too, it has become something very different from its Peircean original—an instrument, not for pursuing objective validity, but rather one for demolishing the very idea of objectivity in these matters. In this way, pragmatism has been transformed step-by-step with postmodern theorists from William James to Richard Rorty into a means for

4. As noted above, Peirce even proposed to rename his doctrine as "pragmaticism" to distance it from what James was up to.

authorizing a free and easy "anything goes" parochialism that casts objectivity to the winds. We have here a total dissolution—a deconstructionism or indeed destruction—of the Peircean approach that saw the rational validity of intellectual artifacts to reside in the capacity to provide effective guidance in matters of prediction, planning, and intervention in the course of nature.

### 3. Postmodern Pragmatism and its Contrary

As these considerations indicate, pragmatism's development has seen an ever widening split between what might be called a "pragmatism of the left" that regards this position as a doorway to flexibility and variability—to cognitive relativity and pluralism—and a "pragmatism of the right" that sees the position as a source of stability, a pathway to cognitive security and uniformity. The latter is the pragmatism of C. S. Peirce, C. I. Lewis, and, among contemporaries, of Hilary Putnam, Susan Haak, and the present writer; the former is the pragmatism of William James, F. C. S. Schiller, and Richard Rorty. Although they share a common label, the two approaches represent diametrically opposed tendencies of thought.

The pragmatism of the left is inexorably drawn to the Jamesean approach of "what works for the satisfaction of people's variable wishes and preferences." That of the right, by contrast, is concerned with what is efficiently / effective for the satisfaction of universal needs (general human desiderata). The one views the aim of the enterprise as a matter of loosening things up, of overcoming delimiting restraints; the other as a matter of tightening things up, of providing for and implementing rationally acceptable standards of impersonal cogency and appropriateness.

The pragmatists of the left take roughly the following line:

> The core of pragmatism is utilization of the standard of "what works." But this splinters apart when we add the question: For whom? Different people have different purposes—different needs, preferences, and goals. They have a different personality-structure (as per William James' tough-minded and tender-minded). And much the same is the case with different groups. Accordingly, pragmatism countenances a live-and-let-live multiplicity of views that is as broad and flexible as the range of human idiosyncrasy and cultural variation.

Such a pragmatism of the left looks to the doctrine as a means of loosening up our thinking—of asserting its idiosyncratic and parochial diversity. It seeks to liberate our thought from impersonal constraints in the interests of achieving an outcome whose acceptability is subjectivistic, personalistic, and relativistic. The crux of such a freewheeling ("postmodernist") pragmatism lies in its abandonment of the ideal of objectivity—its dismissal of the traditional theory of knowledge's insistence upon judging issues by impersonal or of any rate person-indifferent standards. For the objective issue of efficacy in the pursuit of a generic even universal project, this approach to pragmatism substitutes the achievement of the idiosyncratic satisfactions of a person or group. Thus, relativized to matters of individual taste, pragmatic efficacy in now viewed as a matter of either personal preference or social convention—the mores of the tribe.

The pragmatism of the right stands diametrically opposed to these disintegrative tendencies. It sees pragmatism's concern for efficacy as a means of substantiation, solidification, and objectification. The pragmatists of the right take roughly the following line:

> Pragmatism is concerned with what works—with the effective and efficient achievement of purpose. And the purposes at issue are not idiosyncrasies of individuals, but rather those collective, across-the-board human enterprises whose rationale is rooted in the nature of the human condition at large. Our empirical knowledge, in particular, is concerned with the achievement of active (interactionistic) and passive (predictive) *control over nature*. Those ways of proceeding which prove themselves effective and efficient here are *ipso facto* substantiated, so that people engaged in the project are rationally impelled to adopt them. We may propose, but nature disposes—it is reality not we ourselves that is the arbiter of what works in relation to our actions in the world. Pragmatism is a road that leads not to subjectivity but to objectivity; it speaks not for relativistic preferences but for objective constraints.[5]

Such an approach looks to pragmatism as a "reality principle" that imposes rather than abolishes constraints and limitations. Whether the key opens the lock or jams it or whether the mushroom nourishes of kills us is not dependent on the predilections of people but on the modus operandi of impersonal nature in a way that is in practice determinable by anyone and everyone. Its emphasis is on effectiveness in goal attainment. What actually works for the realization of human needs is, after all, something independent of our idiosyncratic wants and preferences. It is this impersonal line of consideration—and it alone—that matters for the universalistic pragmatism of the right, which will hear nothing of variant, alternative, and yet equally appropriate modes of efficacy.

A "pragmatism of the left" is oriented to the local and personal. By contrast, a pragmatism of the right is oriented

---

5. The author's fullest defense of this version of pragmatism is in *Methodological Pragmatism* (Oxford: Basil Blackwell, 1977).

towards the global and universal, seeking to reach out beyond parochial limits towards the community of rational people at large. Its position is that expediency in relation to the teleology of science—explanation, prediction, and control above all—constitutes our best operating criterion for the truth of a belief. And it takes this line because it holds that nature knows no favorites—that in matters of belief and action a decision process that is geared to the impersonal standard of successful applications provides an acid test for the objective cogency which alone affords a correct view of the world and its ways. You can choose your goals, but the effectiveness of the means for their realization is wholly outside your control. Whether those ideas and beliefs actually work or not—whether the engine starts or the bulb lights—is not a matter of social custom but of the world's impersonal ways.

The "pragmatism of the right" therefore pivots on a self-subsistent and person-indifferent reality principle—its cutting edge lies not with people's idiosyncratic convictions but with the world's ways as themselves in principle determinable through rational inquiry. Such a position has its roots in C. S. Peirce's commitment to the idea that, given that our intellectual mechanisms are part and parcel of our evolutionary heritage, it is clear that the prime function of thought is to facilitate effective action in the service of our nature-mandated wants and needs.

Pragmatism is sometimes seen as a *via negativa* philosophy—a mere negation of the quest for certainty: "We cannot get at the real, ultimate truth of things but must settle for what suffices for the needs of practice." This, however, is not pragmatism, but merely academic scepticism revivified. Pragmatism properly understood is a positive doctrine—not one that *substitutes* practical efficacy for truth, but one that involves practice as our best available *evidential test* of truth. This, at any rate, is the stance of a right-oriented (and, one is tempted to add, right-minded) pragmatism.

This harder, less wishy-washy form of pragmatism is accordingly characterized by four key features: (1) it adopts an objectivistic stance that averts the fragmentation of subjectivistic relativism; (2) it is geared universalistically to the needs and interests of human beings at large, and not just to the wants of some small-scale contingently constituted subgrouping (let alone the idiosyncratic preferences of individuals); therefore, (3) it locates the crux for the quality control of our cognitive proceedings, not in the sphere of diversified human wishes and desires but in the impersonal dealings of nature in their (often unwelcome) impact upon us so that pragmatic "success" pivots on the impersonal issue of functional efficacy in the achievement of objectives mandated for us by the inexorable demands of a world not of our own designing—something that we clearly do not make up as we go along but that lies in the objective nature of things.[6] Finally, (4) it places emphasis on an impersonally normative rationality that enables it to implement this pursuit of objectivity.

On this basis, pragmatists of the right tend to follow Peirce into an adherence to metaphysical realism. As they see it, existence precedes knowledge: inquiry does not engender reality but rather yields products that are crucially conditioned by its independent operations. Beliefs that issue from a properly coordinated inquiry are in substantial measure constrained by conditions and circumstances that are themselves belief-independent.

Two very different sorts of pragmatism are therefore at issue, the one conventionalistic and relativistic, the other objectivistic and universalistic. The one is a relativistic pragmatism of personalized wishes and inclinations, the other a rationalistic pragmatism of generic needs and impersonal standards. It seems plausible to describe the latter as being

6. It is important in this connection to note that many of the projects in which we engage are ones that we confront as part of the nonoptimal realities of our situation in this world rather than ones that we voluntarily select: they are *given* rather than *chosen*.

"of the right" because of its essentially conservative nature. It does not call on us to leap into a brand new world of postmodern subjectivity but to maintain allegiance to the cognitive classical virtues of objectivity, reasonableness, universality. Against the arrogance of rationalistic self-sufficiency ("You go your way and I'll go mine") it takes a more humble and collegial line ("let us seek in friendly cooperation for the road that—in view of circumstances beyond our control—it makes sense for all of us to travel together").

## 4. A Return to the Peircean Roots

Richard Rorty's postmodern version of pragmatism is particularly radical in this regard. With Rorty, pragmatism collapses into a freewheeling speculative free-for-all:

> Let me sum up by offering a . . . final characterization of pragmatism: it is the doctrine that there are no constraints or inquiry save conversational ones—no wholesale constraints derived from the nature of the objects, or of the mind, of its language, but only those retail constraints provided by the remarks of our fellow inquirers.[7]

On such a view, clearly, the idea of constraints or standards that root in consideration of impersonal cogency drops altogether from view. The original Peircean insight that the applicative efficacy of its products constitute an objective quality-control standard for our cognitive proceedings is consigned to limbo. Pragmatism is no longer an impersonal standard of objective cogency but an instrumentality of conversational etiquette.

In a recent essay, Rorty writes that "it is essential to my view that we have no prelinguistic consciousness to which language need be adequate."[8] This may be true enough, but only because it aims at that comparatively easy target: "prelinguistic consciousness." Yet, if for this we substantiate "language-independent constraints" the situation is no longer quite that simple. And it is exactly to these language-detached realities—rainstorms and heatwaves, airplane crashes and dam collapses, and such like events and occurrences and processes that pragmatism concerns itself.

It is just at this point that there is a parting of the ways between the two modes of pragmatism. Pragmatism of the left views our scientific knowledge as a mere human contrivance, an unfettered invention devised for practical purposes that it serves more or less well, but without any claims to actual or approximate truth. Pragmatism of the right, by contrast, rejects such negativism and in its place substitutes a fallibilism that takes our scientific knowledge to represent *the best currently available estimate* of the actual truth of things. It maintains the linkage of scientific assertion to truth via the idea of *rationally warranted claims* to being true.

It was, after all, only on the basis of some rather confused thinking that William James was able to take his distinctly cavalier attitudes about truth in saying that "truth is made, just as health, wealth, and strength are made."[9] Consider a truth on the order of "Lead is heavier than copper." Are such truths indeed man-made? What certainty is man-made is the *conception* of lead, copper, and weight. Those English words and the ways in which they collect things together are human artifacts. But once

---

7. Rorty, *Consequences of Pragmatism*, p. 165.
8. Richard Rorty, "The Contingency of Language" in *Contingency, Irony, and Solidarity* (Cambridge: Cambridge University Press, 1989), pp. 3–22; see p. 22.
9. James, *Pragmatism*, p. 104.

those ideas that we characterize as "meanings" are in place, the rest of the situation—that is, the fact that lead outweighs copper—is actually outside the sphere of human control. At that point, however,—after those communicative conventions are in place—the rest of the story is a matter of the world's ways. Neither our piety nor our wit can have any influence from here on in. Those meanings are up to us, but the "facts" that we are able to formulate by their means are beyond our power. They are something we do not *make* but at best learn or discover. When James says that "Truth happens to an idea. It becomes true, is made true by event,"[10] he no longer maintains the needful distinction between the discovery of a fact on the one side, and on the other the fact that is discovered.

In the end, then, there is no question that pragmatism at large encompasses a spectrum of positions, and table 2.1 gives a survey of them in order of their placement in the softness / subjectively spectrum of increasing "hardness," so that descending order reflects the movement from left to right that has been at issue in the present discussion.

**Table 2.1**
**Forms of Pragmatism**

- *Individuality / Subjectivistic Pragmatism*
  - — Voluntaristic [James]
  - — Personalistic [Schiller]
- *Social / Communitarian Pragmatism*
  - — The political community [Dewey]
  - — The ideal community (rational/ultimate-scientific) [Peirce]
- *Functionalistic Pragmatism* (an objectivistic pragmatism of the right as sketched above)

10. Ibid., p. 97.

## 5. Three Traditional Objections to Pragmatism

Yet what advantages does that harder pragmatism of the right enjoy—just where do its claims to superiority lie? The answer here turns on its capacity to deal effectively with the sorts of objections to which pragmatism has traditionally been subject, prominently including the following three:

1. Pragmatism is too indefinite, equivocal, and many-sided to constitute a definite philosophical position: there is not one pragmatic philosophy; there are many. (A. O. Lovejoy)
2. A Peirce-style pragmatism to truth is too closely geared to science: it leaves other important domains of human experience out of account. (William James)
3. Pragmatism is too "materialistic," too grossly "American" in its emphasis on success and practical efficacy; it is the philosophical equivalent of dollar imperialism. (Numberless European critics)

Let us examine these objections more closely to see how they can be dealt with in the setting of rightist pragmatism's objectivistic perspective.

The first objection goes back to Arthur Lovejoy's provocative 1908 paper on "The Thirteen Pragmatisms," which stressed that pragmatism suffers a serious identity crisis.[11] Lovejoy complained that there seemed to be as many pragmatisms as pragmatists—and perhaps even more if he was right regarding the equivocation at work among pragmatist thinkers. To all appearances, pragmatism is not a unified theory but a grab bag of very different doctrines which bear only remote similarities to one another.

There is no question that, from the standpoint of the present deliberations, Lovejoy's classical objection still

11. Lovejoy, "The Thirteen Pragmatisms," pp. 5–12, and 29–39.

holds good. Indeed all the more so, seeing that the spectrum of pragmatist theses and doctrines has even expanded since his day. It is clearer than ever that pragmatism as a whole is a tendency that comprises a collection of rather different doctrines and that if one is to be a pragmatist one must make a choice among them. But, of course, it constitutes no valid objection to any one particular version of pragmatism that there exist alternatives to it! And that existence of an inadequate pragmatism does not impede the prospect of an adequate version of the theory. This issue has already been addressed in the preceding chapter. We saw there that no real shortcoming is at issue here that need faze the pragmatist who maintains the tenability not of pragmatism in general, but of one particular version of the doctrine.

We next turn to the James-style objection that a classical (Peircean) pragmatism is too narrow and that its focus on the *epistemic* success of factual theories in engendering consensus through effective prediction and application and leaves the whole normative-ideological sector of faith and morals out of account. As James has it, Peirce's more narrowly focused pragmatism geared to success in the specifically *cognitive* area is simple too restrictive in its operation. The success at issue must (so James insisted) be construed in its broadest sense, as relating to the "pursuit of happiness" in general, and so also extends to the *affective* area of human feeling and satisfactions.

But this position also faces major obstacles. Already in 1909, Bertrand Russell, who then knew pragmatism only in its Jamesean version, urged exactly the objection that troubled Peirce himself. "Success" and "working out" in cognitive and above all in *scientific* contexts relates to effective experiential / discordant prediction and control in relation to *observational* matters, and here a relationship to cognitive adequacy is clear. But James understands "working" on the very different sense that the belief in question has good affective, emotional, and psychological effects.[12] And this leaves the linkage to cognitive adequacy obscure. Any such psychologistic pragmatism is, of course, very different from what Peirce had in view—and is something whose bearing on the matter of actual truth is, effectively nonexistent. (James himself later ultimately came to recognize this when he acknowledged that he had earlier on confused "consequences of have ideas per se and consequences of ideas *qua believed by us*.")[13] But be this as it may, the fact remains that the circumstance that a Jamesian *religious* pragmatism may be in difficulty affords no objection to a Peircean *cognitive* pragmatism. There is no reason why a pragmatist should not, like anyone else, proceed one step at a time. There is no rational objection to any narrowing of scope that is required in the interests of adequacy. Here, as elsewhere, the use of limited claims betokens not their futility but of their constructive precision.

There yet remains the "European" objection to pragmatism's supposed reflection of "Yankee" dedication to the ideal of the "self-made man" with its focus on a successful pursuit of crass, materialistic ends. Europeans (and especially Germans) often maintained in response to pragmatism that philosophy cannot properly pivot on people's commonplace wants and base desires; it must be geared towards elevated ideas and higher ideals. To hinge philosophical deliberations upon concrete and practical issues is to degrade the subject.[14]

---

12. Russell, "William James' Conception of Truth," pp. 127–49.
13. Ralph Barton Perry, *The Thought and Character of William James*, 2 vols. (Boston: Little Brown and Co., 1935), vol. II: 481. This objection goes back at least to A. O. Lovejoy's "The Thirteen Pragmatisms."
14. Thus, Martin Heidegger asserted the "Dewey is not worthwhile; his thought lacks philosophical substance" (*Dewey ist nicht die Mühe wert weil er ohne eigene philosophische Substanz ist*). And he maintained that: "Americanism . . . is an as-yet-uncomprehended species of the gigantic. . . . The American interpretation of Americanism by

Now this sort of thing is a conceivable objection to a Jamesean extension of a personal-satisfaction pragmatism into the domain of faith and morals. Conceivable—but certainly arguable, since it can and should be argued that pragmatic success can encompass merely crass materialistic well-being but also the realization of higher values—not Epicurean or utilitarian *happiness*, but rather the sort of higher-level satisfaction at issues with Aristotelian *rational contentment* (reflective satisfaction, *eudaimonia*). (And exactly this is the picture that will develop in detail in chapters 7, and 8.) But be this as it may, the complaint at issue is clearly no sensible objection to a classical (Peirceanly objectivistic) pragmatism of a criteriology of factual truths, where success over the correlatively narrower range of cognitively relevant purpose to wit, the scientific desiderata of prediction and effective application—objectives that are clearly appropriate given what is at issue in matters of scientific inquiry.

The salient consideration, then, is that an objectivistic pragmatism of the right is well-situated to meet and overcome the traditionally prominent objections to which pragmatism has been subjected over the years.

## 6. The Turn to Methodological Pragmatism

There yet remains, however, another rather more subtle objection addressed specifically to the classical pragmatism's practicalistic approach to matters of meaning and truth. This objection turns on the contention that a pragmatic theory of

---

means of pragmatism still remains outside the metaphysical realm." *The End of Philosophy*, tr. Joan Stambaugh (New York: Harper and Row, 1973), p. 99.

truth is defeated by the fact that applicative success is achievable without getting it right—that the application and implementation of an erroneous belief can—nevertheless—yield success, and that applicatively successful theories will not ipso facto be true. In Bertrand Russell's hands, this criticism of the pragmatists was bolstered by various quaint examples—among them this:

> Dr. Dewey and I were once in the town of Changsha during an eclipse of the moon; following immemorial custom, blind men were beating gongs to frighten the heavenly dog, whose attempt to swallow the moon is the cause of the eclipses. Throughout thousands of years, this practice of beating the gongs has never failed to be successful; every eclipse has come to an end after a sufficient prolongation of the din.[15]

In such cases, it is not the epistemic merit of the beliefs at issue, but rather, luck alone to which the pragmatic successes are to be attributed.

Perhaps, then, pragmatism's truths are no more than Nietzschean "errors that we can get by with in this life." After all, we do sometimes find ourselves in the happy position that it can readily occur that all goes well in circumstances where we are far off the mark—where success in applications prevails despite our mistakes. You need nourishment. And nature confronts you with something and asks "Is it edible?" in circumstances where success hinges on getting *this* right. You say "yes" because you think it is a pear. You are wrong—it is an apple. But since apples, too, are edible, "all's well that ends well." Still, it is certainly *not* the case that what you are dealing with is *approximately* an apple. But the crucial point is that you are wrong in ways that are (*ex hypothesi*) immaterial to the application in

15. Bertrand Russell, "Dewey's New Logic," in *The Philosophy of John Dewey*, ed. P. A. Schilpp (La Salle, IL: Open Court, 1939), pp. 143–56.

question—this item is edible. Your error just does not matter for the question in view. After all, Ptolemaic astronomy underwrote many successful applications, but this does not show that it is true. All it means is that there is a better theory (Newtonian astronomy) that explains how it was able to achieve those "unmerited" successes. Galenic medicine with its complex congeries of humors actually enjoyed many therapeutic successes in its prescriptions and treatments. But that does not establish its claims to truth. (All we can say is that there is a superior theory—modern scientific medicine—which can be used to explain how it is that those Galenic remedies were therapeutically useful.)

To overcome this eminently cogent-seeming objection to cognitive pragmatism it will be necessary—and sufficient—to make a transition from *thesis* pragmatism to *method* pragmatism. This stratagem of a methodological perspective means that instrumental / pragmatic considerations are to be deployed not on *theses* at all (be they of particular or of generalized bearing), but rather upon the *methods* and procedures by which the acceptance of theses is validated. The justificatory situation comes to be very different here. For methodological pragmatism does not look to individual theses but deploys the pragmatistic standard as a validating resource for those generalized instrumentalities.

After all, an inquiry procedure is by its very nature a method having a uniquely vast range and comprehensiveness: it represents an effectively *boundless* methodology for the verification of theses. These considerations lay bare a critically important aspect of the generality of such a methodological approach to pragmatism—an approach whose generality is crucial to its capacity to overcome the shortcomings inherent in thesis-pragmatism. By its very nature as such, a thesis-oriented pragmatism cannot afford to concede possible discrepancies between success and truthfulness. However, a methodological pragmatism is something else again. Theses will perish in unfavorable circumstances, but methods can live on to fight another day. For the success of a method is a factor whose *systematic* nature gives it great probative weight in spite of occasional failings. A cognitive methodology is something so general and so open-ended in its orientation that gratuitously lucky success in the implementation of its products on a *systematic* basis can be ruled out as a genuine prospect. But the issues that arise here are complex, and require the more elaborate treatment that will be accorded to them in the next chapter.

And so, to summarize. The most serious of the problems and difficulties that pragmatism has encountered during the century of its existence all issue from the same basic circumstance: an ill-advised departure from the original Peircean concern for purposive adequacy as the hallmark of rational cogency. Not only can a return to this concern for applicative efficacy in matters of inquiry and practice protect pragmatism against the sorts of objections that have become prominent in the subsequent philosophical dialectic, but in its recorrelation to methods and principles it can also countervail against the presently fashionable postmodernist disintegration of pragmatism into relativistic vacuity.

As these deliberations indicate, three steps are needed to arrive at a viable version of pragmatism:

1. With Peirce one should construe pragmatic "success" as success in the essentially *epistemic* sector of effective prediction, explanation, and control. Affective success in the *conduct* of everyday life affairs is *not* the issue.
2. The sort of success to which one should look in developing an objectivistic pragmatism in the epistemic domain is neither an individual's personal success nor a particular group's success in the management of collective affairs. Rather, it is a person-indifferent or impersonal success in scientific matters (effective prediction, explanation, and control).
3. One should adopt a method-oriented rather than a thesis-oriented version of the doctrine: The objects of pragmatic

> assessment must be the methods of inquiry rather than individual contention.

The present-day crisis of pragmatism can be met effectively by adopting not a revisionary but a reconstructive understanding of what pragmatism is all about—one that keeps the doctrine close to its Peircean roots in the criteriology for assessing meaning and truth in matters of fact regarding the world's ways. That putative crisis does not, in the end, militate against the pragmatic program's viability, but rather provides a productive occasion for sharpening our understanding of the direction in which the program can and should be developed.

## Appendix

The presently operative distinction between opposed modes of pragmatic doctrine is drastically different from that of H. O. Maunce's interesting and instructive book on *The Two Pragmatisms*.[16] Maunce, too, distinguishes between an earlier (Peircean) and a later (Deweyan) pragmatism, but he does so on a very different basis—that of an orientation in the realism / idealism debate:

> Dewey holds that there can be nothing in reality which transcends the categories of the human mind . . . [a position that] achieved a full flowering in the work of Rorty. . . . [this] is not a new philosophy but is a variation of Positivism, a form of extreme empiricism. It is in conflict with the first [Peircean] Pragmatism, not at incidental points but in essentials. (P. 231.)

---

16. H. O. Maunce, *The Two Pragmatisms* (London: Routledge & Kegan Paul, 1997).

For Maunce the crucial question is whether pragmatic philosophy permits or prohibits going beyond the findings of science. As he sees it, there is the idealistic ("thought is all") pragmatism of thinkers like Rorty and the scientifically realistic pragmatism à la Peirce that is reality-oriented and thereby in a way "metaphysical." Maunce's two pragmatisms therefore consist of an older, more tolerant version (Peircean, Jamesian) prepared to accept that pragmatism can provide for philosophical insights apart from substantive science, and a postmodern, post-philosophically positivistic scientism which he attributes to Dewey and Rorty. But this is emphatically *not* the distinction that is at issue in the present deliberations. For in the present context, the salient distinction is that between a relativistically, sceptical standards-dismissing pragmatism that disdains theory in favor of praxis, and a standard-admitting pragmatism that sees in praxis itself the source and basis of a viable basis for testing the validity of theory. Substantially different categorizations are thus at issue.

CHAPTER THREE

# *Methodological Pragmatism in the Cognitive Domain*

## *Synopsis*

*(1) Pragmatism's focus on functional efficacy reflects the natural and optimal way for assessing the acceptability of methods in general. (2) It is, therefore, also appropriate specifically with respect to the* inquiry *methods that we deploy in the endeavor to resolve our questions. However, the pragmatic approach does not address our question-resolving answers directly. Rather, it appraises them mediately via the merit of the processes and procedures that we employ in making such* estimates *of the truth. (3) For, at this methodological level, we must suppose a linkage between pragmatic success with thesis implementation in matters of prediction and control, and the reliability of our thesis-validating methods. (4) The inherent generality of a methodological approach serves to meet various objectives that are historically made to epistemic pragmatism. (5) In prioritizing* praxis *over* theoria, *methodological pragmatism uses applicative practice as a quality control arbiter with respect to rational theorizing. It thereby effects an inversion in the method-to-thesis relationship that is usually envisioned, since on its*

*basis it is not that cognitive methods are better because they deliver more true theses, but rather that theses are more credible—better qualified for acceptance as truths—because they issue from the use of pragmatically superior methods. (6) Unlike Peirce, who saw the superiority of appropriate methods in their yielding greater synchronic and diachronic uniformity of opinion, the present methodological pragmatism prioritizes their capacity to engender superior applications in matters of prediction and control. (To be sure, to whatever extent people are* rational *the two will in the end come to much the same thing.)*

---

## 1. Aspects of Methodology: Teleology

There is no doubt that we humans make our beliefs—and therefore that we make our true beliefs—but that, of course, does not mean that *we make them true*. We make our beliefs even as we make our soap bubbles—but whether and where they fly depends not on us but on how the world's winds blow. The *truth* of a belief regarding matters of fact will—once this belief is made—depend, not on its maker but on the world's ways. When made, those beliefs and bubbles take on a life of their own—their status from here on in is no longer at the disposition of their makers. And it is this fact that enables us to establish a thought-independent quality control over our beliefs.

Pragmatism's characteristic mode of validation proceeds in functionalistic, that is to say *instrumental* terms. To be validated instrumentally is to be justified in the way natural and proper for an instrument, tool, method, procedure, modus operandi, technique, or the like. The governing idea here is that of effective agency at the generic level of ways of doing or accomplishing things. After all, an instrumentality of any kind is by nature a means for doing things of a certain sort; so that the inevitably teleological question of the *effectiveness of performance* in the realization of its purpose becomes altogether central to the issue of justification. The proper test of any sort of instrumentality lies in its capacity to realize effectively and efficiently the sort of product that constitutes its purposive reason for being.

The overall process of functional justification that is natural to anything instrumental (method, procedure, modus operandi, etc.) thus has the generic structure exhibited in figure 3.1. There is a cyclic feedback process here that ongoingly monitors the adequacy of our methodological resources.

This process represents what might be characterized as a systems-model of instrumental justification. It proceeds in terms of the key concepts of systems-analysis, *viz.*, *input* (the use of a method), *output* (the results of applying the

**Figure 3.1**
**Structure of the Instrumental Justification of an Instrumentality**

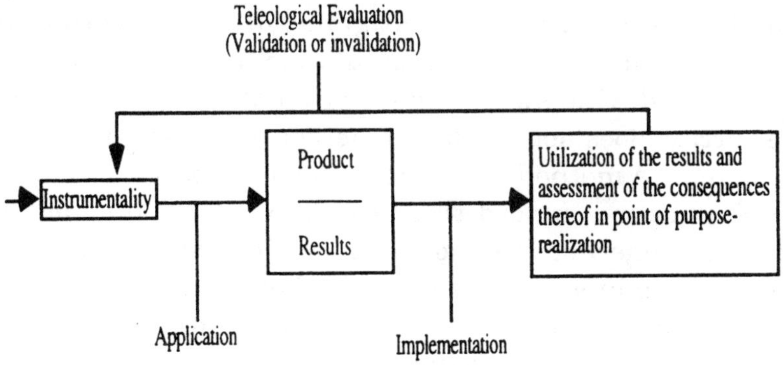


*Note:* The cyclic feedback structure of the process is a pivotal aspect of its approach to quality control.

method), and *quality control* through a feedback assessment process of purpose / realization. Applicative efficacy in realizing the aims of the enterprise becomes the controlling factor. It is clear in the light of such considerations that the natural appraisal standard for the rational evaluation of methods is that of the extent of their systematic success in the performance of heir correlative tasks.

The "validation" of a method therefore resides in an instrumental analysis that determines its suitability to the sort of task that is at issue. The quality-control test that is obviously appropriate here proceeds by determining whether the results of using the method in fact realize the purposes for which it was instituted. "By their fruits shall ye know—or, rather, *evaluate*—them" is the operative motto here. Success in application—its capacity to do its intended work, its performative effectiveness, in short—is the decisive consideration for the validation of a method. Therefore, the rational legitimation of a method is generally not a question of *theoretical* considerations but is essentially *practical* in its bearing. There can be no better or more natural way of justifying a method than by establishing that "it works" in practice with respect to the specific appointed tasks that are in view for it.

However, as Peirce already stressed, isolated or occasional success is relatively insignificant. What matters is *statistical* success—the accumulation of an impressive track record. One swallow does not make a summer, and one success does not validate a method—nor one failure invalidate it. A method is a generic device capable of repetitive application; indeed there can be no such thing as an inherently onetime method (though, of course, occasion for the use of an inherently general method might conceivably arise but once). Moreover, the efficacy of a method (unlike that of a skill or talent) is impersonal—it does not work just for *X* or *Y*, but for anybody. Methodological efficacy is a matter of how things go "across the board" generally and in the long run.[1] Therefore, the instrumental justification at issue in a sensible pragmatism has to be sought at this generic and systematic plane.[2]

Moreover, the salient question will not be "Does the method work wonders?" but rather—and more prosaically and realistically—"Does the method work better than the available alternatives?" A rational pragmatism will opt for that realistic middle road—intermediate between unrealistic idealization and an underambitious settling for the clearly suboptimal. A methodological pragmatism is in this sense true to itself—to its own pragmatic character by insisting upon a realistic (pragmatic) view of the process of rational decision itself. It will be therefore concerned with success, not in an absolute and idealized way but in terms of a comparative assessment of what can be achieved within the sphere of realistically available possibilities.

## 2. The Special Case of Cognitive Methodology: the Methodologically Pragmatic Validation of Knowledge Claims

So much for methods in general, let us now turn specifically to inquiry methods.

---

1. A focus on the specifically *cognitive* methods of inquiry leads to an essentially Peircean perspective in coordinating cognitive rationality with the concerns of the community of inquirers in its "at large" distribution over space and time.
2. The importance for inductive considerations of the inherent generality of methods was clearly perceived by Peirce, who held that "synthetic inferences are founded upon the classification of facts, not according to their characters, but *according to the manner of obtaining them.*" (Quote in Ernest Nagel, "Principles of the Theory of Probability," *International Encyclopedia of Unified Science*, Vol. I [Chicago: University of Chicago Press, 1955], pp. 343–422; see p. 414.)

In barest outline, the "pragmatic theory of truth" takes the success, ensuing on their implementation, as its guide to the acceptability of claims or statements. However, our preceding deliberations indicate that the rationale for a pragmatic criteriology of truth is greatly strengthened when pragmatic considerations are brought to bear not upon specific substantive *theses* at all (be they of particular or of generalized bearing), but rather upon the *methods* used for their substantiation or verification.[3] Our knowledge, it must be stressed, is not just a matter of endorsed theses, of propositional *knowledge-that*, but also, and perhaps even more fundamentally, a matter of guiding us in doing things in the manner of *how-to-knowledge*. Now in the case of specifically cognitive methods, these two seemingly divergent modes of knowledge draw together in linked interaction, since it is now a matter of *how-to-secure-knowledge-that*. Informative knowledge-that must itself be obtained and secured, and the management of this process demands how-to knowledge. But a methodological approach sees the how-to case as primary, approaching propositional knowledge from the direction of its methodological access-way.

It must be acknowledged, of course, that the idea of a cognitive method is rather ramified. There are many sorts of cognitive methods: methods of investigation, methods of explanation, as well as methods for the discovery, acquisition, confirmation, processing, utilization, transmission of information. However, we need focus here on only one group of cognitive methods—*viz.*, those used for the *validation or substantiation of thesis-acceptance*. The methods of present concern are thus specifically those by whose means factual

3. There are, to be sure, ways of connecting theses and methods. But the connections are often loose. Above all, the viability of a method (e.g., "Treat everyone as though they were responsible and intelligent people") does *not* require the truth of the correlative proposition.

theses come to be established: the probative methods of empirical inquiry.

After all, an inquiry procedure is fundamentally *methodological* in character: it seeks to provide a substantiate *method*, a logico-epistemological procedure for warranting acceptance of certain propositions. After all, working well—that is, manifesting effectiveness and efficiency in discharging the tasks for which it is designed—is the key standard for the rational evaluation of methods. The justification of the cognitive modus operandi represented by an inquiry procedure is thus seen in standardly instrumental—that is, purposive—terms.

On this approach, then, the linkage between pragmatic utility and the truth of theses is broken apart, and *methods* are inserted into the gap that opens up. Here pragmatic considerations are not brought to bear on theses directly. The relationship becomes indirect and mediated: a specific knowledge claim is supported by reference to a method, which in its turn is supported on pragmatists lines. Methodological pragmatism in the context of cognitive methods becomes a matter of effectiveness for the attainment of specified cognitive ends—specifically the classic quartet of description, explanation, prediction, and control.[4]

Therefore a methodological pragmatism has it that effectiveness and efficiency in discharging the tasks for which it is designed—is the key standard for the rational evaluation of methods. And the justification of the cognitive modus operandi represented by an inquiry procedure should therefore also be seen in just these standardly instrumental—that is, purposive—terms. On this basis, a successful method is one that yields successfully implementable theses. The rational structure of a pragmatic justification of a methodology of inquiry thus exhibits the format outlined in

4. This version of pragmatism, here sketched only briefly, will be set out in fuller detail in the next chapter.

**Figure 3.2**
**The Pragmatic Justification of an Inquiry Methodology**

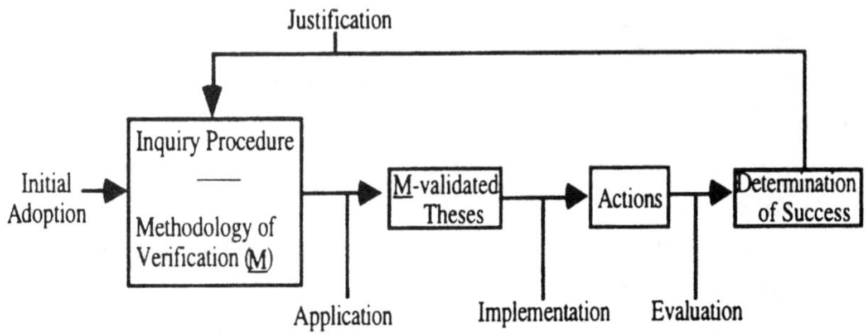


figure 3.2, which implements the general structure of instrumental validation as depicted in figure 3.1 in the specific case of question-resolving inquiry.

Naive thesis pragmatism has it that: "a proposition *means* what we do about it in practice, and a proposition *is true* if this practice is successful." Now from the very start, opponents of pragmatism, wanted for reasons of dialectical convenience to construe this in the most naive (and thus most vulnerable) way. And on this basis they liked to point out that this construction of meaning and truth encounters great difficulty when the passage of time is taken into consideration.[5] Thus, the implications for our actual practice of a proposition about what Caesar ate for breakfast on that fateful Ides of March are virtually nil: this is something that has effectively no practical bearing for us. There is little if anything that we can nowadays do about it, successfully or otherwise. And the

5. See Lovejoy, "The Thirteen Pragmatisms," and also Russell, "William James' Conception of Truth."

same thing with future-oriented propositions, such as, "The U.S.A. will continue to exist as a nation and hold a Presidential election in the year 4,000 A.D." Surely—those critics complained—such propositions are meaningful and have a truth status independently of anything that we might do about the matter here and now. And if this is so, then the pragmatic account of the matter has it wrong. One of the tasks of a methodological pragmatism of the sort to be articulated here is to counter this line of objection. By targeting the pragmatic standard at methods we bypass the problem of the potential intractability of individual cases.

There is no *hors de texte* says Derrida. The only reason for a belief is yet another belief says Davidson. But this sort of "wisdom" is error. The world of thought is not self-contained; it is integral to the wider world of nature, part of a realm in which events happen and experiences occur. A perfectly good reason for believing that the cat is on the mat is that we experience (i.e., observe) it to be there. The acceptability of beliefs lies not with other beliefs but with experience—and experience must here be understood in rather general and broadly inclusive terms.

On this approach, then, the linkage between pragmatic utility and the truth of theses is broken apart, and *methods* are inserted into the gap that opens up. Pragmatic considerations are *not* brought to bear on theses directly. This mediation of methods between pragmatic considerations and thesis-acceptance is central to, and indeed definitive of, the specifically *methodological* pragmatism at issue here.

Such a Peirce-inspired method-pragmatism contrasts sharply with the thesis-pragmatism of the historical tradition represented by William James—for whom the serviceability of specific beliefs was the crux. But it is certainly not out of tune with the motivating spirit of the doctrine. For by focusing upon *cognitive methods*—methods of inference, testing, checking, and other ways and means of task accomplishment in the area of cognitive substantiation—we take the pragmatic turn and come to see how-to knowledge as more fundamental than knowledge-that, since the latter is held to be ultimately rooted in the former.

Methodological pragmatism accordingly stands in sharp contrast to a more naive thesis-pragmatism, holding that claims of the form "*p* is true" should be abandoned and ones of the form "it is [pragmatically] well advised to accept *p*" should be employed in their place. This version of pragmatism seeks to substitute pragmatic acceptability for truth. Methodological pragmatism, by contrast, proposes to retain truth claims as such, but insists that their status brings in no more (but also no less) than what is provided for by the ruling of an acceptability criterion that we are well advised to employ.

A methodological pragmatism of this sort may well meet with the following objection:

> This pragmatic approach to cognitive quality control exhibits the characteristic flaw of all instrumentalism, because, in effect, it simply abandons *truth* for *utility* in pivoting the issue of quality-control on goal-attainment in the practical rather than theoretical area.

This objection is gravely mistaken. For at the level of particular claims and theses, the theory is not "instrumentalistic" at all: it continues the orthodox commitment to the truth and sees its pursuit as the pivotal object of the enterprise of inquiry subject to the usual standards of the scientific method. Only at a remove, at the methodological level where that method itself is under evaluation, do pragmatic considerations enter in, since it is here alone that successful praxis seen as the appropriate adequacy-control criterion. The link between truth and praxis is therefore not seen as direct, but as mediated by the methodology of inquiry. The operative process is one of validating claims to truth *via* methods and then the appropriateness of methods *via* praxis.[6]

Cognitive pragmatism has it that even in matters of theory the pivot of rational belief lies in the of guidance of action (communicative action—that is, thought-coordination among individuals—included). Thus, it leads to what might be called the "pragmatic inversion" of epistemology. The operative inference is now one that moves not from "better claim to truth" to "more effective guidance of action" but in the exactly reverse direction. Such an inversion sees any effort to validate an inquiry procedure in terms of the truthfulness of its products as picking up the wrong end of the stick. For warrant should be taken as the independent variable and truthfulness as the dependent variable, with our inquiry procedures not seen as warranted because truth-producing, but rather presumed to be truth-producing because of their rational warrant. The linkage between presumptive truth and adequate action-guidance is preserved all right, but the respective fundamentality of these two factors is reversed. The position at issue has it that we should not evaluate an inquiry procedure by the truth of its results, but conversely, assess the truthfulness of the results in terms of rational merits of the procedure that underwrites them.

Again, methodological pragmatism may seem to be vulnerable to another objection:

> In some circumstance one instrumentality is instrumentally useful but in another setting yet another very different instrumentality may well be so. Utility is by nature an opportunistic standard. It will not yield anything general, definite, use indifferent. And this opportunistically variable aspect of utility prevents pragmatism from achieving any stable doctrinal position. It may, nay probably will,

6. A fuller account of the validation process at issue in this section is presented in the author's *Methodological Pragmatism* (Oxford: Basil Blackwell, 1977).

> speak not for any one method but for a diversified plurality of different methods.

The response here lies in urging the question: Just exactly what is it whose utility is to be at issue with our pragmatism? The answer here is: rules, principles, methods, and other such like process of inherent generality. The individual whose modus operandi is subject to the procedure "In circumstance of type 1 follow rule no. 1 and those of type 2 follow rule no. 2" is not a person who has *abandoned* rules, but rather simply one who has *adopted* a complex rule. And there is no reason why, in a complex world, our rules, principles and methods have to be simple. This is something that pragmatism can and does accept and recognize. Its position is not one of doctrinal avoidance but one of the acceptance of doctrinal complexity.

It emerges against the background of these considerations that there are three sorts of cognitive pragmatism, namely, those proceeding at the level of individual theses, of thesis-clusters, and of thesis-certifying methods, respectively. And so we obtain:

- thesis pragmatism (particularistic). William James, F. C. S. Schiller.
- system pragmatism (locally systemic). C. I. Lewis, R. Carnap.
- system pragmatism (holistic). W. V. Quine.
- method pragmatism (procedural). C. S. Peirce.

## 3. Why This Link Between Pragmatic Efficacy and Truthfulness?

But just why should the pragmatic success engendered by its deliverances be taken to justify an inquiry method and count towards establishing its legitimacy as a criterion of acceptability or verification? Why should its endorsement by an inquiry method with a good track record of applicative success speak for the acceptability of a proposition as at least a good estimate of the truth?

It must be recognized and acknowledged from the outset that no inevitable and failproof connection between truth and successful implementation obtains where individual beliefs are concerned. The literature of the subject is replete with examples of the following sort: A man mistakenly believes he has a certain disease and mistakenly believes a certain medication is called for by way of treatment. However, he actually has another, more serious malady against which—unbeknownst to anyone—this medicine is highly effective. If he "knew the truth" about his malady he would suffer badly, being altogether ignorant of any remedy for his actual condition. But, as it is, that erroneous belief saves his life. In theory, accepting a falsehood could be enormously benefit-conducive in matters of application and implementation. This sort of example illustrates the traditional objection against pragmatism that it might well prove highly successful to act on some (quite incorrect) thesis. After all, action that proceeds on beliefs that are false and fail to capture "what is actually the case" can on occasion—or even frequently—eventuate as pragmatically successful, due to chance or good luck or kindly fate or whatever.[7]

All this is true enough as far as it goes. None the less, the situation is radically altered when what is at issue is

7. In the first decade of this century, this line of objection was heavily pressed against William James by A. O. Lovejoy in "The Thirteen Pragmatisms" and by Russell in *Philosophical Essays*. Even John Dewey, James' pragmatist ally, criticized him for confounding the intellectual issues of what can satisfy the inquiring mind with the issue of genuinely pragmatic values.

not the isolated case of a particular accepted thesis (or even a cluster of them), but rather a general, across-the-board process or policy of belief-validation. Individual theses may well manage to slip through the pragmatic net singly or in groups. But comparatively greater effectiveness of a method in delivering more successfully implementable theses into our hands systematically and in a wide variety of contexts is clearly an indication of its comparative superiority as a means of inquiry. Just here lies the crucial competitive advantage of a specifically *methodological* pragmatism.

The systematic success of an inquiry method cannot plausibly be dismissed as a sheerly fortuitous piece of luck owing to the inherent generality of methods. After all, the applicability range of an inquiring methodology is literally boundless: no factual issue is to lie outside its intended province. Here it is effectively assured that probatively irrelevant side effects by way of fortuitous benefits or disasters will become canceled out in the larger scheme of things. That inappropriate processes might prove pervasively successful at this synoptic level of generality is theoretically possible but affectively unlikely—a prospect so farfetched that it can be dismissed with confidence. Fundamental mistakes at *this* level of generality are bound to have applicative repercussions across a limitless frontier that would not only be discernible but also ultimately would prove catastrophic in implementation. These considerations indicate a critically important aspect of the generality of the such a methodological approach to pragmatism—an approach whose generality is crucial to its capacity to overcome the shortcomings inherent in thesis-pragmatism.

To be sure, the use of generally effective methods can underwrite no categorical guarantees, be it in motorcycle maintenance or in belief formation. The relation of cognition and reality accordingly remains subject to the epistemic mediation of a sort best characterized in terms of the idea of reliable *estimation*. And reliable here does not mean failproof. Even as I know that most Americans will survive the present year without being able to say with categorical certainty that this will be the case with any particular one of them, so at the level of scientific complexity, I can know that the information at my disposal is generally reliable without being able to say with unqualified categorical certainty to what extent this is so in this or that particular case. Precisely because the later, "progressive" stages of the application of our inquiry procedures are more fully warranted on the basis of the ampler and more successful body of praxis that they underwrite, we can take the stance that is *rational to view their deliverances as better qualified for endowment with the presumption of truth*. It is on this basis alone that we can be increasingly confident that our currently accepted picture of nature affords a comparatively *better estimate* than our past pictures do. Our rationally formed beliefs about the world should therefore be seen as having two interrelated aspects: on the one hand, they are indeed *estimates* of the truth and not definitive demonstrations thereof, but on the other hand they are not *mere* estimates: they are *responsible* estimates of the truth that rest on the most amply authenticated methodological basis that it has been within our power to devise. As Peirce emphasized, in matters of scientific theorizing there are no categorical guarantees—we have to maintain a fallibilistic view of things.

By its very nature as such, a thesis-oriented pragmatism cannot afford to concede possible discrepancies between success and truthfulness. But a methodological pragmatism is in a very different position here. Theses perish in unfavorable circumstances, but methods can live on to fight another day. For the success of a method is a factor whose *systematic* nature gives it great probative weight in spite of occasional failings. A cognitive methodology is something so general and so open-ended in its orientation that gratuitously lucky success in the implementation of its products on a *systematic* basis can be ruled out as a genuine prospect.

## 4. The Generality of the Methodological Approach Overcomes Various Objections

In treating methods as basic, the pragmatism advocated here does *not* take the circular route of evaluating the adequacy claims of cognitive methods in terms of the claims to truth of the theses they validate. Instead, it would have us judge the adequacy of a method in terms of the applicative efficacy of its products. The result of the applicatively most effective inquiry methods are seen as providing our best rationally warranted estimates of the actual truth of things. The first priority now is to identify the performatively best method we can find; subsequently proceeding to determine the presumptive truth in its terms.

It would indeed be problematic to go about justifying theses in terms of further theses in term of further theses, and thus ever onwards. But there is no need to take such this homogeneous approach to the issue of validation. For we can, fortunately, monitor tour acceptance of theses via the methods that substantiate them, and then validate these methods by pragmatic tests—specifically considering how well we fare *in applying and implementing its professed claims in matters of prediction and control*. It thus becomes possible to break the regress of justifying theses by theses: a thesis can be justified by application of a method, the adoption of this method itself being justified by reference to certain *practical* criteria (preeminently, its success in matters of prediction and control). Applicative technology, so to speak, comes to be the key here.

Such a theory-external quality control upon cognition is ultimately vital to our justificatory deliberations because it blocks the prospect of a futile spinning around in reality-detached cycles of purely theoretical gyrations, with ideas and beliefs chasing after ideas and beliefs. Someplace along the line of justification there must be provision for a correlative contact with a self-sustained and largely unmanipulable reality—an agency that furnishes a "reality principle" quite independently of the drift of our thoughts and wishes. This crucially requisite principle is provided for in the framework of the present methodological approach by the factor of the success consequent upon implementing action. Goal-attainment—successful goal-pursuing *praxis* (prescinding for the moment from the intrinsic character of these goals)—is the ultimate guarantor of validity of the products of man's endeavors at the acquisition of empirical knowledge.

To be sure, everyone is familiar with the occasional surfacing, even today, of some occult or pseudoscientific methodology leading to views of the world that substantiate fact-purporting theses of the strangest sort. (Think here of the flat-earth theorists.) It is often striking here how beautifully everything meshes at the theoretical level—one bit of strangeness being supported by others. A seamless fabric of self-supportive absurdities is readily imagined. The crunch comes only with the tough question: Does this approach to the warranting of claims actually enable its proponents to navigate more effectively amid the rocks and shoals of this world by underwriting a complex and diversified body of successful applications in matters of prediction and control?

Therefore, the turn to *methodological* pragmatism at once overcomes objections along the lines of Bertrand Russell's well known complaint: "The chief criticism one would then have to make on pragmatism [for its adopting usefulness as a standard of truth] would be to deny that utility is a useful criterion because it is so often harder to determine whether a belief is useful than whether it is true."[8] Whatever the merit this complaint may have against pragmatism as a criteriology for thesis assessment, it has none whatsoever against a *methodological* pragmatism for which the utility of specific beliefs is an essentially irrelevant matter.

A. C. Ewing once offered essentially the following objection to pragmatism: "Even 'success' on a vast scale need not provide a sound warrant for truth claims. For suppose that a railway bridge were built on odd and unsound engineering principles, but that this led to a train-crash in which Hitler was killed (near the outset of his career) and millions of lives saved."[9] Here an obvious concession is at once in order. Action which proceeds on beliefs that are false and fail to capture "what is actually the case" can on occasion—or even frequently—eventuate as pragmatically successful, due to chance or good luck or kindly fate or whatever. However, the situation must be different when what is at issue is not an isolated action or a particular believed thesis (or even a cluster of them), but rather a general policy of acting based on alignment with a *methodologically universalized standard* of belief-validation. Individual theses may well manage to slip through the net of disconfirmation singly or in groups, but *methods* for factual inquiry are something else again. The objection in view thus fails to do justice to the generality of a methodological approach by viewing the matter of truth determination far too narrowly. What is at issue in the present context is vastly more universalized, namely, an inquiry procedure for the determination of (presumptive) truth

8. Russell, "William James' Conception of Truth," p. 138.
9. In a discussion in Geneva, Switzerland in March of 1973, not long before the death in June of that year of this charming septuagenarian (b. 1899) of spry intellect. The subsequent commentary will overlook the fact that the relevant issue is one of epistemic success in prediction and control rather than success in enhancing the quality of people's lives. The example is readily reconfigured to accommodate this consideration.

across the entire factual board, and not just in one narrow area (e.g., bridge building). Methodological systematicity of the sort at issue is so comprehensive that probatively irrelevant side effects by way of fortuitous bonuses or disasters become canceled out in the larger scheme of things. Fundamental mistakes at *this* level of generality would have repercussions across a limitless frontier and would be bound to come to unwelcome manifestation.

## 5. How the Present Methodological Approach Contrasts with that of Peirce

It is instructive to consider just how the presently contemplated methodological pragmatism compares with the position of Charles Sanders Peirce. Defining inquiry as the generic process by which we move from doubt to belief, Peirce—as we have seen—recognized a plurality of available methods of inquiry, there being not only the *scientific* method, but also, such alternative as, for example, the *traditionary* (method of tenacity), the *dogmatic* (method of authority), and the *metaphysico-speculative* (a priori method). The scientific method emerges as the best of these—so Peirce argued—for two interconnected reasons: (1) it is *self-corrective*: if it leads us into missteps it will itself discover these in due course and put them to rights in the long run; and (2) it is *stabilitarian*: it alone leads to the establishment of stable beliefs—beliefs that will stand up over the long run. Thus, Peirce, too, takes an approach that is methodological in spirit.

But while Peirce is both a pragmatist in his theory of meaning and a methodologist in his theory of methods of inquiry, he is not quite a methodological pragmatist in the sense of the present discussion when truth is concerned.

This is so because for Peirce the decisive consideration in truth determination is stability—or "fixity" as Peirce himself characterized it—and *not* pragmatic efficacy of any sort. For Peirce saw the critical merit of the scientific method to lie in its capacity to provide for an eventual convergence of opinion on particular theses—a stable uniformity of thought within the community of scientific inquirers. And this approach flows smoothly into his conception of truth. For, according to Peirce, the mark of a true belief—one constrained by an external and independent reality—is implicit in its destiny as fated to be underwritten by the operation of scientific method.[10] And so, while Peirce saw the superiority of appropriate methods in terms of their yielding greater synchronic and diachronic uniformity of opinion, the present methodological pragmatism, by contrast, pivots matters on their superior criteriological efficacy with regard to applications in matters of prediction and control. (To be sure, to whatever extent people are rational the two will come to much the same thing, since they will be brought together in a common position through their universal preference for what works.) Only if one presupposes a community of people who are pragmatically rational will Peirce's approach and that of the present methodological pragmatism come into close alignment.

10. In the essay "What Pragmatism Is" (*Collected Papers*, vol. V: sects. 5.416–434), Peirce proposes "to define the 'truth' as that to which belief would lead if it were to tend indefinitely toward absolute fixity." Thus, Bertrand Russell was—as regards Peirce—quite wrong in saying that the crucial difference between the pragmatist's theory and his own is that he defines truth in terms of the *causes* and they in terms of the *effects* of beliefs. (*An Inquiry into Meaning and Truth* [London: G. Allen and Unwin, 1940]; [1963 reprint, Hammondsworth: Penguin Books]; see p. 308 of the reprint.) Peirce's conception of truth is realistic and correspondistic; for him, true beliefs are "satisfactory" in virtue of their consonance with reality, and in no danger of subsequent overthrow once properly arrived at.

To be sure, when all this is said and done the question remains: just what sort of inquiry method does a methodological pragmatism endorse? And the answer is pretty well a foregone conclusion—at any rate in the realm of matters of factual inquiry. At this time of day, such a pragmatism must award the palm of victory to the inductive methods of science. Be their faults what they may, we have no better—no more pragmatically effective—way of obtaining answers to our questions about how things work in the world. And so in this regard, too, the methodological pragmatism contemplated here carries us back to the doctrinal position of C. S. Peirce with regard to the centrality—and the limitations!—of science. This important issue demands a chapter unto itself.

# CHAPTER FOUR

# *Fallibilism and the Pragmatic Epistemology of Science*

Synopsis

*(1) The quest for a pragmatically optimal inquiry method issues (unsurprisingly enough) in acknowledging the primacy of natural science in this regard. For applicative efficacy in matters of prediction and effective intervention in nature is clearly the key to quality control here, seeing that* this *sort of "pragmatic success" lies at the heart of the scientific enterprise. (2) This circumstance serves both to betoken and to explain the emergence of the scientific method through an evolution-analogous process of* rational *(rather than* natural*) selection. (3) While one key aspect of pragmatism's view of science relates to the potential fallibility of our scientific theorizing, a pragmatic approach nevertheless provides for a substantial degree of objectivity and realism; it is certainly not tantamount to a nihilistic scepticism in scientific matters.*

## 1. Monitoring the Adequacy of Science

Applicative efficacy is the natural standard of pragmatism, whose approach to validation therefore has an indelibly *empirical* cast, seeing that actual experience is generally the best guide to practical efficacy. On this basis, the question, "What sort of inquiry method does a pragmatic approach in epistemology endorse?" has an answer that is almost anticlimactic, seeing that it is—clearly and obviously—the scientific method evolved over recent centuries that leads the field of available prospects of success with respect to matters of inquiry.

The mission of the cognitive enterprise—and of natural science in particular—is to provide us with information about how matters stand in the world by way of useful and reliable estimates as to the truth of things. But this perspective nevertheless still invites the question: Can we actually ever tell how good an estimate of "the real truth" science actually provides?

Any sensible attempt to assess how successful our cognitive efforts are in their intended mission of telling the truth must confront the fact that it is not possible to determine the adequacy of our theorizing *directly* by seeing how well inquiry manages to get at the truth of things. For—obviously—we have no inquiry-independent way of telling what this truth is so as to compare the products of our inquiries with it. Any attempt to appraise the adequacy of our theorizing on its own, purely theoretical terms is thus ultimately futile. And this indicates the need for a belief-independent control of the correctness of ourtheorizing, some theory-external reality principle to serve as a standard of adequacy.[1] And just here is where pragmatism can come to the rescue.

1. Compare the discussion of the so-called Wheel Argument (*diallelus*) in the author's *Methodological Pragmatism* (Oxford: Blackwell, 1977), pp. 15–17 and *passim*.

As we have seen, methodological pragmatism's position is (to put it in a nutshell) that while base-level issues are to be resolved in terms of *standards*, those standards themselves are to be evaluated in terms of their efficacy and efficiency with respect to the teleology of the domain in question. To be sure, this matter of goal realization calls for different modes of implementation, depending on the domain at issue. In the case of formal sciences like logic and mathematics, the superiority of one method over another may becomes manifest through purely theoretical considerations of problem-solving effectiveness in theoretical matters. Here we need never leave our armchairs. But with other enterprises—inquiry in the natural sciences, for example, or the management of political and public affairs—there is no substitute for experiencing the results of our actual efforts "out in the field," so to speak.

Now the aim of natural science is represented by the traditional quartet of description, explanation, prediction, and control, in line with the following picture:

Theoretical Goals

- *description* (answering *what*? and *how*? questions about nature)
- *explanation* (answering *why*? questions about nature)

Practical Goals

- *prediction* (successful alignment of our expectations regarding nature)
- *control* (effective intervention in nature)

In this way, the teleology of factual inquiry is internally diversified and complex, extending across both the cognitive / theoretical and active / practical sectors. Truth-acceptance is, on the one hand, the determining factor for belief in purely intellectual and theoretical regards, and, on the other, a guiding standard for the practical conduct of action. Our inquiry processes thus come to be endowed with a duality of objectives, and the relevant teleology of scientific inquiry is both theoretical and practical. The two are inseparably interrelated; where we cannot take hold of the one we cannot grasp the other. And it is in the practical sector of actual application that—on pragmatism's telling—we find our best available prospect for a belief-external quality control regarding theoretical matters.

To be sure, historical experience indicates there are various alternative approaches to determining how things work in the world. The examples of such occult cognitive frameworks as those of numerology (with its benign ratios), astrology (with its astral influences), and black magic (with its mystic forces) indicate that alternative explanatory frameworks exist, and that these can have very diverse degrees of merit. Now in the Western, Faustian[2] intellectual tradition, the ultimate arbiter of rationality is represented by a very basic concept of knowledge-wed-to-practice, and the ultimate validation of our beliefs lies in the combination of theoretical and practical *success*, with "practice" construed in its pragmatic and affective sense. Here the governing standards of scientific rationality are implicit in the description-transcending goals of *explanation*, *prediction*, and preeminently *control* over nature. (And thus the crucial factor is not, for example, sentimental "at-oneness with nature"—think of the magician *vs.* the mystic *vs.* the sage as cultural ideals.) These standards revolve about considerations of *practice* and are implicit in the use to which our conceptual resources are put in the management of our affairs. And it is here, in the belief transcending domain of our predictive and interventionist praxis that the quality-controlling monitor of our scientific claims ultimately roots. The arbitrament of practice over theory—whether our engineered-designed bridges stand or fall, and whether our aerodynamics-designed airplanes fly or plummet—provides for theory-external check on the adequacy of our theorizing.

2. *Im Anfang war die Tat*, as Goethe's *Faust* puts it.

Such a pragmatic approach to science does not take an instrumentalistic stance which abandons the pursuit of truth and sees the practical issues of prediction and control as the sole goals of the enterprise. Rather, it sees *praxis* as paramount because there just is no prospect of any more direct alternative, any immediate comparison of these claims with the science-independent "real-truth" of things. The capacity of our cognitive tools to meet their *theoretical* goals can be monitored *obliquely*, by appraising their realization of our *practical* goals. The practical and *purposive* aspects of cognition thus comes to the fore. The governing quality controls of our mechanisms of inquiry—its methods, concepts, and so forth, that furnish the whole machinery by which we build up our world picture (knowledge, *epistêmê*, science)—emerge as fundamentally pragmatic. We are led to the recognition that here effective *praxis* is the ultimate quality-control arbiter of acceptable *theoria*: that we must monitor the adequacy of our scientific knowledge by way of assessing the efficacy of its applications in guiding our expectations and actions in matters of prediction and control.

One point needs emphasis here. In speaking of the "success" of the methods of science we take into view only the issue of comparative success in providing information for the effective guidance of *praxis*. The orientation of that *praxis* itself—be it for good or evil—is in *this* limited context altogether irrelevant. Conceivably we may use our knowledge to destroy the species in war, genocide, or an otherwise contrived cataclysm of some sort. But *this* sort of failure (or "nonsuccess") is simply irrelevant from the angle of present purpose. What matters for success in point of control is simply the factor of effectiveness in achieving *chosen objectives*, be they themselves good, indifferent, or bad.

Yet is successful control itself not something merely theoretical, the object of a mere judgment that also lies in the eye of the beholder? As one critic has put it:

> But while the actual occurrence of happiness or unhappiness, pleasure or pain, etc., is indeed beyond our control . . . the same does not seem obviously to hold for our beliefs about such matters. . . . Thus beliefs or judgments about pragmatic success turn out not to constitute genuine input from the world, but instead . . . can . . . be arbitrarily manipulated at will, so long as the other elements are appropriately adjusted.[3]

It would thus be contended that, while *the actual occurrence* of pain, suffering, disappointment (etc.) may be extra-theoretical, nevertheless a person's *awareness* of such things is not, but rather lies only in the area of belief—of mere opinion.

But this seems very dubious. With such inherently affective factors as pain, suffering, disappointment, and so forth, the fact cannot obtain without its realization—the feeling without its recognition. Here awareness of the experience is part of the experience itself. One cannot separate the pain from the feeling of pain, the surprise from the feeling of surprise. The belief is not something separate and additional that we may or may not add to the experience; it is integral to the experience itself: intelligent creatures are designed by nature (i.e., evolution) to have propositionalized experiences. Since "states of consciousness" are involved, they function in a way that is largely impervious to manipulation. And, in any case, actual *survival* is not a matter of belief at all. Nor is the negative reaction to actual bodily injury and physical harm something markedly susceptible to variation in the beliefs of individuals. "Mind over matter" is a precept whose range of effectiveness has its limits: the "power of positive thinking" is rather feeble in these regards. In human affairs, we are, after all, dealing with a conscious being for whom the affective negativities of actual mishap—and indeed even of merely disappointed ex-

3. This objection is raised in Laurence BonJour, "Rescher's Idealistic Pragmatism," *The Review of Metaphysics* 39 (1976): 702–26; see p. 721.

pectations—can neither be overlooked nor, in the normal course of things, appraised as other than the negatives that they are. The idea that—outside the laboratory setting of Pavlovian conditioning—we can manipulate arbitrarily and at will the sorts of things that cause people happiness or unhappiness, pleasure or pain is surely implausible. A powerful dictator can certainly get people to *do* things, but what he can get them to *think* in line with his wishes is something a good deal less plastic (George Orwell's *1984* notwithstanding).

It is also instructive to contrast the present approach with that of Hilary Putnam's "explanatory realism."[4] On Putnam's approach, the veridicality of the products of our inquiry methods turns on pragmatic argumentation of the format:

- Our epistemic criteria endorse the claims of the corpus *S* (i.e., of science).
- The endorsements of our epistemic criteria—namely, the claims of *S*—are successfully implementable.

*Therefore*: The claims of the corpus *S* are indeed true. Now as Putnam sees it, this argument's conclusion that the theses of science are veridical is to be seen as itself a quasi-scientific theory that effectively and optimally *explains* the successful implementability of these scientific claims in prediction and intervention. The presumptive truth of our scientific claims—their authenticity vis-à-vis the real world—is therefore an inductive product, a scientific theory, an inference to the best explanation.

However, the present methodological pragmatism takes a very different approach. Its reasoning is rather deductive than inductive. The conclusion is seen as

4. See Hilary Putnam's *Meaning and the Moral Sciences* (Oxford: Blackwell, 1978).

emerging from the first premiss alone (since that's exactly how epistemic criterial function). After all, if our epistemic criteria authorize us to assert a thesis, then the truth of this thesis is thereby something to which we stand committed, just because that's exactly what is at issue in these epistemic standards for acceptance *as true*. To be sure, the further question of the *appropriateness or validity* of those epistemic criteria still remains to be considered. And it is on *this* supplemental issue alone that the methodological approach sees the pragmatic efficacy of the second premiss as having an important inductive and evidential bearing.

## 2. The Arbitrament of *Praxis*

From the very outset, pragmatism has taken the position that the paradigm of rational inquiry is not the isolated individual's quest for the certainty of the immediate experience of a Cartesian ego, but the social effort of a community of inquirers striving across the generations to obtain and, improve the answers to enduring questions. And this is emphatically so with a methodological pragmatism, seeing that while beliefs may be something personal, methods are inherently general. Moreover, pragmatism accepts the fallibilistic view that *perfected* performance is always a matter of hope and not achievement. At any particular juncture one simply does the best one can. The cognitive methods and substantive procedures we deploy for forming our view of reality thus evolve selectively by an historic, evolutionary process of "trial and error"—analogous to the mutations affecting the bodily mechanisms by which we comport ourselves in the physical world. Therefore, cognitive methods develop dynamically subject to ongoing revision in response to the element of "success and failure" in point of the teleology of the practice of rational inquiry.

The success-reflecting progressiveness that lies at the root of quality control in scientific inquiry is not something arcane, sophisticated, and extensively theory-laden. It turns on the elemental fact that virtually *any* enhancement in control—any growth of our technological mastery over nature—is bound to have some results that are also discernible at the *grosso modo* level of our everyday life conceptions and dealings. Understanding *how* our capacities are extended in the course of "scientific progress" will generally be a very sophisticated matter, but any fool can see *that* they are extended in certain ways. For it is transparently clear to even the most unsophisticated observer that as regards "control over nature" science has for centuries been moving from strength to strength. The progressiveness of science appears most strikingly and decisively in its ever-expanding predictive and physical control over nature. The old conception of *scientia propter potentiam* provides a perfectly workable basis for taking the widening horizons of technological capacity as an index of scientific progress.[5]

The historical development of methods is a matter of "survival of the fittest" with *fitness* assessed in terms of the practical objectives of the rational enterprise—particularly in the guidance of man's practical affairs. The ways and means of inquiry have been built up by an historic, evolutionary process of selection based on "trial and error," much as has happened with the evolutionary selection bodily mechanisms by which we comport ourselves in the physical world. At this stage, we are carried back to a Darwinian perspective on cognitive evolution. But it is rational rather than natural selection is now critical. The governing standards of

5. This view of science was a philosophical commonplace in the initial era of modern science spanned by the work of Bacon, Hobbes, and Leibniz.

the Western tradition of human rationality are represented by those characteristic goals of science (description, explanation, prediction and control). (And thus not, for example, sentimental "at-oneness with nature"; think of the magician *vs.* the mystic *vs.* the sage as cultural ideal.) The standards of cognitive rationality are therefore viewed in the light of a very basic concept of knowledge-wed-to-practice, and their ultimate validation lies in realizing a combination of theoretical and practical *success*. Their evolutionary development therefore proceeds by explicitly *rational selection*, rather than by some purpose-indifferent process analogous to the *natural selection* of the standard biological case.[6] Elimination is now something that occurs by choice, not by physical annihilation. It turns on what people adopt and transmit—in general because they find it to be serviceable. As changes are entertained (under the pressure of necessitating circumstance), one methodological instrument may eventuate as more fit to survive than another, because it answers better to the range of relevant purposes. And as with any tool or method or instrument, the question of evaluation here takes the instrumentalist form: Does it work? Does it yield desirable results? Is it successful in practice? Legitimation along these lines is found in substantial part in the fact of survival through historical vicissitudes in the context of questions of this sort. The pivotal issue is that of "working out best."

As pragmatism sees it, in a community of rational agents, there is bound to be a parallelism between applicative efficacy and substantiative justification. This circum-

---

6. Of course, even in the most orthodox and rigoristic of biological evolutionisms one cannot but recognize that with the historical emergence of man the purposive aspect must be given a role upon the evolutionary stage, since purpose and final causation here overshadow efficient causation and introduce a "Lamarckian" aspect into evolution. See G. G. Simpson, *The Meaning of Evolution* (New Haven: Yale University Press, 1949), pp. 289ff.

stance has far-reaching ramifications, since pragmatism here becomes conjoined to evolutionism. And control is a pivotal factor here. To be sure, if a bounteous nature satisfied our every whim spontaneously, without effort and striving on our part, the situation would be very different. For then the beliefs which guide and canalize our activities would generally not come into play—they would remain inoperative on the sidelines, never being "put to the test." There would then be no need for active (and thought-guided) intervention in "the natural course of things" within an uncooperative (at best indifferent, at worst hostile) environment. But as things stand, we are constantly called upon to establish varying degrees of "control over nature" to satisfy even our most basic needs (to say nothing of our virtually limitless wants).

The developmental perspective and the pragmatic approach thus join together into a seamless whole. A continuous thread links together the entire tradition of realistic pragmatism in its conviction that the ongoing work of an enduring community of rationally competent inquirers will be self-monitoring—that mistakes will be detected and reduced in the course of time. The guiding conviction is that the community will, over the course of time, learn how to improve its procedures of inquiry through the processes of inquiry itself so that rational inquiry is in this sense self-monitoring and self-corrective. And here we cannot reasonably look on nature as a friendly collaborator in our human efforts, systematically shielding us against the consequences of our follies and crowning our cognitive endeavors with a wholly undeserved success that ensues for reasons wholly independent of any actual adequacy vis-à-vis the intended range of purpose.

An essentially Darwinian perspective is crucial here. It is no more miraculous that the human mind can *understand* nature more or less adequately than it is miraculous that the human eye should be able to *see* it more or less correctly. Peirce's insight holds good: Our cognitive methods are able to earn credit as giving a trustworthy picture of the world precisely because they evolve under the casual pressure of that world.[7] In sum, science stands forth as superior in its claims to providing an appropriate inquiry method on grounds that are essentially pragmatic. And this pragmatic superiority of science as a resource in matters of effective description, explanation, prediction and control both manifests and serves to explain its emergence in cognitive evolution by rational selection.

One crucial point must be emphasized at this stage. In speaking of "the scientific method" in relation to pragmatic endorsement it must, of course, be recognized that what is at issue is not a single and uniform mode of procedure but a vast manifold of thought-tools—of different, albeit interrelated experiential, observational, and inferential methods. And this, of course, means that the scientific method is something that is not fixed (save at the very highest level of generality—but a procedural organon that is itself evolving under the pressure of considerations of pragmatic efficacy. This points to yet another important consideration.

## 3. The Fallibilist Perspective

Methodological pragmatism stands committed to the improvability of our cognitive processes, and thereby acknowledges that our putative knowledge will generally represent no more than a best-available *estimate* of the truth. The proper stance here is that of fallibilism, a philosophical

7. On these issues see also the author's *Methodological Pragmatism*, and *A Useful Inheritance* (Savage MD: Rowman and Littlefield, 1989).

doctrine regarding natural science—most closely associated with Charles Sanders Peirce—maintaining that our scientific knowledge claims are vulnerable and may well turn out to be false. On this view, complex beliefs, and above all our sophisticated scientific theories cannot be asserted as true categorically, but can only be maintained provisionally subject to future revision. Fallibilists insist that we must acknowledge an inability to attain the final and definitive truth regarding the theoretical concerns of natural science—in particular at the frontier of theoretical science. We should and must come to terms with the fact that—at any rate at this level of generality and precision—*each* of our accepted scientific beliefs *may* turn out to be deficient, and *many* of our accepted beliefs *will* turn out to be so.

William James sensibly affirmed that "all our theories are *instrumental*, are mental modes of adaptation to reality."[8] We devise and accept theories with a view to purposes and the appropriateness of those devisings and acceptances has to be construed in purposive terms. But circumstances change. And the conditions which render a theory acceptable at one juncture can—and in the scientific course of things generally do—give way to other conditions which give a different look to the lay of the land. Fallibilism, unlike scepticism, does not insist on the falsity of our scientific contentions but rather on their tentativity as estimates: it does not hold that knowledge is flatly unavailable here, but rather that it is always provisional and that the line of separation between real and merely purported knowledge is imperceptible for us save with the wisdom of hindsight.

Peirce, its most prominent exponent, has not been alone is holding such a fallibilistic position. Other twentieth-century philosophers who have espoused scientific fallibilism in one form or another include Gaston Bachelard, Rudolf Carnap, Pierre Duhem, and Karl Popper.

8. James, *Pragmatism*, p. 94.

In antiquity, the mitigated sceptics of the middle academy were the precursors of this position, since they taught that we can never achieve certain knowledge (*epistêmê*) in matters regarding the world's ways but have to make do with what is nearly probable or plausible (*to pithanon*). Thomas Kuhn's picture of scientific progress, which envisions a repetitive cycle of periods of normal science punctuated by revolutionary revisions, also lends itself naturally to such a construction.[9]

What is it that speaks for fallibilism? Why should we see our most sophisticated claims to knowledge of the world—even in our best state-of-the-art scientific theories—as being vulnerable?

One of the most basic lessons of modern epistemology is that the available observational data will *underdetermine* theories, because theories always outreach the data. Theories always transcend the data and project beyond them, so that there is an inevitable evidential gap between the universal claims of a theory and the particular facts that afforded its supporting data. (The fitting of a continuous curve to discrete data points provides a somewhat oversimplified analogy.) Observations are always discrete, finitely enumerable, and episodic. They deal in specific information-yielding

---

9. Regarding fallibilism and its ramifications see: Gaston Bachelard *Essai sur la connaissance approchóee* (Paris: J. Vrin, 1929); Rudolf Carnap *Logical Foundations of Probability* 2nd rev. ed. (Chicago: University of Chicago Press, 1962); John Dewey *Experience and Nature* (Chicago: Open Court, 1926); Pierre Duhem *La théorie physique, son object et sa structure* (Paris: A. Hermann, 1980). Engl. trans. by P. P. Wiener, *The Aim and Structure of Physical Theory* (Princeton: Princeton University Press, 1954); Thomas Kuhn *The Structure of Scientific Revolutions* (Chicago: University of Chicago Press, 1962); Charles Sanders Peirce *Collected Papers of C. S. Peirce*, eds. C. Hartshorne and P. Weiss, vol. I, "Principles of Philosophy" (Cambridge, MA: Harvard University Press, 1931), see esp. sect. 1.120, "The Uncertainty of Scientific Results"; K. R. Popper *The Logic of Scientific Discovery* (New York: Basic Books, 1959); Nicholas Rescher *The Limits of Science* (Berkeley and Los Angeles: University of California Press, 1984).

episodes that transpire at particular spatiotemporal locations. Theories, on the other hand, are general and non-finite in their bearing: they deal in how certain features of a generic sort characterize situations of a certain kind always and everywhere. As Pierre Duhem already emphasized, scientific theories lie beyond the possibility of definitive confirmation by our limited data.

This data-transcendence of all theoretical claims means that there will always be various alternative ways of rounding the data off into generalized theories. Our actually available information can never constrain unique theoretical resolutions. For observed data are finite; possible hypotheses infinite; and the finite cannot constrain the infinite. The concrete realities we experience observationally are always to some extent ambiguous. In principle they always admit of alternative theoretical rationalizations. Theorizing without data is futile. But even theorizing on the basis of ample data involves risks and carries in its wake the prospect of ambiguity, diversity, and discord.

There is much in such a picture of the cognitive situation that rings true. The fact is that the equilibrium between them and data that is achieved by natural science at *any* given stage of its development is always an unstable one. The subject's history indicates that scientific theories have a finite lifespan; they come to be modified or replaced under various innovative pressures, in particular the enhancement of observational and experimental evidence (through improved techniques of experimentation, more powerful means of observation and detection, superior procedures for data processing, etc.). As philosophers of science have insisted for many years, we must acknowledge an inability to attain the final and definitive truth in the theoretical concerns of natural science—in particular at the level of theoretical physics. Our present-day science cannot plausibly claim to deliver a definitive picture of physical reality—irrespective of what the date on the calendar may be.

Consider an analogy. How do we extract objective factual information from subjective personal experience? Naively by what seems to be an inference from the particular premiss:

> (C) I take myself to be seeing a cat on the mat (i.e., I have the experience of "seeing" a cat on the mat).

via the general premiss:

> (P) Visual experiences are veridical: What I apparently see is in fact the case.

to the conclusion: "There is a cat on the mat." But if this naive account were right, we would be in real difficulty. For the fact of the matter is that premiss (P) is simply false. We know perfectly well—from optical illusion and the trickery of "magicians"—that (P) is unacceptable.

There is, of course, the possibility of replacing (P) by

> (P′) Visual experience is *usually* veridical: What I apparently see is *generally* the case.

But this, unfortunately, does not lead to the desired conclusion but only to "There is *probably* a cat on the mat." And this result, however useful, fails to answer the question of what is on the mat. For there just is no cognitively secure route from probability to fact.

The most sensible line to take here is that what is at issue is not an *inference* at all, but the *implementation of a practical policy*:

- (Experiential fact) I take myself to be seeing a cat on the mat
- (Practical policy) To accept visual experience as veridical

---

∴ There is a cat on the mat.

We thus reach our result not just via "reasoning from experience" but rather through *the experience-imprinted prompt-*

*ing* of taking of something to be so. What is thus at issue is *an experience-imprinted* practical policy resulting in a process that is, to reemphasize, one not of *inferring* but of *taking*.

To be sure, there remains the questions of *justifying* the policy. And it is exactly at this point that earlier premiss (P') comes into play once itself is established through an imprinting by due experiential substantiation. The positive policy at issue is appropriate because experience shows that it is generally successful. It is here—at this methodological / procedural point—that pragmatic considerations come into decisive operation.

One this basis, then, what is at issue in the cognitive exploitation of experience is *a practical policy of procedure* that is itself backed by a probabilistic validation. The upshot, however, is that we do—and must—come to terms with the unpleasant reality of fallibilism. Exactly as experience teaches, we are left with a course of procedure that can occasionally go wrong. Like our best-made plans our best-grounded beliefs are nowise failure-proof. But we nevertheless validate that practical policy on the essentially practical ground that it offers us what is—as best we can tell—the best available means of realizing our ends.

As fallibilism sees the matter, our scientific theories are no more than the best we can do here and now to resolve our question regarding nature's modus operandi. New theoretical knowledge does not just supplement but generally upsets our knowledge-in-hand. Any scientific theory or system is the product of human contrivance, and like any such contrivance—be it a house, a dam, or a knowledge-claim—is ultimately bound to encounter conditions that its constructors did not—and could have—anticipated and which render its ultimate failure likely. Changed social conditions destabilize social systems; changed physical conditions destabilize physical structures; changed experiential (i.e., experimental and observational) conditions—changed scientific technology, if you will—destabilize scientific theories. Rational inquiry links the products of our understanding to the experienced conditions of a world in which chance and chaos plays an ineliminable role, so that there will always be new conditions and circumstances that ultimately threaten our rational contrivances.

We would like to think of our science as money in the bank—as something safe, solid, and reliable. Unfortunately, however, history militates against this comfortable view of our scientific theorizing. In the sophisticated reaches of natural science, new knowledge does not just supplement but generally upsets our knowledge-in-hand. We learn by empirical inquiry about empirical inquiry, and one of the key things we learn is that at no actual stage does science yield a final and unchanging result. We have no responsible alternative to supposing the imperfection of what we take ourselves to know. (And there is no reason to see the posture of our successors as fundamentally different from our own in this respect.) We occupy the predicament of the "Preface Paradox" exemplified by the author who apologizes in his preface for those errors that have doubtless made their way into his work, and yet blithely remains committed to all those assertions he makes in the body of the work itself. We know or must presume that (at the synoptic level) there are errors, though we certainly cannot say where and how they arise.

It may seem strange at first thought, but is nevertheless true, that fallibilism is a more plausible doctrine with respect to *scientific* knowledge than with respect to the less demanding "knowledge" of everyday life. For our ordinary-life generalizations are actually less vulnerable than scientific theories. Someone who asserts (say) that peaches are delicious, means to be saying something like, "Most people will find the eating of suitably grown and duly matured peaches a rather pleasurable experience." Such a statement has all sorts of implicit safeguards, that can be cashed in through such guarding locutions as "more or less," "in ordinary circumstance," "by and large," "normally," "if all things are equal," and so on. They are thus so well hedged that it is eminently implausible that contentions such as these should be overthrown. And an analogous situation obtains even in those sectors of descriptive science where sophisticated precision and detail are not at issue. In theoretical science, however, we willingly accept greater cognitive risks because we ask much more of the project. Here the objectives are primarily theoretical and governed by the aims of disinterested inquiry. Therefore, the claims of informativeness—of generality, exactness, and precision—are paramount in science. Here we deliberately court risk by aiming at maximal definiteness and thus at maximal informativeness and testability.

With any sort of estimate, there is always a characteristic trade-off relationship between the evidential *security* of the estimate on the one hand (as determinable on the basis of its probability or degree of acceptability), and its contentual *definiteness* (exactness, detail, precision, etc.) on the other. But technical science forswears the looseness of vague generality or analogy or approximation. It has no use for qualifiers such as "usually," "normally," or "typically"; universality and exactness are its touchstones—it declares not merely that roughly such-and-such generally occurs in certain sorts of circumstances but exactly what happens in exactly what circumstances. The law claims of science involve no hedging, no fuzziness, no incompleteness, and no exceptions; they are strict: precise, wholly explicit, exceptionless, and unshaded. In making the scientific assertion "The melting point of lead is 327.5°C," we mean to assert that *all* pieces of (pure) lead will unfailingly melt at *exactly* this temperature. We certainly do not mean to assert that *most* pieces of (pure) lead will probably melt at *somewhere around* this temperature. In technical science we always aim at the maximum of universality, precision, accuracy, and exactness. And this commitment to generality and detailed precision renders the claims of science highly vulnerable. We realize that none of the hard claims of present-day frontier natural science will move down the corridors of time untouched. Fragility is the price that we pay in science for the sake of generality, precision, and sophistication. We therefore have little choice but to acknowledge the vulnerability of our scientific beliefs, subject to the operation of the security definiteness trade-off. Ironically, then, the common sense of everyday life is securer than the more sophisticated claims of frontier science.

But does fallibilism not make science as we have it into a matter of "the mere opinion of the day"—of mere social consensus in the scientific community? To protect scientific realism in the face of the prospect of unending scientific change, it is tempting to adopt Peirce's stratagem of a resort to *convergent approximation*. This calls for envisaging a situation where, with the passage of time, the theories we successively arrive at grow increasingly concordant and their claims less and less differentiated. In the face of such a course of successive changes of ever-diminishing significance, we could proceed to maintain that the world really is not as *present* science claims it to be, but rather is as the ever more clearly emerging science-in-the-limit claims it to be. The reality of ongoing change is now irrelevant as with the passage of time the changes matter less and less. We increasingly approximate an essentially stable picture.

This prospect is attractive and it is certainly a theoretically possible one. But neither historical experience nor considerations of general principle provide reason to think that it is actually possible. Indeed, quite the reverse!

In any convergent process, later is lesser. But since scientific progress on matters of fundamental importance is generally a matter of replacement rather than mere supplementation, there is no reason to see the *later* issues of science as *lesser* issues in the significance of their bearing upon science as a cognitive enterprise—to think that nature will be cooperative in always yielding its most important secrets early on and reserving nothing but the relatively insignificant for later on. The fact is that a very small-scale effect—even one that lies very far out along the extremes of a "range exploration" in terms of temperature, pressure, velocity, or the like—can force a far-reaching revolution and have a profound impact by way of major theoretical revisions. (Think of special relativity in relation to aetherdrift experimentation, or general relativity in relation to the perihelion of Mercury.) Given that natural science progresses mainly by substitutions and replacements that go back to fundamentals and lead to comprehensive overall revisions of our picture of the phenomena at issue, it seems sensible to say that the shifts across successive scientific "revolutions" maintain the same level of overall significance—it is neither a convergent nor a divergent process. Thus, if we are to be realistic fallibilists we must hold a position more radical than that of Peirce. His approximationism is simply too optimistic to accommodate the harsh realities.

However, fallibilism is an invitation not to scepticism but to doing the very best we can manage in the circumstances. We may not be able to *perfect* our knowledge but we can certainly *improve* it. In human inquiry, the cognitive ideal is correlative with the striving for definitive systematization. And this is an ideal which, like other ideals, is worthy of pursuit despite the fact that we must recognize that its full attainment lies beyond our grasp.

The partisans of purely theoretical disciplines like mathematics may wonder if pragmatism does not simply abolish necessity altogether. The answer is: No. A sensible pragmatism will take a complex, multi-stage line of approach which holds that: (1) Necessity is always contextual, that is, relative to the conceptual framework of a certain modality of cognitive deliberation. (2) Such deliberation is always purposive: it proceeds within certain problem-posing structures. (3) The issue of the extent to which a conceptual framework is appropriate hinges upon its effectiveness within the problem-solution at issue. On this basis a thesis is necessary in a manner that is not absolute but contextual, with the appropriateness of necessity imputations hinging on the question of whether the concept framework within which that necessity obtains is (relative to the available alternatives) optimally effective for the problem solutions at issue. Thus, for example, the proponents of arithmetic are necessary propositions that acknowledged as such even by pragmatists. And this is so because they are contextually necessary within the standard arithmetic that is optimally efficacious for dealing with quantitative matters within the range of cases at issue (in ordinary life, accounting, science, etc.).

In general, however, a pragmatically realistic fallibilism insists that we would do well to temper our claims to categorical knowledge with a Cognitive Copernicanism. The original Copernican revolution made the point that there is nothing *ontologically* privileged about our own position in space. The fallibilistic doctrine now at issue effectively holds that there is nothing *cognitively* privileged about our own position in time. A kind of intellectual humility is in order—a diffidence that abstains from the hubris of pretentions to cognitive finality or centrality. Realism calls for the humbling view that just as we think our predecessors of a hundred years had a fundamentally inadequate grasp on the furniture of the world, so our successors of a hundred years hence will almost certainly take the same view of *our* purported knowledge of things. It is not that natural science as we have it is the *best possible* cognition about the world, but rather that it is *the best that is available to us*, here and now.

It yet remains to be considered more closely how, despite its espousal of fallibilism, a sensible pragmatism is nevertheless able to overcome the relativistically negative tendency so often attributed to pragmatism—and rightly so in the case of what our earlier discussion characterized as the "pragmatism of the left." How, given its fallibilistic stance, can pragmatism possibly provide for realism and objectivity? It is to this task that the next chapter will be addressed.

CHAPTER FIVE

# *Metaphysical Realism and the Pragmatic Basis of Objectivity*

## Synopsis

*(1) Metaphysical realism is not a position that one can establish on the basis of mere observation. Being a precondition for rather than a consequence of our empirical knowledge, it is something that we presuppose for our inquiries rather than learn or infer from them. (2) However, the legitimation of this presuppositional precommitment can proceed smoothly on practical and instrumentalistic lines. (3) For without it, communication about and inquiry into the world about us would become infeasible, and the project of information acquisition that is so crucial to meeting our needs would thereby become impracticable. (4) The validation of our commitment to realism is ultimately retrospective, resting on the pragmatic consideration of its applicative and implementational efficacy. In this way, realism's prime support lies in the pragmatically utilitarian consideration of what it manages to do for us.*

## 1. The Existential Component of Realism

Realism has two indispensable and inseparable constituents—the one existential and ontological, the other cognitive and epistemic. The former maintains that there indeed is a real world—a realm of mind-independent, objective physical reality. The latter maintains that we can to some extent secure adequate descriptive information about this mind-independent realm—that we can validate plausible claims about it. This second contention obviously presupposes the first, seeing that behind the question "Are our claims about an item correct?" there unavoidably stands the question "Are our claims about this item at all?" But how can that first, ontological thesis of metaphysical realism be secured within a generally pragmatic approach?

The answer here lies in the consideration that realism represents a commitment that we *presuppose* for our inquiries rather than *discover* as a result of them. For we do not—cannot—discover as a result of (mind-managed!) inquiry and investigation that a totally mind-detached reality actually exists. This is clearly not an inductive inference issuing from the scientific systematization of our observations, but rather represents a regulative, thought-guiding presupposition that makes empirical inquiry possible in the first place. How could we ever learn from observation that our mental experience is itself largely the causal product of the machinations of a mind-independent manifold—that all those phenomenal appearances are causally rooted in an altogether mind-external physical realm? What is at issue here is a practice-enabling presupposition that experience is indeed objective. That what we *take* to be evidence indeed *is* evidence, that our sensations yield information about an order of existence outside the experiential realm itself, and that this experience is not just a mere phenomenon but represents the appearance of something extramental, belonging to an objectively self-subsisting order—all this is something that we must always *presuppose* in using experiential data as "evidence" for how things stand in the world. For if we did not presume from the very outset that our sensations somehow relate to an extramental reality so as to be able to evidentiate claims about its nature, then we could clearly make no use of them to draw any inference whatever about "the real world."

The commitment to a mind-independent reality is, all too clearly, a *precondition* for empirical inquiry—a presupposition we have to make to be able to use observational data as sources of objective information. We really have no alternative but to *presume or postulate* it. Objectivity represents a postulation made on *functional* (rather than *evidential*) grounds: we endorse it in order to be in a position to learn by experience. What is at issue here is not so much a product of our experience of reality as a factor that makes it possible to view our experience as being "of reality" at all. As Immanuel Kant clearly saw, objective experience is possible only if the existence of such a real, objective world is an available given from the outset rather than the product of experience—an ex post facto discovery about the nature of things.[1]

Our endorsement of the reality of observation-engendering causs in nature—which as *causes of experience* in the

---

1. Immanuel Kant held that we cannot experientially learn through perception about the objective reality of outer things, because we can only recognize our perceptions as *perceptions* (i.e., representations of outer things) if these outer things are supposed as real from the first (rather than being learned or inferred from representations). As he summarizes the matter in the "Refutation of Idealism": "Idealism assumed that the only immediate experience is inner experience, and that from it we can only *infer* outer things—and this, moreover, only in an untrustworthy manner. . . . But in the above proof it has been shown that outer experience is really immediate. . . ." (*CPuR*, B276). Here "is really immediate" is to be construed as: "must be accepted noninferentially from the very outset, because inference could not accomplish what is needed to arrive at those outer things from mere experience."

order of being also do double duty as inferences from it in the order of learning—is not based on empirical investigation but on general principles of a procedural character. What we learn from science is not and cannot be *that* an inherently unobservable subobservable order of physical causality undergirds nature as we observe it, but rather *what*—with their reality taken as given—these underlying and preliminarily presumed agencies must specifically be like. Science does not (cannot) teach us that the observable order emerges from underlying unobserved causes and that the phenomena of observation are signs betokening this extra- and sub-phenomenal order of existence. For this is something that we must presume a priori of any world in which *observation* as we understand it can transpire. What science does teach us (and metaphysics cannot) is what can plausibly take to be the descriptive character of this phenomena-engendering order.

Of course, once we have postulated an objective reality and its concomitant causal operation, then principles of inductive systematization, of explanatory economy, and of common cause consilience can work wonders in exploiting the phenomena of experience to provide the basis for plausible claims about the nature of the real. But we indispensably need that initial existential presupposition to make a start. Without that natural commitment to a reality serving as ground and object of our experience, its cognitive import will be lost. Only on this basis can we proceed evidentially with the exploration of the interpersonally public and objective domain of a physical world order that we share in common. Only by way of a facilitating presupposition that is ultimately retrovalidated through its applicative utility and efficacy can we ever hope to establish that our observational experience—unlike our dream experience—is ever *evidence* for anything objectively mind-external, that is, is ever able to provide information about a "real world."

That second, descriptive (evidential) component of realism thus stands on a very different footing from its first, existential (presuppositional) component. For reality's *nature* is something about which we can only make warranted claims through actually examining it. Substantive information must come through inquiry—through evidential validation. Once we are willing to credit our observational data with objectivity,—with reality-orientation and thus with evidential bearing—then we can, of course, make use of them to inform ourselves as to the nature of the real. But the objective bearing of observational experience is not something that we can preestablish; it is something we must presuppose in the interest of honoring Peirce's pivotal injunction never to bar the path of inquiry. And the functional nature of this practice-enabling presupposition means that the validation process at work must—at this fundamental level—be altogether pragmatic. It represents a step we take prospectively—in order to put ourselves into a position to satisfy our goals.

## 2. Realism in its Regulative / Pragmatic Aspect

The preceding deliberations point clearly in the direction of a pragmatic justification for our realistic stance toward our experience as intensionally indicative of something beyond itself. The commitment to realism is the possibilizing instrumentality for a certain practical modus operandi. We therefore have good reason—good *pragmatic* reason—for standardly operating on the basis of the "presumption of objectivity" reflected in the guiding precept: "Unless you have good reason to think otherwise (that is, as long as nothing impedes: *nihil obstat*) treat the materials of inquiry and communication as veridical—as representing the nature of the real." The ideal of objective reality is the focus of a family of convenient regulative principles—a functionally useful instrumentality that enables us to transact our cognitive business in the most satisfactory and effective way. And so, bearing this pragmatic perspective in mind, let us consider this issue of utility and ask: What can this postulation of a mind-independent reality actually do for us?

The answer is straightforward. The assumption of a mind-independent reality is essential to the whole of our standard conceptual scheme relating to inquiry and communication. Without it, both the actual conduct and the rational legitimation of our communicative and investigative (evidential) practice would be destroyed. To be evidentially meaningful, experience has to be experience of something. And nothing that we do in this cognitive domain would make sense if we did not subscribe to the conception of a mind-independent reality. And since this is not a learned fact it is—and must be!—an assumption whose prime recommendation is its utility.

To begin with, we indispensably require the notion of reality to operate the classical concept of truth as "agreement with reality" (*adaequatio ad rem*). Once we abandon the concept of reality, the idea that in accepting a factual claim as true we become committed to how matters actually stand—"how it really is"—would also go by the board. The very semantics of our discourse constrains a commitment to realism; we have no alternative but to regard as real those states of affairs that are affirmed by the contentions we are prepared to accept. Once we put a contention forward by way of serious assertion, we must view as real the states of affairs it purports, and must see its claims as facts. We need the notion of reality to operate the conception of truth. A factual statement on the order of "There are pi mesons" is true if and only if the world is such that pi mesons exist within it. By virtue of their very nature as truths, true statements must state facts: they state what really is so, which is exactly what it is to "characterize reality." The conception of *truth* and of *reality* come together in this notion of *adaequatio ad rem*—the venerable principle that to speak truly is to say how matters stand in reality, in that things actually are as we have said them to be.

In the second place, the nihilistic denial that there is such a thing as an objectively mind-independent realm would destroy once and for all the crucial Parmenidean divide between appearance and reality. And this would exact a fearful price from us, since we would then be reduced to talking only of what we (I, you, many of us) *think* to be so. The crucial contrast notion of the *real* truth would no longer be available: we would only be able to contrast our *putative* truths with those of others, but could no longer operate the classical distinction between the putative and the actual, between what people merely *think* to be so and what actually *is* so. We could not take the stance that, as the Aristotelian commentator Themistius put it, "that which exists does not conform to various opinions, but rather the correct opinions conform to that which exists."[2]

The third point relates to the issue of cognitive coordination. Communication and inquiry, as we actually carry them on, are predicated on the fundamental idea of a real world of objective things, existing and functioning "in themselves," without specific dependence on us and so equally accessible to others. Intersubjectively valid communication can only be based on common access to an objective order of things. All our ventures at communication and communal inquiry are predicated on the stance that we communally inhabit a shared world of things. They presuppose there is a realm of "real objects" among which we live and into which we inquire as a community, but about which we ourselves as

2. Maimonides, *The Guide for the Perplexed*, trans. M. Friedlander (London: George Routledge and Sons, 1904), vol. I:71, 96a.

individuals presumably have only imperfect information that can be criticized and augmented by the efforts of others.

This points to a fourth important consideration. Only through reference to the real world as a *common object* and shared focus of our diverse and imperfect epistemic strivings are we able to effect communicative contact with one another. Inquiry and communication alike are geared to the conception of an objective world: a communally shared realm of things that exist strictly "on their own" within which and, more importantly, with reference to which inquiry proceeds. We could not proceed on the basis of the notion that inquiry estimates the character of the real if we were not prepared to presume or postulate from the very outset a reality for these estimates to be estimates of. It would clearly be pointless to devise our characterizations of reality if we did not stand committed to the proposition that there is a reality to be characterized.

The fifth consideration is that the very idea of inquiry as we conceive it would have to be abandoned if the conceptions of "actual reality" and "the real truth" were no longer available to serve their crucial contrasting roles. We could no longer assert: "What we have there is good enough as far as it goes, but it is presumably not 'the whole real truth' of the matter." Without the conception of reality we could not think of our knowledge in the fallibilistic mode we actually use—as having provisional, tentative, improvable features that constitute a crucial part of the conceptual scheme within whose orbit we operate our concept of inquiry. For our commitment to the mind-independent reality of "the real world" stands together with our acknowledgment that, in principle, any or all of our *present* scientific ideas as to how things work in the world, at *any* present, may well prove to be untenable. The information that we may have about a thing, be it real or presumptive information, is always just that—information *we* lay claim to. We recognize that it varies from person to person. Our attempt at communication and inquiry are thus undergirded by the stance that we communally inhabit a shared world of objectively existing things, a world of "real things" among which we live and into which we inquire (but about which we do and must assume that we have only imperfect information at any and every particular stage of the cognitive venture). Our conviction in a reality that lies beyond our imperfect understanding of it (in all the various senses of "lying beyond") roots in our sense of the imperfections of our scientific world picture—its tentativity and potential fallibility. In abandoning our commitment to a mind-independent reality, we would lose the indispensably objective impetus of inquiry.

After all, reality (on the traditional metaphysicians' construction of the concept) is the condition of things answering to "the real truth"; it is the realm of what really is as it really is. The pivotal contrast is between "mere appearance" and "reality as such," between "our picture of reality" and "reality itself," between what actually is and what we merely think (believe, suppose, etc.) to be. Our allegiance to the conception of reality, and to the appearance / reality contrast that pivots upon it, roots in the fallibilistic recognition that, at the level of the detailed specifics of scientific theory, anything we presently hold to be the case can possibly turn out otherwise—indeed, certainly will do so if past experience give any auguries for the future.

Sixth and finally, we need the conception of reality in order to operate the causal model of empirical inquiry regarding the real world. Our standard picture of our place in the scheme of things is predicated on the fundamental idea that there is a real world (however imperfectly our inquiry may characterize it) whose causal operations produce *inter alia* causal impacts upon us, providing the basis of our world picture. Reality is viewed as the causal source and basis of the appearances, the originator, and determiner of the phenomena of our cognitively relevant experience. "The real world" is seen as causally operative both in serving as the external moulder of thought and as constituting the ultimate arbiter of the adequacy of our theorizing.

In summary, then, we need that postulate of an objective order of mind-independent reality for at least six important reasons.

- To preserve the distinction between true and false with respect to factual matters and to operate the idea of truth as agreement with reality.
- To preserve the distinction between appearance and reality, between our *picture* of reality and reality itself.
- To serve as a basis for intersubjective communication.
- To furnish the basis for a shared project of communal inquiry.
- To provide for the fallibilistic view of human knowledge.
- To sustain the causal mode of learning and inquiry and to serve as basis for the objectivity of experience.

What is at stake is ultimately a principle of practice—though, to be sure, it is thought-practice that is at issue. And the justification for this fundamental presupposition of objectivity is not *evidential* at all; postulates as such are not based on evidence. Rather, it is practical and instrumentalistic—pragmatic, in short. It is procedural or functional efficacy that is the crux. The justification of this postulate lies in its utility: we need it to operate our conceptual scheme. We could not form our existing conceptions of truth, fact, inquiry, and communication without presupposing the independent reality of an external world. In its absence, we simply could not think of experience and inquiry as we actually do. (What we have here is a "transcendental argument" of sorts, namely, one that from the character of our conceptual scheme to the unavoidability of accepting its inherent presuppositions.)

And so, our commitment to the mind-independent reality of "the real world" stands alongside our fallibilistic acknowledgment that in principle any or all of our *present* scientific ideas as to how things work in the world, at *any* present, may well prove to be untenable. Our conviction of a reality that lies beyond our imperfect understanding of it (in all the various senses of "lying beyond") roots in our sense of the imperfections of our scientific world picture—its tentativity and potential fallibility. In abandoning this commitment to a mind-independent reality, we would lose the impetus of inquiry. And yet realism's epistemic status is not that of an empirical discovery, but that of a presupposition whose ultimate justification is a transcendental argument from the very possibility of the projects of communication and inquiry as we standardly conduct them.

The presuppositional conception of a mind-independent reality therefore plays a central and indispensable role in our thought about matters cognition. It is seen as the epistemological *object* of veridical cognition, in the context of the contrast between "the real" and its "merely phenomenal" appearances. Moreover, it is seen as the target of *telos* of the truth-estimation process at issue in inquiry, providing for a common focus in communication and communal inquiry. (The "real world" thus constitutes the *object* of our cognitive endeavors in both senses of this term—the *objective* at which they are directed and the *purpose* for which they are exerted.) And, further, reality is also to be seen as the ontological *source* of cognitive endeavors, affording the existential matrix in which we live and move and have our being—and whose impact upon us is the prime mover for our cognitive efforts. All of these facets of the concept of reality are integrated and unified in the classical doctrine of truth as it corresponds to fact (*adaequatio ad rem*), a doctrine that not merely invites but indeed requires a commitment to mind-independent reality as constituting at once the framework and the object of our cognitive endeavors in science. And their ultimate ratification lies in their role as indispensable presuppositions for our unavoidable practices.

## 3. Realism and Objectivity as a Requisite of Communication

In matters of communication too the idea of mind-independent reality is functionally pivotal. For subscription to an objective reality is indispensably demanded by any step into the domain of the publicly accessible objects essential to communal inquiry and interpersonal communication about a shared world. We could not establish communicative contact about a common objective item of discussion if our discourse were geared to our own idiosyncratic experiences and these conceptions bound up with them. But the objectivity at issue in our communicative discourse is a matter of its very *status* as putatively communicative, rather than somehow depending upon its specific *content*. For the substantive content of a claim about the world in no way tells us whether it is factual or fictional. This is something that we have to determine from its *context*, which means, in effect, that in general it is provided for by a preestablished conventionalized intention to talk about "the real world." This intention to take real objects to be at issue, objects as they actually are, our potentially idiosyncratic conceptions of them quite aside, is fundamental because it is overriding—that is, it overrides all of our other intentions when we enter upon the communicative venture. Without this conventionalized intention we should not be able to convey information—or misinformation—to one another about a shared "objective" world that underlies and connects those variable experiences of ours.

If it were not reality as it actually is that we are concerned to discuss, but merely "reality-as-I-conceive-it-to-be," then we could not really manage to agree or disagree with one another. Indeed we then just could not communicate successfully in the informative mode. We are able to say something about the (real) moon or the (real) Sphinx, because of our submission to a fundamental communicative convention or "social contract" to the effect that we *intend* (mean) to talk about the very thing itself as it "really" is—our own personal conception of it notwithstanding. We adopt the standard policy in communicative discourse of letting the communally established language rather than whatever specific informative notions and conceptions we may actually "have in mind" on particular occasions, be the decisive factor with regard to the things at issue in our discussions. When I speak about the Sphinx (even though I do so on the basis of my own conceivably strange conception of what is involved here), I will be discussing "the *real* Sphinx" in virtue of the basic conventionalized intention governing our use of referring terms within the wider community.

Any effective venture in communication must be predicated on the fundamental intention to deal with the objective order of this "real world."

This fundamental intention of objectification, the intention to discuss "the actual Sphinx" or "the moon itself"—regardless of how untenable one's own ideas about it may eventually prove to be—is in fact a basic precondition of the very possibility of communication. If our assertoric commitments did not transcend the information we have on hand, we would never be able to "get in touch" with others about a shared objective world. It is crucial to the communicative enterprise to take the egocentrism-avoiding stance that rejects all claims to a privileged status for *our own* conception of things. In the interests of this stance, we are prepared to "discount any misconception" (our own included) about things over a very wide range indeed—that we are committed to the stance that factual disagreements as to the character of things are communicatively irrelevant within very broad limits. No claim is made for the *primacy* of our own conceptions, for their *correctness*, or even for their mere *agreement* with those of others. The fundamental intention to discuss "the thing itself" predominates and overrides any mere dealing with the thing as we conceive it to be. Certainly, that reference to "objectively real things" at work in our discourse does not contemplate a peculiar sort of *thing*—a new *ontological* category of "things-in-themselves." It is simply a shorthand formula for a certain communicative presumption or imputation rooted in an a priori commitment to the idea of a commonality of objective focus—a presumption that is allowed to stand unless and until circumstances arise to render this step untenable.

And the possible incorrectness of our conceptions is venial in this regard. For if we were to set up our own conception of things as somehow definitive and decisive, we would at once erect a barrier not only to further inquiry but—no less importantly—to the prospect of successful communication with one another. Communication could then only proceed with the wisdom of hindsight—at the end of a long process of tentative checks. "Aha," I can say at the end of a long exchange—and then only—"*now* I can see (or, at least, can plausibly *conjecture*) what it is that was talking about." Communicative contact would be realized only in the generally problematic situation where extensive exchange indicates retrospectively that a consilence of views exists so that there has been an *identity* of conceptions all along. And we would always stand on very shaky ground. For no matter how far we push our investigation into the issue of an identity of conceptions, the prospect of a divergence lying just around the corner—waiting to be discovered if only we pursued the matter just a bit further—can never be precluded. One could never advance the issue of the identity of focus past the status of a more or less well-grounded *assumption*. And then any so called communication would no longer be an exchange of information but a tissue of frail conjectures. The communicative enterprise would become a vast inductive project—a complex exercise in theory-building, leading tentatively and provisionally toward something which, in fact, the imputational groundwork of our language enables us to presuppose from the very outset.[3]

The fundamental convention of a shared social insistence on communicating—the commitment to an objective world of real things—affords the crucially requisite common focus indispensable to any genuine communication. What links my discourse topically with that of my interlocutors is our common subscription to the a priori presumption (a defeasible presumption, to be sure) that we are both talking about a shared thing, our own possible misconceptions of it notwithstanding. The commitment to objectivity is based to any prospect of our discourse with one another about a shared world of "real things," to which none of us in a position to claim privileged access. This commitment establishes a need to "distance" ourselves from things, that is, to recognize the prospect of a discrepancy between our (potentially idiosyncratic) conceptions of things and the true character of these things as they exist objectively in "the real world." And the conception of a mind-independent reality is the ever-present mechanism by which this crucially important distancing is accomplished.

However, maintaining this stance means that we are never entitled to claim to have exhausted a thing *au fond* in cognitive regards, to have managed to bring it wholly within our epistemic grasp. For to make this claim would, in effect, be to *identify* "the thing at issue" purely in terms of "our own conception of it," and identification which would effectively remove the former item (the thing itself) from the stage of consideration as an independent entity in its own right, by endowing our conception with decisively determinative force. And this would lead straightway to the unacceptable result of a cognitive solipsism that would preclude reference to intersubjectively identifiable particulars,

3. The justification of such imputations is treated more fully in chapter IX of the author's *Induction* (Oxford: Blackwell, 1980).

and would thus block the possibility of interpersonal communication and communal inquiry.

Any and all pretensions to the primacy and predominance, let alone the definitive correctness, of our own conceptions, regarding the realm of the real must be set aside in the context of communication. In communication regarding things, we must be able to exchange information about them with our contemporaries and to transmit information about them to our successors. And we must be in a position to do this on against the background of the recognition that *their* conceptions of things may not only be radically different from *ours*, but conceivably also rightly different. Thus, it is a crucial precondition of the possibility of successful communication about things that we must avoid laying any claim either to the completeness or even to the ultimate correctness of our own conception of any of the things at issue. This renders critically important *that* (and understandable *why*) conceptions are not pivotal for communicative purposes. Our discourse *reflects* our conceptions and perhaps *conveys* them, but it is not substantively *about* them. Thus, we deliberately abstain from any claim that our own conception is definitive if we are to engage successfully in discourse. We deliberately put the whole matter of conceptions aside—abstracting from the question of the agreement of my conception with yours, and all the more from the issue of which one of us has the right conception. This sort of epistemic humility is the price we pay for keeping the channels of communication open.

But why embark upon the objectivity-presupposing projects of inquiry and communication at all? Why not settle back in comfortable abstention from this whole complex business?

The answer is straightforward. The impetus to inquiry for knowledge-acquisition reflects the most practical of imperatives. Our need for *intellectual* accommodation in this world is no less pressing and no less *practical* than our need for physical accommodation. But in both cases, we do not want just some house or other, but one that is well built, that will not be blown down by the first wind to sweep along. Sceptics from antiquity onward have always said, "Forget about those abstruse theoretical issues; focus on your practical needs." They overlook the crucial fact that an intellectual accommodation to the world is itself one of our deepest practical needs—that in a position of ignorance or cognitive dissonance we cannot function satisfactorily.

After all, the project of cognitive development is not optional—at any rate not for us humans. Its rationale lies in the most practical and prudent of considerations, since it is only by traveling the path of inquiry that we can arrive at the sorts of good reasons capable of meeting the demands of a "*rational* animal." Homo sapiens has evolved within nature into the ecological niche of an intelligent being. In consequence, the need for understanding, for "knowing one's way about," is one of the most fundamental demands of the human condition. The practical benefits of knowledge, on the other hand, relate to its role in guiding the processes by which we satisfy our (noncognitive) needs and wants. The satisfaction of our needs for food, shelter, protection against the elements, and security against natural and human hazards all require information. And the satisfaction of mere desiderata comes into it as well. We can, do, and must put knowledge to work to facilitate the attainment of our goals, guiding our actions and activities in this world into productive and rewarding lines. And this is where the practical payoff of the information we secure through inquiry and communication comes into play. Here again, pragmatic considerations are paramount.

Only by subscribing to that fundamental reality postulates can we take the sort of view of experience, inquiry, and communication that we in fact have. Without it, the entire conceptual framework of our thinking about the world and our place within it would come crashing down. And the validation of those communication-enabling presuppositions thus lies in this very fact. It is a practical validation. The utility of a commitment to objective reality within the context of our cognitive and practical endeavors is such that even if it were not there, we would have to invent it. Did we perhaps do so? Can it be that nothing more than an intellectual artifact is at issue? Does that underlying *praxis* itself admit of some further and deeper justification? But how can the pragmatic basis of our concept of reality by itself provide an adequate validation for this crucial resource of communication and inquiry? A "validation" in terms of functional utility establishes our claims to mind-independent reality not by the cognitive route of learning but by the pragmatic route of an indispensably useful postulation. Crucial though this may be, it clearly cannot be the *entire* story.

## 4. Retrojustification: The Wisdom of Hindsight

The consideration that we *must* proceed in the way of objectivity-presuming cognition as a matter of the functional requisites of our situation because there is just no viable alternative if our aims are to be attained and our needs and purposes served, stops short of being altogether conclusive. For it does not offer us any assurance that we will actually succeed in our endeavor if we do proceed in this way; it just has it that we will not if we do not. And so, the issue of actual effectiveness remains undecided and a nagging doubt still remains, one which roots in the challenge: "Let it be granted that this line of approach provides a cogent practical argument. All this shows only that realism is *useful*—perhaps so much so as to be effectively indispensable for us. But does that make it *true*? Is there any rational warrant for it over and above the mere fact of its utility?"

To respond to this sort of challenge, we have to move beyond presupposed functional requisites to address the issue of actual effectiveness. We must now have recourse to the resources of actual experience. For what *is* learned by experience—and can only be learned in this way—is that in proceeding on this prejudgment our attempts do, by and large, work out pretty well vis-à-vis the purposes we have in view for inquiry and communication.

The starting point of our justifactory reasoning was a basic project-facilitating postulation. Yet this does not tell the whole story. For there is also the no less important fact that this postulation obtains a vindicating retrojustification because the farther we proceed on this basis, the more its obvious appropriateness comes to light. With the wisdom of hindsight, we come to see with increasing clarity that the project that these presuppositions render possible is an eminently successful one. The pragmatic turn does crucially important work here in putting at our disposal a style of justificatory argumentation that manages to be cyclical without vitiating circularity. What is at issue is a matter of unavoidable presumptions whose specific mode of implementation is ultimately retrovalidated in the light of experience.

We want and need objective information about "the real world." This, of course, is not to be had directly without the epistemic mediation of experience. And so we treat certain data as evidence—we extend "evidential credit" to them as it were. Through trial and error we learn that some of them do indeed *deserve* it, and then we proceed to extend to them greater weight—we "increase their credit limit" as it were and rely on them more extensively. And, of course, to use those data as evidence is to build up a picture of the world, a picture which shows, with the "wisdom of hindsight," how appropriate it was for us to use those evidential data in the first place.

Charles Sanders Peirce put the issue with his characteristic clarity: "It may be asked how I know that there are reals. If this hypothesis is the sole support of my method of inquiry, my method of inquiry must not be used to support my hypothesis."[4] Peirce placed his finger on exactly the right question. Yet while this reality-hypothesis is indeed not a product of inquiry, but a presupposition for it, nevertheless, it is one whose justification ultimately stands or falls on the success of the inquiries it facilitates. Its validation cannot be preestablished through evidence but can only be provided ex post facto through the justificatory impetus of successful implementation.

On this basis, the substantive picture of nature's ways that is secured through our empirical inquiries is itself ultimately justified, retrospectively as it were, through affording us with the presuppositions on whose basis inquiry proceeds. As we proceed to develop science there must come a retrojustifactory "closing of the circle." The world picture that science delivers into our hands must eventually become such as to explain how it is that creatures such as ourselves, emplaced in the world as we are, investigating it by the processes we actually use, should do fairly well at developing a workable view of that world. As we saw in the preceding chapter's discussion of "rational selection," the "validation of scientific method" must and can in the end itself become scientifically validated. Though the process is cyclic and circular, there is nothing vicious and vitiating about it.

The rational structure of the overall process of justification accordingly looks as follows:

1. We use various sorts of experiential data as evidence of objective fact, and—
2. We do this in the first instance for purely *practical* reasons, *faute de mieux*, because only by proceeding in this way can we hope to resolve our questions with any degree of rational satisfaction. (Functional validation.)
3. But as we proceed two things happen:
   (*a*) On the pragmatic side we find that we obtain a world

4. Peirce, *Collected Papers*, vol. V: sect. 5.383.

picture on whose basis we can operate effectively. (Pragmatic revalidation.)

(*b*) On the cognitive side we find that we arrive at a picture of the world that can itself provide an explanation of how it is that we are encouraged to get things (roughly) right—that we are in fact justified in using our phenomenal data as data of objective fact. (Explanatory revalidation.)

The success at issue in this pragmatic perspective is twofold—both in terms of understanding (cognition) and in terms of application (*praxis*). And it is this ultimate success that justifies and rationalizes, retrospectively, our evidential proceedings. In the first instance we have to do with pragmatic necessity; in the final analysis we come to the realm of pragmatic efficacy.

Therefore, we arrive at the overall situation of dual "retrojustification" depicted in the systems-theoretic process description of figure 5.1, which shows that all the presuppositions of inquiry are ultimately justified because of a "wisdom of hindsight" enables us to see that by their means we have been able to achieve both practical success and a theoretical understanding of our place in the world's scheme of things. Here, the cycles must—and presumably do—close in smooth loops of systemic justification. And both loops are crucial. Successful practical implementation is needed as an extratheoretical quality-control monitor of our theorizing. And the capacity of our scientifically devised view of the world to underwrite an explanation of how it is that a creature constituted as we are, operating by the means of inquiry that we employ, and operating within an environment such as ours, can ultimately devise a relatively accurate view of the world is also critical for the validation of our knowledge.[5] The closing of these inquiry-geared loops

5. These issues are examined in greater detail in the author's *Methodological Pragmatism* (Oxford: Basil Blackwell, 1977).

**Figure 5.1**
**The Retrojustification of the Presupposition of Inquiry**

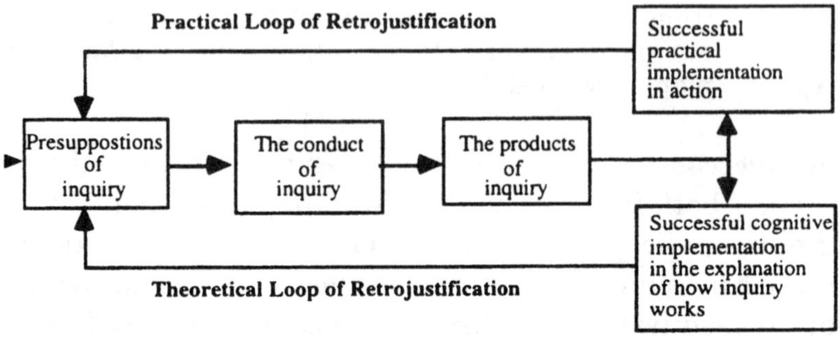


validates, retrospectively, those several realistic presuppositions or postulations that made the whole process of inquiry possible in the first place. Realism thus emerges as a presupposition-affording postulate for inquiry—a postulation whose ultimate legitimation eventuates retrospectively through the results, both practical and cognitive, which the process of inquiry based on those yet-to-be-justified presuppositions is able to achieve.

The retroactive component of the justification at issue is critical for present purposes. That a priori presumption of realism could be validated by the "essential presupposition" argument that if we do not proceed in this way then success in the projects at issue (inquiry and communication) simply becomes impossible. So far so good. But not quite enough. For this pivots the matter on the issue of the mere possibility of success. It does nothing to extend any sort of assurance that success will actually be attained. (We remain at the level of necessary conditions without embarking on the issue of sufficiency.) And this is something that can only be achieved ex post facto—after we actually go on to proceed with the process of inquiring. That this is achievable in a reasonable degree is something that has to be a matter of actual discovery. And it is here that the factor of pragmatic efficacy at issue with such retrojustification comes to play its critical role.

Let us then review the overall line of deliberation. Metaphysical realism—the doctrine that there is a mind-independent reality and that our experience can provide us with a firm cognitive grip upon it—does not represent a learned fact but a presuppositional postulate. As such, it has a complex justification that unfolds in two phases.

The first, initial phase is prospective, proceeding with a view to the functional necessity of *taking* this position—its purpose-dictated inevitability. For this step alone renders possible a whole range of activities relating to inquiry and to communication that is of the highest utility for us—and indeed is a practical necessity. In possibilizing[6] a host of purpose-mandated activities—that is, bringing them within the range of the feasible—the postulate of metaphysical realism obtains its initial justification in the practical order of reasoning.

However, such an initial functional justification of metaphysical realism is good but not good enough. And so, a second phase of justification goes further—indispensably albeit only retrospectively. It proceeds by noting that when (which is to say *after*) we actually engage in the goal-directed practice that the postulate in question possibilizes, our applicative and explanatory efforts are, in fact, attended by success—that making the initial postulate has an immense pragmatic payoff since what is involved is not just pragmatic utility but pragmatic efficacy. This issue of actual efficacy is ultimately crucial for the justification of the practical postulate at issue.

---

6. In English, we have no single-word verb "to make possible" akin to the German *ermoeglichen*, apart from the obsolete *possibilitate*, nowadays known only to readers of the O.E.D. To adopt "possibilize" for this purpose would perhaps be sensible and certainly convenient.

In this way, then, the overall strategy of validation has two phases—the one preliminary and prospective, the other substantiative and retrospective. That we must take on a commitment to realism is presupposed for the conduct of inquiry as we understand it. However, that we fare well through proceeding in this way in matters of communication and inquiry is something that has the status of an ex post facto discovery. Insofar as actual evidentiation is asked for, we have all that we can reasonably hope to obtain, given the inevitable realities of the situation we confront in this domain.

And so, in seeking for the most plausible rationale for realism we enter the region of pragmatic presuppositions retrojustified through their applicative and implementational efficacy. The utility of the conception of reality is so great and the service it renders so important that if it were not already there we would have to invent it. But the pragmatic success that ensues systematically when we put this conception to work goes to show that in doing so we have not proceeded capriciously.[7]

7. The author's *Empirical Inquiry* (Totowa, NJ: Rowman and Littlefield, 1982) offers further perspectives upon some of the themes of this chapter.

# CHAPTER SIX

# *Pragmatism and the Theory of Language: Use Conditions* vs. *Truth Conditions*

*Synopsis*

*(1) The distinction between use conditions and truth conditions is pivotal for the theory of language; both are essential to any adequate account of meaning and its ramifications. (2) These two factors differentiate and at the same time unite the projects of semantics and pragmatics. (3) The requirement for the dichotomy at issue roots in the cognitive opacity of real things. (4) Throughout the realm of our objective factual claim, this opacity makes for a cognitive gap between assertion and evidence. In particular, use conditions provide us with the indispensable means for coping with the unavoidable "inductive" issues that arise here. (5) Although both are required, nevertheless an approach to meaning analysis that prioritizes use conditions over truth conditions has much to be said in its favor. (6) And this circumstance speaks persuasively for the pragmatic approach to matters of linguistic meaning.*

## 1. Truth Conditions *vs.* Use Conditions

Any adequate account of language must come to terms with the difference between pragmatics and semantics, between functional issues of usage and effective communicative procedure on the one hand, and informative issues of linguistic meaning and truth on the other. And it must therefore acknowledge the crucial distinction between use conditions and truth conditions, between conditions of *warrant* and conditions of *truth* in relation to the statements we make. The use conditions encompass the *user-oriented circumstances in which a statement is appropriately and warrantedly assertable* on the basis of the ground rules, governing the communicative employment of the language. The truth conditions, by contrast, detail *the reality-oriented circumstances that must obtain for a statement to be true*. The former provide the operational criteria of usage that govern the processes of language use in conveying information, the latter indicate the entire range of the objective circumstances that must actually obtain for the statement is to be made correctly (i.e, truly).

Truth conditions represent the existential requirements for being true—as, for example, "There are no witches" requires a world without witches. On this basis, any claim whatever that is logically entailed by a given contention will figure among its truth conditions, which thus include the entire gamut of inferential consequences that follow from its assertoric content. For suppose that the consequence *C* follows inferentially from the statement *S*, so that *S* entails *C* with logical strictness. Then, of course, not-*C* would entail that not-*S*, so that the obtaining of *C* would always be comprised among the truth conditions of *S*. A statement's truth conditions are thus ontologically oriented and encorporate the (effectively fathomless) sum-total of what actually must be the case for that initial statement to be true.

By contrast, the use conditions of a language comprise the *authorizing criteria for making particular assertions* by specifying the sorts of cognitive or epistemic circumstances that qualify a statement as being made *appropriately* (i.e., warrantedly). They indicate the circumstances under which the staking of those informative claims by a language user are in order—including on the negative side what sorts of further circumstances would abrogate such entitlements.[1]

Its use conditions look to the evidential situations in which a statement can appropriately be claimed to obtain. Thus, when I see what looks to be an apple in the grocer's bin next to a label reading, "Fresh Macintoshes, 80¢ per pound," I quite appropriately take the *use* conditions for the claim "Those objects are apples" to be fully and amply satisfied. The requisites of warrant are met: no one could take me to task for being careless or irresponsible in making the statement. Use conditions are therefore procedurally oriented, encompassing not only the immediate evidential situation, but also the general setting of the communicative circumstances in which a particular assertion is validated as appropriate within the setting of the communicative practice at issue. But, of course, *truth* conditions are something else again, seeing that they involve a vast deal more over and above all that the information-in-hand enables us to certify. It is, for example, part of the condition of truth for

1. Inferential relationships can, of course, obtain either way—there are both *truth*-implications and *use*-implications. The latter give rise to what H. G. Grice called "conversational implicatures." See his posthumous *Studies in the Ways of Words* (Cambridge MA: Harvard University Press, 1989). To be sure, the important difference between use is conditioned by communicative considerations and by the social proprieties will have to be taken into account in the present context. It is, of course, communicative usage rather than social etiquette that is at issue here.

the claim that objects are (authentic) apples that they have apple cores at their middle rather than sand; that they grew on apple trees rather than being synthesized in an apple replicator; that they are not strangely deformed pears of some sort, and so forth. And so, while truth conditions deal with the (limitless) objective facts being purported, use conditions deal with the (comparatively very limited) demands imposed by communicative proprieties and practices of language employment.

What is involved in the truth conditions of a contention is something far above and beyond the vastly more modest and manageable matter of its use conditions. If the circumstances are such that a proposition's *truth* conditions are not satisfied, then this proposition is false. But if the circumstances are such that a proposition's *use* conditions are not satisfied, then this proposition is not necessarily false, but merely such that its assertion is inappropriate or unwarranted in the circumstances. No secure inference about its truth need be in order one way or the other. The failure here is not an error of commission but an error of omission—of not properly equipping one's claim with an appropriate grounding. When the use conditions are satisfied in the context of a speaker's claim, we might well eventually have to wind up saying that the speaker had spoken *falsely*, but not that the speaker had spoken *inappropriately*, let alone "in reckless disregard to the truth." After all, warrant does—and must—come well short of truth. (If all those truth conditions had to be verified, we could never make a statement at all.)

To be sure, it would be quite mistaken to think that the conditions of use or assertability as consisting in explicitly formalized rules alone. In general, what is at issue is not, strictly speaking, a matter of *rules* at all. The use-conventions of contingency are virtually never formulated and codified; indeed they are doubtless not fully codifiable, any more than are the "rules" for hitting a forehand in tennis or a tee shot in golf. The matter is one of experientially acquired "know how." What is at issue relates to the characterizing conditions of a practice, of how-to-do-it guidelines, of the practical skills and tricks of the linguistic trade of what is learned largely through observation, imitation, and habituation, rather than through mastery of and adherence to explicitly specifiable rules. (There are, obviously, some things we must be able to do without using rules—following rules, for one, since we would otherwise be in the paradoxical situation of needing rules to govern the use of rules.) Language users can observe the proprieties without mastering them via explicitly codified form: here, as elsewhere, one can know the proper thing to do by way of tacit learned mastery of a normative practice without any access to the formal rules (if any) that define this practice.

The difference between *giving* and *taking* becomes pivotal here—between that which my experiences *give* to me and that which I for my part simply *take* them to be—for the idea of a presumptive "taking" is a crucial aspect of our language-deploying discursive practice. For one thing, it is the pivot point for the objectivity of language use—for its intensionality (with an S) in point of application to real-world objects. The actual starting point may be no more than "I take myself to be seeing an apple." But we readily go beyond this idea to "I take it to be an apple that I see," and then move beyond this thought to *claim*: "I see an apple." And these transitions—this move from experiential subjectivity to our objective and factual claims—find their warrant in the established principles and practices of language use, that is, in these "use rules" of language. It is not that that apple is somehow *given* to us in "brute experience." (Wilfrid Sellars' critique of "The Myth of the Given" is perfectly in order.) But beyond that mythological *given* there lies the reality of what is actually *taken* by us: the reality—grounded in the practical politics of communication—of what we ourselves proceed to take to be so subject to the established use rules of linguistic policy and *praxis*.

## 2. The "Logic" of Use Conditions: Pragmatics *vs.* Semantics

As the preceding considerations indicate, a statement's satisfying the conventions of use or assertability emphatically does *not* automatically guarantee its actual truth. The use conditions simply determine the appropriateness (the justifiability or defensibility) of making these statements—the warrant, in context, for staking the claims at issue. And truth always transcends warrant: objective statements always have an assertoric content that claims more than what the information-in-hand assures—and ever could assure given that our actual evidence is always both finite and confined to the past and present. It is therefore perfectly possible that—even when all of the use conditions for some claim are met—things may nevertheless so eventuate that this duly authorized statement will ultimately have to be withdrawn, not (*ex hypothesi*) as having been inappropriate but rather as having unfortunately turned out to be incorrect.

The employment of some symbolism will help to illuminate this characteristic contentual gap that opens up between use conditions and truth conditions:

$u(S, P)$ = "the informative situation $S$ satisfies the use conditions for the claim $P$; the claim is epistemically *authorized*"

$t(S, P)$ = "the informative situation $S$ satisfies the truth conditions for the claim $P$; the claim is informatively *correct*"

There is a fundamental asymmetry here. We do not have $t(S, P)$ unless *all* of *P*'s truth conditions are satisfied in the situation $S$. On the other hand $u(S, P)$ demands no more than that *some* set of duly sufficient assertability conditions for $P$ is satisfied in the situation $S$.

When the truth conditions of a statement are satisfied, any individual sufficiently apprised of this fact will be in a position to stake the claim at issue. The vastness of truth conditions assures that in the ordinary course of things $t(S, P)$ will carry $u(S, P)$ with it. (If the cat actually *is* on the mat, a normal observer will, in ordinary circumstances, see it to be there, etc.) Thus, the transition from $t$ to $u$ is always feasible.

But moving in the opposite direction is distinctly problematic. For, as we have seen, the implicational involvements of $t(S, P)$ generally go well beyond those of $u(S, P)$. Things which look enough like apples that we would be "well within our rights" to think of calling them so often fail to be apples—wax fruit, for example. In practice we unhesitantly (and appropriately) claim that $t(S, P)$ whenever $u(S, P)$ has been determined to obtain, acting on the *presumption* that when the circumstances are such that we are duly authorized (given the rules of language) to assert the $P$, then $P$ is indeed true. Probability rides to the rescue here: we take this stance because with most of the types of objective statements satisfaction of the use conditions ordinarily carries satisfaction of the truth conditions in its wake: given $u(S, P)$ it becomes probable that $t(S, P)$. The warranting use conditions for "the cat is on the mat" will—given how things work in the world—ordinarily and in most cases assure the satisfaction of the truth conditions.[2] Were things otherwise, language would not be able to serve its function in the

2. The hypothetical element is crucial here. If it were appropriate to call someone a witch (which it never is) then it would be true that she would perform magic (which she cannot).

transmission of information since the circumstances of different individuals differs. But the connection at issue is one of functional efficacy rather than logical entailment. It is a matter of operational efficacy—of "what we can get away with" in our actual communicative practice. For the fact is that the body of information that linguistic practice requires for authorizing us in making a statement is always and inevitable far smaller than the body of information that that statement itself authorizes in the way of inference.

Use conditions reflect a practical policy of presumption in the employment of language and thereby form part and parcel of any communicative *praxis*. The legitimation of the practical policy at work here is ultimately the matter of convenience. For as is generally the case with practical policies, cost benefit come to play a crucial role. And the fact is that language simply could not develop as an effective instrument of communication (information transmission) if the coordination of warrant to truth did not generally obtain.[3] The justification of use conditions is thus *pragmatic*, residing in considerations of utility—in the ultimately established practical effectiveness with which they enable us to realize the relevant purposes of the context (which in this linguistic case involve the guidance of our own actions and the connecting of those actions through communication with others).

What is at issue in the transition from *u*-satisfaction to *t*-satisfaction is therefore at best a step authorized by the operative conditions of language use—a quasi-implication that obtains on "practical" rather than "theoretical" grounds. And so while we recognize, *in abstracto*, that this transition is not inferentially legitimate in any automatic way, nevertheless, we proceed *in concreto* as though this were so. Our policy of

3. Some other issues relevant to the present deliberations are discussed in chapter 1 ("Meaning and Assertability") of the author's *Empirical Inquiry* (Totowa NJ: Rowman and Littlefield, 1982).

language employment is such that in practice we take the truth conditions and the use conditions of statement as ordinarily de facto coordinated, and not as merely correlated in a statistical manner. In effect we operate with a *substantive* and *factual* assumption that "coordinates" the criteria for applying our concepts with the inferential consequences that—given the meaning of these concepts—ensue upon their application. In actual practice we effectively allow the use conditions to do duty for truth conditions, seeing the negativity of a risk of error is here offset by the communicative advantages of being able to make communicatively efficient claims.

## 3. Semantics, Pragmatics, and the Issue of Meaning

The truth conditions of a statement are a matter of the informative *semantics* of a language; the use conditions are a matter of what has come to be called its operative *pragmatics*. And these use conditions are intrinsic components of the language—a part of what children learn about the use of their native tongue "at mother's knee." Truth conditions do not have a monopoly on "meaning"—this concept is broad enough to encompass both sorts of conditions. After all, the use conditions and their correlative imputational ground rules are every bit as much an aspect of the "meaning" of our words as are the truth conditions. These two approaches to "meaning" (*viz.* through consequences via truth-condition and through antecedents via warranting or use conditions) stand in a symbiotic intertwining. For a crucial part of learning what a word *means* is to learn how it is *used*—that is, to get a working grasp of the sorts of conditions and circumstances under which its use in certain ways is *appropriate*. And here it is necessary to realize that this involves an "inductive" component—and implicit view of "the way in which things work in the world."[4]

Linguistic pragmatism, a pragmatism of meaning elucidation, is predicated in the idea that meaning pivots on use. To be sure, the matter of context plays a pivotal role here. For it will only be contexts of assertion, of information-consequence, that matter, not, for example, poetry or the language of affection. (The ardent lover's "little peach" would scarcely welcome being called his small *prunus persica.*) Thus, even as a truth-pragmatism must focus upon utility for specifically *cognitive* purposes, so a meaning-pragmatism must focus upon use for specifically *informative* purposes.

"But surely it is the truth conditions that are the pivotal factors for meaning? Surely you don't really know what a statement means if you don't know fully and exactly what follows from it." This objection seems altogether plausible on first look—but only because we theorists have by long-standing custom and habituation become deeply invested in the "logical" (rather than "practical") sense of meaning. Semantics has long dominated over pragmatics in language studies. But both are in fact needed. Without access to the truth conditions of a statement, we would not know exactly what it claims, but without access to its use conditions, we would not know when it is actually in order to stake this claim when operating in the linguistic community at issue. Neither aspect is dispensable.

The fact is that "meaning" is a wideranging and comprehensive concept that embraces both semantical and pragmatic issues. To gain an adequate grasp of a language we must learn *both* what follows from its statements *and* what authorizes them—what conditions allow us to take them to be in order. Any exclusivistic doctrine along the

4. Cf. the author's *The Primacy of Practice* (Oxford: Basil Blackwell, 1973), pp. 107–123.

lines of "meaning is use" or "meaning is a matter of truth conditions" is one-sided, dogmatic, and inappropriate in its very claim to exclusiveness.

## 4. The Duality of Truth and Usage Roots in the Cognitive Opacity of Real Things

It lies in the nature of use conditions that they must inevitably differ substantially from truth conditions where statements of objective matter of fact are at issue. Nevertheless, when communicating with one another about the real world, we have no choice but to settle in practice for letting $u(S, P)$ do duty for $t(S, P)$. For the crucial fact is that use conditions have to be experientially manageable. But truth conditions, by contrast, are always experience-transcendent where matters of objective fact are at issue. Here we can never be in a position to claim that the information at our disposal is sufficient. Only with purely subjective, self-referential claims—"I have a headache"; "I am under the impression that that is a cat"; "It displeases me that he might come"—do use and truth conditions come into close convergence, with no possibility of a slip between the lip of cognitively accessible circumstance and the cup of actual fact.

Let us consider the situation more closely.

To be able to serve their function, use conditions will have to operate within the orbit of the discernible features of our experience. But, of course, truth conditions in the case of matters of objective fact always have to go far beyond this. To begin with, it is clear that, as we standardly think about things within the conceptual framework of our fact-oriented thought and discourse, *any* real physical object has more features than it will ever actually manifest in experience. For every objective property of a real thing has involvements of a dispositional character and these are never surveyable *in toto* because the dispositions which particular concrete things inevitably have endow them with an infinitistic aspect that cannot be comprehended within experience. This desk, for example, has a limitless manifold of phenomenal features of the type: "having a certain appearance from a particular point of view." It is perfectly clear that most of these will never be actualized in experience. Moreover, a thing *is* what it *does*: entity and lawfulness are coordinated correlates—a good Kantian point. And this fact that real things involve lawful comportment means that the finitude of experience precludes any prospect of the *exhaustive* manifestation of the descriptive facets and features of any real things.[5]

The world's component furnishings not only have more characterizing properties than they ever *will* overtly manifest, but they have more than they possibly ever *can* manifest. This is so because the dispositional properties of things always involve what might be characterized as *mutually preemptive* conditions of realization. A cube of sugar, for example, must as such have the dispositional property of reacting in a particular way if subjected to a temperature of 10,000°C and of reaching in a certain way if placed for one hundred hours in a large, turbulent body of water. But if either of these conditions is ever realized, it will destroy the lump of sugar as a lump of sugar, and thus block the prospect of *its* ever bringing the other property to manifestation. The perfectly possible realization of a thing's various dispositions may fail to be mutually *compossible*, so that the dispositional properties of a thing cannot ever be mani-

5. This aspect of objectivity was justly stressed in the "Second Analogy" of Kant's *Critique of Pure Reason*, though his discussion rests on ideas already contemplated by Leibniz, *Philosophische Schriften*, ed. C. I. Gerhardt, vol. VII (Berlin: Wiedmann, 1890), pp. 319 ff.

fested completely—not just in practice, but in principle. Our objective claims about real things always commit us to more than we can actually ever determine about them.

The very concepts at issue—namely, "experience" and "manifestation"—are such that we can only ever *experience* those features of a real thing that it actually *manifests*. But the preceding considerations show that real things always have more experientially manifestable properties than they can ever actually manifest in experience. The experienced portion of a thing is like the part of the iceberg that looms above water. All real things are necessarily thought of as having hidden depths that extend beyond the limits, not only of experience, but also of experientiability. To say of something that it is an apple or a stone or a tree is to become committed to claims about it that go beyond the data we have—and even beyond those which we can, in the nature of things, ever actually acquire. The "meaning" inherent in the assertoric commitments of our factual statements is never exhausted by its verification. Real things are cognitively opaque—we cannot see to the bottom of them. Our knowledge of such things can thus become more *extensive* without thereby becoming more *complete*. And this consideration has far-reaching implications.

## 5. The Inductive Aspect

The cognitive opacity of the real means that our objective factual claims always have more contentual ramifications (and thereby more truth conditions) than we can ever bring under secure cognitive control. For the use conditions of our claims will, in the very nature of things unavoidably fall far short of what the truth conditions require. There is always an "inductive gap" here that actual usage and -

real-life discourse management does not fill in but simply leaps over.

Consider the following course of reasoning:

It looks like a duck.

It quacks like a duck.

It waddles like a duck.

---

Therefore: It is a duck.

This reasoning is clearly not deductively valid. There is a substantial gap between the premiss-provided information and the conclusion-claimed contention. (Mechanical "ducks" can do all those things as well.) Nor is the inference enthymematically valid. For any premisses that we might add which actually manage to close the deductive gap fully and completely—"Whatever looks, quacks, and waddles like a duck will actually *be* a duck," for example—will simply not be true. And nothing that we can add by way of epistemically *available* truth will close the deductive gap. Such tenability as the argument has it obtains from a certain *practical policy*, namely: *As long as no counterindications come to light, to treat as a duck anything that (sufficiently) behaves like one*. And this embodies a *praxis* rather than a factual claim of some sort. We know full well that it is false to claim "Whatever looks, quacks, and waddles like a duck, will actually be a duck." But in ordinary circumstances (in the absence of visible counter indications) we feel free to implement the policy at issue with an inferential leap, not because in doing so we cannot possibly go wrong, but rather because we will generally go right.

And so when those indicated premisses obtain and no further specific indications to the contrary are at hand, we do not hesitate to affirm that conclusion; its use conditions are in sound shape. But, of course, the truth conditions—that its cells contain duck DNA, for example—will largely lie outside our ken. We commit ourselves to them via an inductive leap across the vast information-gap that obtains because warrant for use inevitably falls well short of truth requirements.

This experience-ampliating aspect of use conditions is simply part and parcel of an inductive process built into the use of language as our instrumentality for communicating with one another about the world we live in. The validation of these extensively presumption-predicated communicative resources is ultimately pragmatic rather than semantical in nature. Cognitive utility is the crux here. For without reliance on use conditions as distinct from truth conditions, linguistic communication about a shared world would become infeasible. And without our commitment to a fundamentally inductive stance, use conditions would become impracticable. Only by recourse to conditions of use in contrast to conditions of truth can the gap between the warrant for our objective assertions and their assertoric content be bridged over. What is at issue here is a matter of communicative policy—a pragmatic resort validated by a track record of effectiveness in the service of our practical objectives. And in justifying this policy, probabilities grounded in our experience of real-world conditions have to come into it. We unhesitatingly leap across that information gulf because ample experience shows that we can get away with it.

## 6. Advantages of a Pragmatic Approach to Meaning

In various contexts of linguistic communication use conditions become paramount for deliberations about meaning—less on utilitarian grounds than because the matter of truth as such often retreats into the background. This occurs in particular where no statement making is at issue, for example, with questions and commands. Truth as such is not at issue here, but questions of appropriateness and correctness of usage certainly remain. And counterfactual conditionals also constitute a case in point. Consider the somewhat problematic conditional: "If Napoleon had won at Waterloo, he would still have lost in the end by overreaching himself."[6] It is not just hard to say whether this conditional contention is true but seriously questionable if the characterization of truth is even applicable here. And the reason is simple: truth as a semantical concept turns on how matters actually stand in the real world—factuality is in some manner or other a matter of *adaequatio ad rem*. But counterfactuals will, by their very nature, leave the real-world situation behind. Thus, in many contexts—questions, commands, and counterfactual conditionals prominent among them—there are linguistic properties to be observed and communicative purposes to be served even though semantics of truth conditions does not naturally come into play here. For with communicative resources of this nature, where the linkage of truth as such is rather tenuous, a truth-conditional analysis as standardly practiced would involve a commerce with merely possible worlds. The utility of a pragmatical (use-conditional) rather than a semantical (truth-conditional) approach to meaning analysis is thus particularly manifest in non-declarative contexts such as those arising with questions, commands, and suppositions.

In the end, then, it is only natural and to be expected that resort to a praxis-oriented, use-conditional approach is required for securing an adequate theoretical grip on the communicative operations of a language. And the pragmat-

6. "If 'through' were spelled 'thru' it would have four letters" is less problematic but represents an extreme case. On these issues see the author's "Counterfactuals in Pragmatic Perspective," *The Review of Metaphysics* 50 (1996):35–61.

ics of use conditions is a resource that elucidates aspects of meaning-theory that the more orthodox approach of semantics that looks to truth conditions alone is unable to accommodate. Pragmatism, with its characteristic approach to validation in terms of what works in practice, therefore has a pivotal and in fact indispensable part to play in the theory of linguistic meaning.[7]

---

7. Further perspectives upon some of the themes of this chapter are presented in the author's *Communicative Pragmatism and Other Philosophical Essays on Language* (Lanham, M.D.: Rowman and Littlefield, 1998).

# CHAPTER SEVEN

# *Pragmatism and Value*

*Synopsis*

*(1) Values too are practical instrumentalities—thought-tools that serve us in our endeavor to achieve satisfying lives. This purposive aspect of evaluation renders it part and parcel of the pragmatic enterprise, thereby placing value deliberation into the sphere of practical rationality. (2) David Hume's narrowly value-excluding conception of reasoning is profoundly misguided. Reason can and must be evaluative. (3) And rational evaluation does not pivot on mere preferences. Irrespective of other features, the rational legitimacy of values can root in their capacity to serve our needs and interests effectively. (4) Moreover, this pragmatic aspect of the matter is not in conflict with a commitment to higher values but is in fact integrally bound up with it.*

## 1. Purposiveness and Values

Pragmatism is a multipurpose resource. For a pragmatic approach to validation can, of course, be implemented in *any* purposive setting. Given any aim or objective whatever, we can always provide a correlative validation in terms of effectiveness and efficiency its realization. But a really thorough pragmatism must dig more deeply. It cannot simply take purposes as given—as gift horses into whose mouths we must not look. For purpose-adoption, too, has to be viewed in a pragmatic perspective as an act or activity of sorts that itself stand in need of legitimation. What is thus needed is an *axiology of purposes*, a normative methodology for assessing the legitimacy and appropriateness of the purposes we espouse.

Now this is an issue that a thoroughgoing pragmatism, one which is altogether true to itself, needs to and can address in pragmatic terms. And the terms of reference at issue here will in the natural course of things have to be those of philosophical anthropology. We are humans, members of Homo sapiens—that is an inescapable given for us. And given along with it are the conditions needed by us humans to lead not just *survivable* lives (requiring air, food, and shelter) but also those conditions needed by us to live satisfying lives (requiring self-respect, companionship and a feeling of belonging, and a sense of control over major elements of our life, and the like). And the pragmatic validation of aims and purposes can be established pragmatically in point of their efficiency and effectiveness in the realization of such life-maintaining and life-enhancing requirements that are mandated to us by our position in the world's scheme of things as rational beings.

By virtue of their very nature as purposive instrumentalities, value claims fall within the domain of reason. For values are functional objects that have a natural teleology themselves, namely, that of helping us to lead lives that are personally satisfying (meet our individual needs) and communally productive (facilitate the realizations of constructive goals to the community at large). This state of things has far-reaching implications because it indicates that our assessment of values themselves can and should be ultimately pragmatic. Our evaluations are appropriate only insofar as their adoption and cultivation are efficiently and effectively conducive to the realization of human interests—our rationally appropriate ends, personally and communally.

A pragmatism that is consistent, coherent, and self-sustaining will not just proceed pragmatically with respect to achieving unevaluated ends and purposes but must also apply its pragmatic perspective to the issue of validating ends and purposes themselves in terms of their capacity to facilitate the realization of those considerations which, for us humans, are simply "facts of life."

## 2. Evaluative Rationality and Appropriate Ends: Against the Humean Conception of Reason

Pragmatism's standard of adequacy pivots on procedural efficacy. But can this seemingly crass prioritization of utility possibly provide grounds for even acknowledging the significance in human affairs of higher, less crassly utilitarian sorts of values? Can it ever reach beyond the sphere of the bare basic necessities of life?

To resolve this question we must go back to basics. Pragmatism pivots the validation of our instrumentalities of thought and action on their effectiveness in goal realization. But goals are certainly not created equal; they clearly have different degrees of merit. There are impersonally valid modes of evaluation by which goals themselves can be assessed, so that the rational evaluation that pragmatism envisions can be implemented in an objectively cogent way. The capacity for intelligent choice makes us humans into rational agents, but it is only through our having *appropriate* values that the prospect of *intelligent* choice becomes open for us. The human situation being what it is, existential circumstances spread a vast range of possibilities out before us. At many junctures, life confronts us with alternative directions in which to proceed. And only through the evaluation of such alternatives can we effect a sensible (rationally appropriate and acceptable) choice among them. On this basis, values are instrumentalities that serve to make the satisfactory conduct of life possible. And a commitment to values not only aids in making our lives as intelligent agents possible, but they also make it meaningful. For the life of the human individual is brief: here today, gone tomorrow. It is through our commitment to values that we can reach out beyond the restrictive limits of the space and time available to us as individuals in this world, moving towards the realization of something larger and more significant.

To be sure, it is often said that values are just matters of taste—of mere personal predilection. If this were indeed the case, then any and all claims to value objectivity would at once become untenable. But is it so? Evaluation certainly is not—and should not be—a matter of taste. People who are not prepared to back an option of *X* over *Y* by *cogent reasons* of some sort are merely evincing a preference and not actually making any sort of meaningful evaluation at all. Tastes, as usually understood, represent unreasoned preferences and purely subjective predilections. There is consequently no disputing about them: *de gustibus non disputandum est*. If I prefer *X* to *Y*, then that's that. But values are something quite different. They are by nature functional instrumentalities since their mission is to canalize our action via our rational choices. They have objective impact, relating not to what we *do prefer* but to what we *can and should appropriately deem preferable*—that is, worthy of preference. And preference worthiness is something that is always discussible, something that needs to be reasoned about. To be in a position to maintain—in a manner that is sensible and reasonable—that *X* is preferable to *Y*, one must be in a position to back one's claim up with some sort of rationale. And this reason-boundedness of sensible evaluations carries them outside the range of mere matters of taste.

Moreover, our values themselves are not—and should not be—arbitrary and haphazard. For in the final analysis, they pivot not on wants but on our best interests and real needs—on what is necessary to or advantageous for a person's well being. We humans, being the sorts of creatures we are, have need-based interests which as such should (insofar as we are rational) control the validation of our wants and preferences. Validating an evaluation thus is not and cannot be a matter of mere subjectivity. The projects into which our nature impels us—the medical project, say, or the alimentary, or the cognitive—carry certain value commitments in their wake. Just here is where the pragmatic impetus comes into play. For once a goal is given, other connected goals can come to be validated with reference to it. It is thus a grave mistake to think that one cannot reason about values on the supposed ground that values are simply a matter of taste and thus beyond the reach of reason because "there's no reasoning about tastes." Such a position founders on the distinction between mere wants and real needs. For the fact is that values are valid just exactly to the extent they serve to implement and satisfy our needs and our correlatively appropriate interests. (The seeming harshness of this view is mitigated by the circumstance that for us humans the satisfaction of some of our mere wants—seen not in specific but in statistical generality—is itself a need.)

A good way to exhibit the inappropriateness of the view that where values begin reason is at an end is through a pragmatic appraisal that regards values as *practical* instrumentalities, tools that aid us in the best approach to understanding what valuation *is* is to proceed by examinating what valuation *does*. This purposive aspect of evaluation renders it part and parcel of the pragmatic enterprise, thereby making room for value deliberation within the sphere of practical rationality. And this means that a rational critique of values is not only possible but necessary. In particular, values that impede the realization of a person's best interests are clearly inappropriate. A priority scheme that sets mere wants above real needs or sets important objectives aside to avert trivial inconveniences is thereby deeply flawed from the rational viewpoint.[1] And even as with needs and interests in general, so even great values may well have to yield to the yet greater. (Some things are rightly dearer to sensible people than life itself.)

David Hume drew a sharp contrast between "reason," which he construed narrowly as concerned solely with means and wholly indifferent to ends, and a very different, entirely reason-detached faculty of motivation that concerns itself with ends—namely, *the passions*. As Hume saw it, the exposition of formal relationships in logic and mathematics apart, reason merely deals with experiential information about the world's states of affairs and the associative relationships that lie at the root of cause and effect. Reason is strictly instrumental: it can inform me about what I must do *if* I wish to arrive at a certain destination, but only "passion"—desire or aversion—can make something into a destination for me. Thus, Hume regarded an impetus toward or away from some object—any sort of pro- or con-reaction—as simply the wrong sort of thing to be rational or sensible, an

1. And what other viewpoint would it possibly make sense for us to adopt here?

autonomous force operating entirely outside the realm of reason. And he therefore considered those directive passions as entirely arational. Rationality is totally disconnected from matters of evaluation. When one asks what is to be done, reason as such has no instructions—in its exclusive concern for rationally arbitrary ends, it is wholly a matter of what one happens to want.

As Hume thus saw it, reason is a "slave of the passions" where evaluation is concerned. Its modus operandi is strictly conditional: it dictates hypothetically that if you accept this, then you cannot (in all consistency) fail to accept that. But, all this is a matter of the hypothetical if-then. The categorical "accept this!" is never a mandate of reason, but of those extra-rational passions. Reason herself initiates no commitments; it is inherently conditionalized, never saying what one should (or should not) opt for, but only what one is consequentially committed to if one *already* stands committed to something else. The assessment of fundamentals, be they cognitive or evaluative, lies beyond the reach of reason. On this basis, Hume insisted:

> It is not contrary to reason to prefer the destruction of the whole world to the scratching of my finger. It is not contrary to reason for me to choose my total ruin. . . . It is as little contrary to reason to refer even my own acknowledged lesser good to my greater, and to have a more ardent affection for the former than the latter.[2]

But all this is obviously very strange stuff. Any conception of reason that has these consequences is deeply problematic. For a "rationality" that excludes the critique of harmful affections and desires is no rationality at all. On any plausible view of the matter, reason cannot simply beg

2. David Hume, *A Treatise on Human Nature*, bk. II. pt. iii., sect. 3. For Hume, the only inappropriate desires are those that depend on irrational beliefs.

off from considering the validity of ends. Our motivating "passions" can surely themselves be rational or otherwise: those that impel us towards things that are bad for us or away from things that are good for us go against reason, those that impel us away from things that are bad for us and towards things that are good for us are altogether rational. There is certainly such a thing as evaluative, appraisal-oriented reasoning.

Meeting people's needs is (by hypothesis) an imperative necessity. And even meeting their mere desires is a rationally warranted desideratum as long as no larger obstacle (their interests in those of others, for example) stands in the way. But some such sort of qualification is always necessary in adjudging the role of preferences.

As this perspective indicates, rationality involves two sorts of issues—means and ends. The rationality of means is a matter of factual information alone—of what sorts of moves and measures lead efficiently to objectives. But the rationality of ends is a matter not of *information* but of *legitimation*. It is not settled just by factual inquiry, but involves appraisal and evaluative judgment. And in the larger scheme of things both aspects are needed: ends without requisite means are frustrating, means without suitable ends are pointless. Accordingly, rationality has two sides: an *axiological* (evaluative) concern for the appropriateness of ends and an *instrumental* (cognitive) concern for effectiveness and efficiency in their cultivation. The conception of rationality fuses these two elements into one integral and unified whole, seeing that the inherent purposiveness of values makes them part of the rational enterprise. Evaluation is not at odds with reason but is a crucial component of its work. People's ends and purposes are certainly not automatically valid: they can be self-destructive, self-defeating impediments to the realization of their true needs and best interests. For ends do not lie outside the domain of value but rather serve to define it.

The rationality of ends inheres in the simple fact that we humans have various valid *needs*—that we require not only nourishment and protection against the elements for the maintenance of health, but also information (cognitive orientation), affection, freedom of action, and much else besides. Without such varied goods we cannot thrive as fulfilled human beings. The person who does not give these manifold desiderata their due—who may even set out to frustrate their realization—is clearly not being rational.

The pivotal fact is that there is not only inferential (logical) reason but also evaluative (axiological) reason. Just as rational people only believe what is belief-worthy under the circumstances, so they only value what is value-worthy—*deserving* of being valued under the circumstances. And the determination of value-worthiness requires the sensible application of appropriate standards—in short, reasoning.[3] For, it is quintessentially the work of reasoning to determine what sorts of commitments are rational (reason-conforming) and what sorts are not. (And this is so whether the "commitments" at issue be beliefs or evaluations.) Only when we make an evaluative commitment contrary to the requirements of reason do we thereby enter into the realm of the strictly subjective.[4]

A common complaint against pragmatism is that it is an instrumentalistic philosophy that cares only for means and not ends. But this is a travesty. It is certainly not how things need to be. A sensible pragmatism is emphatically not a matter of efficient means to arbitrary ends. The sort of instrumentalism that matters to such a pragmatism is one that cares not just for the *efficiency* of means but for their

3. On rational *vs*. irrational ends see Kurt Baier, *The Moral Point of View* (Ithaca NY: Cornell University Press, 1958); and Bernard Gert, *The Moral Rules* (New York: Harper and Row, 1973).

4. Some theorists would change the "contrary to" of this sentence to "above and beyond." But for the already indicated reasons this would be inappropriate. Reason is no self-sufficient be-all and end-all for us.

*appropriateness*, which is a matter of combining a whole range of evaluative factors—not efficiency and effectiveness alone but also their broader normative nature. Inappropriate ends contaminate efficient means even as inherently positive ends can be undone through being pursued by inappropriate means. Requiring a proper coordination of means and ends is an essential facet of any sensible pragmatism.

Evaluation thus lies at the very heart and core of rationality. For, rationality is a matter of best serving our overall interests. The person who expends more effort in the pursuit of ends than they are worth is not just being wasteful but foolish, which is to say irrational. The rationality of our actions hinges critically both on the appropriateness of our ends *and* on the suitability of the means by which we pursue their cultivation. Both of these components—the *cogently cognitive* ("*intelligent* pursuit") and the *normatively purposive* ("*appropriate* ends")—are alike essential to full-fledged rationality.

To be sure, the springs of human agency are diverse. We frequently act not for *reasons* alone, but from "mere motives"—out of anxiety, cupidity, habit, impulse. In such cases, we also have ends and purposes in view—but generally not *appropriate* ones. If rationality were merely a matter of unevaluated goals and purposes as such—if it were to consist simply in the "technical rationality" of goal-efficient action—then the established line between the rational and the irrational would have to be redrawn in a very different place, and its linkage with what is intelligent and well advised would be severed. But where there is no *appropriate* and thus no meaningful end, rational agency ceases. (There may, of course, still be room for goal-directed action, but without *appropriate* goals it is bound to be problematic from the standpoint of rationality.) And, of course, while all people are (hopefully) *ca-*

*pable* of reason, no well-informed person thinks they generally exercise this capacity.

The rationality of ends is an indispensable component of rationality at large for two principal reasons. Rationally valued ends must be evaluatively appropriate ones: if we adopt inappropriate ends we are not being rational, no matter how efficiently and effectively we pursue them. The sensible attunement of means to ends that is characteristic of rationality calls for an appropriate balancing of costs and benefits in our choice among alternative ways of resolving our cognitive, practical, and evaluative problems. Reason therefore demands determination of the true value of things. Even as cognitive reason requires that in determining what we are to accept we should assess the evidential grounds for theses at their true worth, so evaluative reason requires us to appraise the values of our practical options at their true worth in determining what we are to choose or prefer. And this calls for an appropriate cost-benefit analysis. Values must be managed as an overall "economy" in a rational way to achieve overall harmonization and optimization. Economic rationality is not the only sort of rationality there is, but it is an important aspect of overall rationality. Someone who rejects such economic considerations—who, in the absence of any envisioned compensating advantages, deliberately purchases for millions benefits he recognizes as being worth only a few pennies—is simply not rational. It is just as irrational to let one's efforts in the pursuit of chosen objectives incur costs that outrun their true worth as it is to let one's beliefs run afoul of the evidence. And the evaluative rationality at issue here is the pragmatic one of the efficient pursuit of appropriate ends.[5]

5. Some of these issues are also treated in the author's *Rationality* (Oxford: Oxford University Press, 1986).

## 3. The Crucial Role of Interests and Needs: Wants and Preferences are not Enough

Pragmatism's concern for success and effectiveness in matters of goal attainment is something very different from mere preference utilitarianism. Economists, decision theorists, and utilitarian philosophers often maintain that rationality turns on the intelligent cultivation of one's *preferences*. But this is problematic in the extreme. We cannot extract judgmental rationality from preferences because mere preferences as such are *unevaluated* wants, and there is no such rationality without evaluation. After all, what I want or merely *think* to be good for me is one thing; what I need and what actually is good for me is another. To move from preferences and perceived interests to genuine benefits and real interests I must engage in a rational critique of ends—to examine in the light of objective standards whether what I desire is desirable, whether my actual ends are rational ends, whether my putative interests are real interests. The genuinely rational person is the one who proceeds in situations of choice by asking not the introspective question "What do I prefer?" but the objective question: "What is to be deemed preferable? What *ought* I to prefer on the basis of my best interests?" Rational comportment does not just call for desire satisfaction, it demands desire management as well. The question of *appropriateness* becomes crucial here. And this is an issue about which people can be—and often are—irrational; not just careless but even perverse, self-destructive, and crazy. We pursue mere will-o'-the-wisps when we impute to our ends a weight and value they do not in fact have.

An objectivistic pragmatism will—if at all reasonable—certainly not deny the personalistic element of subjectively originating tastes, desires, inclinations, and personal involvements. But it insists that they must ultimately have a footing in our genuine needs. Wants and preferences as such are not enough; legitimate values must have a *rationale*. Consider the contrast between:

- *professed wants*: what I say or declare that I want or prefer;
- *felt wants*: what I (actually) do want or prefer;
- *real (or appropriate) wants* and *actual needs*: what the reasonable (impartial, well-informed, well-intentioned, understanding) bystander would maintain that I ought to want on the basis of what is "in my best interests."

It is this last item—namely, what is in my "real" or "best" interests—that is decisive for rationality. Rationality, then, is not just a matter of doing what we *want* (if this were so, it would be far simpler to attain!), but a matter of doing what we (rationally) *ought*, given the situation in which we find ourselves.

The rationality of ends is essential to rationality as such; there is no point in running—however swiftly—to a destination whose attainment conveys no benefit. It is useless to maintain "rational consonance" with what we believe or do or value if those items with respect to which we relativize are not themselves rational in the first place. Principles of relative rationality are pointless in the absence of principles of categorical rationality. Wants per se (wants unexamined and unevaluated) may well provide impelling *motives* for action, but will not thereby constitute good *reasons* for action. To be sure, it is among our needs to have some of our wants satisfied. But, it is needs that are determinative for interests, and not wants as such. A person's *true* interests are not those he *does have* but those he *would have* if he conducted his life's affairs properly (sensibly, appropriately). A person's *welfare* is often ill served by his *wishes*—which may be altogether irrational, perverse, or pathological.[6] This distinction of appropriateness of *real*, as opposed to *merely seeming*, wants and interests—is crucial for rationality. The latter turns on what we merely happen to want at the time, the former on what we *should* want, and thus on "what we would want if"—if we were all those things that "being intelligent" about the conduct of one's life requires: prudent, sensible, conscientious, well-considered, and the like.[7]

Clearly, there is nothing automatically appropriate—let alone sacred—about our own ends, objectives, and preferences as such. We can be every bit as irrational and stupid with the adoption of ends as with any other choice. Apparent interests are not automatically real, getting what one wants is not necessarily to one's benefit, goals are not rendered valid by their mere adoption. People's ends can be self-destructive, self-defeating impediments to the realization of their true needs. For rationality, the crucial question is that of the true value of the item at issue. What counts for rational validity is not preference but preferability—not what people do want, but what they *ought* to want; not what *people* actually want, but what *sensible* or *right-thinking* people would want under the circumstances. The normative aspect is ineliminable here. Rationality calls for objective judgment—for an assessment of preferability, rather than for a mere expression of preference, no questions asked. The rationality of ends, their rational appropriateness and legitimacy, is therefore a crucial aspect of rationality. More is at issue with rationality than a matter of strict instrumentality—mere effectiveness in the pursuit of ends no matter how

---

6. See the author's *Welfare* (Pittsburgh: University of Pittsburgh Press, 1972). Cf. John Rawls, *A Theory of Justice* (Cambridge MA: Harvard University Press, 1971), p. 421. Rawls traces this line of thought back to Henry Sidgwick.
7. The contrast goes back to Aristotle's distinction between *desire* as such and *rational preference*. Many aspects of Aristotle's ethical theory bear usefully on the present discussion.

inappropriate they may be. When we impute to our ends a weight and value they do not in fact have, we pursue mere will-o'-the-wisps. There is an indissoluble connection between the true value of something (its being good or right or useful) and its being rational to choose or prefer this thing. Being desired does not automatically make something desirable, nor being valued valuable. The pivot is how matters *ought* to be—a region where needs come to dominate over wants.

And so, the crucial question for rationality is not that of what we prefer, but that of what is in our best interests—not simply what we may happen to desire, but what is good for us in the sense of fostering the realization of our needs. The pursuit of what we want is rational only in so far as we have *sound* reasons for deeming this to be want-deserving. The question whether what we prefer is preferable, in the sense of *deserving* this preference, is always relevant. For it is not just beliefs that can be stupid, ill-advised, and inappropriate—that is to say, *irrational*—but ends as well.

Valuation can be sensible or perverse, well-oriented or ill-advised, interest-enhancing or interest-retarding in sum, rational or irrational. The fact is that we can be every bit as irrational in the adoption of ends as in any other choice. Apparent interests are not automatically real, getting what one wants is not necessarily to one's benefit, goals are not rendered valid by their mere adoption. Rationality calls for critical judgment—for an assessment of preferability, rather than for a mere expression of preference. More is at issue with rationality than a matter of strict instrumentality—mere effectiveness in the pursuit of arbitrarily selected ends, no matter how inappropriate they may be. When we impute to our ends a weight and value they do not in fact have, we pursue mere will-o'-the-wisps. The rational appropriateness and legitimacy of ends is thus an indispensable aspect of rationality at large.

Contentions like "Smith is selfish, inconsiderate, and boorish" therefore do not lie outside the sphere of rational inquiry—nor for that matter do contentions like "Behavior that is selfish / inconsiderate / boorish is against the best interest of people." The issue of *appropriate* action in the circumstances in which we find ourselves is pivotal for rationality. Be it in matters of belief, action, or evaluation, we want—that is to say, often do and always *should* want—to do the best we can. One cannot be rational without due care for the desirability of what one desires—the issue of its alignment with our *real*, as distinguished from our *putative*, or merely seeming interests.

But just what is it that is in a person's real or best interests? Partly, this is indeed a matter of meeting the needs that people universally have in common—health, satisfactory functioning of body and mind, adequate resources, human companionship, and affection, and so on.[8] Partly, it is a matter of the particular role one plays: cooperative children are in the interests of a parent, customer loyalty in those of a shopkeeper. Partly, it is a matter of what one simply happens to want. (If John loves Mary, then engaging Mary's attention and affections are in John's interests—some sorts of things are in a person's interests simply because he takes an interest in them.) But these want-related interests are valid only by virtue of their relation to universal interests. Mary's approbation is in John's interest only because "having the approbation of someone we love" is *always* in *anyone's* interest. Any valid *specific* interest must fall within the validating scope of an appropriate *universal* covering principle of interest legitimation. (The development

8. The issue goes back to the specification of the "basics" (*principiae*) of the human good in the Middle Academy (Carneades)—things like the soundness and maintenance of the members of the body, health, sound senses, freedom from pain, physical vigor, and physical attractiveness. Compare Cicero, *De finibus*, V: vii, 19.

of my stamp collection is in my interest only because it is part of a hobby that constitutes an avocation for me and "securing adequate relaxation and diversion from the stress of one's daily cares" is something that is in *anyone's* interests.)

But what of "mere whims and fancies." If I have a yen for eating crabgrass, then is my doing so not a perfectly appropriate "interest" of mine? Yes it is. But only because it is covered by perfectly cogent universal interest, namely, that of "Doing what I feel like doing in circumstances where neither injury to me nor harm to others is involved." A specific (concrete, particular) interest of a person is valid as such only if it can be subordinated to a universal interest by way of having a basis in people's legitimate needs. It is these higher-level principles that are the controlling factors from the standpoint of reason. Only through coming under the aegis of those larger universal needs can our idiosyncratic want come to be validated.

The person who does not give such manifest desiderata their due—who may even set out to frustrate their realization—is clearly not being rational. This certainly can—and does—happen. Like various beliefs, various evaluations are palpably crazy.[9] Reason, after all, is not just a matter of the compatibility or consistency of pre-given commitments, but of the warrant that there is for undertaking certain commitments in the first place. An *evaluative* rationality which informs us that certain preferences are absurd—preferences which wantonly violate our nature, impair our being, or diminish our opportunities—fortunately lies within the human repertoire.

Xenophanes of Colophon was doubtless right. Even as different creatures may well have different gods so they

9. For strict consistency, a rigorous Humean should, by analogy, hold that cognitive reason, too, is only hypothetical—that "it only tells us that certain beliefs must be abandoned *if* we hold certain others, and that no beliefs are contrary to reason as such, so that "it is not contrary to reason to think one's finger larger than the entire earth."

might well have different goods. But no matter. The preeminently appropriate sort of good for us humans is *our* sort of good—the human good. In this regard, Aristotle did indeed get to the heart of the matter. For us, the human good is indeed an adequate foundation for substantive, practical rationality. Given that we are what we are, it is this that is decisive for us. We have to go on from where we are. It is in *this* sense alone that there is no deliberation about ends. The universally appropriate ends at issue in our human condition are not somehow freely *chosen* by us; they are fixed by the (for us) inescapable ontological circumstance that—like it or not—we find ourselves to exist as human beings, and thus are able to function as free rational agents. Their ultimate inherence in (generic) human needs determines the appropriateness of our particular, individual ends.

We humans are so situated that from *our* vantage point (and who else's can be decisive for us?) various factors can and should be seen as goods—as aspects or components of what is in itself a quintessentially good end in its relation to us. Without achieving such goods we cannot thrive as human beings—we cannot achieve the condition of well-being that Aristotle called "flourishing." Flourishing as *humans*, as the sorts of creatures we are, patently is *for us* an intrinsic good (though not, to be sure, necessarily the supreme good). It "comes with the territory" so to speak, being mandated for us by our place in nature's scheme of things. And this desideratum is itself many-faceted in serving as an umbrella goal that can carry others in its wake. It must, after all, come to be particularized to the concrete situation of specific individuals and thereby becomes complex and variegated. On this basis, the rationality and objectivity of evaluative ends inheres in the simple fact that we humans have various valid *needs*—that we require not only nourishment and protection against the elements for the maintenance of health, but also information ("cognitive orientation"), affection, freedom of action, and much else besides. Without achieving such varied goods we cannot thrive as human beings.

To be sure, a person's "appropriate interests" will have a substantial sector of personal relativity. One person's self-ideal, shaped in the light of his own value structure, will—quite appropriately—be different from that of another. And, moreover, what sorts of interests a person has will hinge in significant measure on the particular circumstances and conditions in which he finds himself—including his wishes and desires. (In the *absence* of any countervailing considerations, getting what I want is in my best interests.) All the same, there is also a large body of real interests that people share in common—for example, as regards standard of living ( health and resources) and quality of life (opportunities and conditions)—and it is these factors of life sustainment and enrichment that are ultimately determinative of the validity of individualized interests. Both sorts of interests—the idiosyncratic and the generic—play a determinative role in the operations of rationality. And both must therefore figure in a sensible pragmatism's concern for the realization of our objectives.[10]

## 4. The Pragmatic Aspect

Peircean pragmatism was directed in the first instance to issues of meaning and truth—to questions of *matters of fact* regarding how things stood in the world.

But, of course, we human are not creatures of inquiry alone. We pursue not only knowledge but happiness and

10. The author's *The Validity of Values* (Princeton: Princeton University Press, 1993) offers further perspectives on some of the themes of this chapter.

meaning as well. We need not only information about the world but guidelines for the conduct of our own lives within it: principles and values to live by. And here, too, a pragmatic approach makes sense—an enlarged pragmatism of not merely *observational* experience but of experience in general. Here, too, the proof of the pudding is in the eating, but the payoff at issue is not better understanding of nature but better, more satisfying lives for ourselves.

There is, accordingly, room both for a pragmatism of theoretical inquiry and for a pragmatism of satisfying living. The rational economy of ends and means is operative throughout.

But what is at issue here are two purposively different ventures that must not be conflated. For we must neither base our values on observational principles nor fix our beliefs on affective principles.

At this point, we come to Arthur Lovejoy's old objection that pragmatists (i.e., James) confused:

1. the empiricist (experiential consequences following from the *assertoric substance* (i.e., content) of a belief, and
2. the empirical / experiential consequence following from the adoption and implementation of a belief.

For questions of fact, of course (1) is determinative. But for principles of action (2) is perfectly appropriate. As long as there is no conflict, that is, as long as the two criteria are directed at *different issues*, there should be no problem about these being two different criteria.

Pragmatism pivots validation on the efficacy and effectiveness of action, with the question "Effectiveness and efficacy at what?" answered: "In point of attaining the correlative ends and purposes—that is, in teleological terms." The rational evaluation of ends is therefore of the essence here, seeing that the pivot must be not merely what ends a person has but what ends a person should have. A reasonable pragmatism will, of course, have to orient itself to sensible goals—not to satisfying arbitrary human desires but rather to meeting human interests, and specifically those real or true interests that are defined through our needs. And, of course, the issues are nowise opposed. For an intelligent being that makes its way in the world by the exploitation of information there can be no conflict between the needs of knowledge and the needs of life—it is all a matter of the rational balance of costs and benefits.

The teleology on which a sensible pragmatism can be based will be contextualistically pluralistic. It does not say "Here is one all-predominant goal, a *summum bonum* on whose effective pursuit everything pivots." Rather it says, "Human beings are complex organisms, creatures of many needs and valid desires whose circumstance in this world commits them in projects of various sorts: physical, epistemic, social, and so forth. And it is the particular context of a given issue or problem that determines the nature of the relevant teleology." And so, while effectiveness in *praxis* relating to goal attainment is pragmatism's uniform standard throughout, there is also a clear recognition that different goals are relevant in different contexts. Pragmatic appropriateness is always contextual and situationally conditioned. Even as the proper instrument depends on the task at hand and the proper answer on the question at issue, so the matter of what concrete objective is appropriate will depend on the nature of the situation.

And here we come to the point at which James and Dewey went astray. For insofar as pragmatism is part of the "revolt against dualism"—against splitting the world into scientific and a humanistic hemispheres—the proper route is not that of a reconciliatory monism that negates distinctions or papers over them, but rather that of a pluralism which acknowledges the many-sided complexity and diversity of human purposes.

But does not a pragmatism geared to the multiplicity of human purpose disintegrate into an anarchistic relativism? Not necessarily. It all depends on the view one takes regarding the nature of human purposes. There is, to be sure, the nihilistic view of intended chaotic diversity—you have your purposes and I have mine and never the twain need meet. But this view is unrealistic in both senses of the terms ("untrue to the facts" and "oblivious to something that is—or should be supposed to be—real"). Human purposes are not arbitrary; they root in the facts—in the realities of the human situation. Some of them are outright needs (food, shelter, companionship, self-respect)—in conditions without which leading a satisfying human life becomes impossible. Others indeed are optional and person variable. You order chocolate ice-cream, I order vanilla. Different purposes indeed, but both subordinated to the common desideratum of palatable nourishment. You like romantic novels and I prefer adventure films. Different purposes again, but both subordinate to the common desideratum of spending some time at a diversion one enjoys. In this light, it can be seen that a purpose-geared pragmatism need not be anarchically relativistic. It can—and should—be understood that the issue of "valid human purposes" on which a viable pragmatism pivots stands coordinate with authentic needs imposed by the given realities of the human condition.

One issue that has been of particular concern here relates to the supposed crassness of pragmatism. Pragmatism is indeed committed to prioritizing the factors of success, efficacy, and efficiency. But has been repeatedly stressed here it is important to recognize and emphasize there is nothing inherently crass or materialistic about this prioritization as such. For efficacy as such can characterize any sort of purposive enterprise, be is a low or high, contemptible or noble. There is nothing inherently unworthy about it. And the proper heed of human interests that is demanded by any rationally viable sort of evaluation will have to give to the higher, nobler goals the weight that is their proper due. In consequence there need be nothing crass or materialistic about a sensibly designed version of pragmatism.

The fact that we have various higher interests outside the crass "material" realm—interests bearing on those larger projects that make life not only possible but satisfying—renders unsustainable the traditional objection that pragmatism is by nature crassly materialistic. There is, to be sure, a self-serving aspect to this matter of facilitating a *satisfying* life. But this is attenuated when *meaningful* satisfactions are at issue. For an indelibly idealistic aspect of values emerges when they bear on the achievement of a truly satisfactory life. Given our nature, satisfaction and meaning are inseparable because we humans cannot be fully content with a life that we cannot regard as somehow meaningful. In consequence, a value pragmatism is not at odds with a concern for higher values but is in fact integrally connected to it. And—above all—an idealistic pragmatism is no contradiction in terms. Once pragmatism is construed in methodological terms with reference to purposive adequacy in general, there is no good reason whatever why pragmatism cannot be normatively principled.

It deserves note that the pragmatic process of value validation avoids the circularity—or, at any rate, apparent circularity—of validating values with reference to values. For as indicated above, its procedure is to validate values—ultimately, at least—with reference to *needs*. And needs are rather different in nature from values as such. For while values are something that we adopt, and so have an aspect of voluntary commitment, needs are externally imposed, being inherent in our condition and circumstances as fixed by the place we occupy in the world's scheme of things. Needs, that is to say, are situationally mandated, imposed by the ontological realities of our given condition.

But are not needs themselves somehow evaluative in nature? Well, in a way—yes. Yet the sort of "circularity" at issue here is not vicious, but inevitable and altogether rational. For the evaluative realm is probatively closed, just like the factual realm: even as facts can be substantiated only by the invocation of facts so evaluations can be substantiated only by the invocation of values. (The conclusion of a cogent argument must be thematically homogeneous with its premisses which alone is still, after all, to provide for what the conclusion claims: *ex nihilo nihil.*)

In sum, three points require particular emphasis with regard to a pragmatic approach to values: (1) The values we subscribe to are themselves something that requires being evaluated and justified. (2) Since values themselves are purposive instrumentalities that serve us in the conduct of affairs, the natural way to proceed in their evaluation is pragmatically, in terms of their efficacy in guiding us toward the of human ends. (3) And the purposes at issue here are our genuine needs and authentic best interests as defined through needs inherent in the given realities of the human condition. A sensible pragmatism must therefore be geared to efficacy and effectiveness in the realization of *appropriate* purposes, that is to say in the service of our real, true, best interests—those that themselves can sustain the scrutiny of reason. The pragmatic approach is thus not at odds with a rational axiology but rather represents an inherent aspect of its modus operandi. In this way, the rational appropriateness of the larger human projects at issue in such spheres as cognition, evaluation, and action provides the footing on whose basis pragmatism becomes a comprehensively viable philosophical pragmatism.

CHAPTER EIGHT

# *Morality, Pragmatism, and the Obligations of Personhood*

*Synopsis*

*(1) Morality is a functional enterprise whose characterizing mission is to provide for principles and rules of conduct that safeguard the interests of people—a project in which all of us decidedly have a stake. (2) This functional / purposive dimension means that rational deliberation about moral matters can—and should—proceed in an essentially pragmatic mode. (3) The ethics of science and communication affords a good example of this. (4) The obligatoriness of morality does not, however, reside in its advantages for us humans, real though they are. Instead, it arises from an ontological duty to self-realization and pivots on our mode of emplacement in the world's scheme of things. (5) Moreover, the pragmatic / functional aspect of morality, while indeed geared to human advantage, certainly does not root is people's crass and materialistic desires. The "success" at issue in a pragmatic morality is something whose basis is, can, and should be larger and deeper—a gearing to the realizing the goods inherent in the human condition. (6) In view of such considerations it would be quite wrong to think that a pragmatic approach to morality must*

*degrade the enterprise into a crassly materialistic egocentrism.*

---

## 1. The Functional Nature of Morality

Even as a sensible pragmatic approach to value in the case of individuals pivots matters of legitimation upon efficacy in the service of *their* real or genuinely best interests, so a sensible pragmatic approach to morality pivots matters on efficacy in the service of the best interests of people-in-general. Pragmatism is, in fact, closely linked to one prominent moral theory, namely, utilitarianism, the doctrine that proposes to appraise moral rules and codes by the standard of what optimally conduces to "the greatest good of the greatest number." For when pragmatism's standard of "what works out for the best" is construed as being *collectively* optimific at the communal level, then "the best" simply and directly comes to "the greatest good of the greatest number." From this standpoint, utilitarianism is straightforwardly tantamount to one particular version of moral pragmatism.

Nevertheless, pragmatism has long had a bad name among moral philosophers. And for good reason. For William James (to some extent), and some of his more bohemian-minded followers such as F. C. S. Schiller (to a greater extent), have taken the line that pragmatism's standard looks to the achievement of success in "the pursuit of happiness." In reacting against this, pragmatism's more ethically minded opponents then objected—not without justification—that such a position is simply a crass hedonism that diminished all normative, and, in particular, all *moral* concern to the level of success in pleasure seeking and the pursuit of material goods. In this way, pragmatism was given a self-oriented, and relativistic construction and regarded as a matter of success in "doing one's own thing" in a crassly self-serving way that set the position at odds with a morally meaningful concern for the well being and interests of others.

The blatantly hedonistic approach of such a pragmatism reflects the currently widespread but nevertheless unfortunate tendency to deny the possibility of rational controversy about moral issues—to relegate morality to the relativistic never-never land of matters of taste, feeling, or otherwise unsupportable opinion. Extensive approval nowadays greets a moral subjectivism that takes roughly the following line:

> In moral judgments, as in judgments of taste, it is impossible to be mistaken. Whatever a social group deems to be right is thereby rendered right for it. In matters of moral obligation and permission agreement is everything, collectively thinking something to be so makes it so (even as in matters of taste, thinking something to be pleasing means that it *is* pleasing).

But this consensualistic view of the matter is deeply problematic, since it is very much mistaken to hold that a certain practice is rendered morally acceptable simply because people chose to have it so. For it lies in the very nature of the concept at issue that *moral* appropriateness hinges on how actions affect the real interests of people-in-general, and obviously the particular individuals concerned will not automatically be the decisive arbiter here.

Moral evaluation as standardly conceived turns on how actions actually affect people—on the negative side, for example, by doing them unwarranted harm, violating their rights, needlessly endangering their well-being, wantonly undermining their welfare, or otherwise injuring their interests. And it is clear that, from such a functional viewpoint, the moral project stands alongside the cognitive project or the practical project as yet another enterprise to which intelligent and rational creatures are bound to be committed in the cause of satisfying their needs and their interests. The moral enterprise is by its very nature simply one more goal-directed endeavor defined by a characteristic teleology of its own—to delineate and encourage—modes of action and interaction that conduce to the best interests of people in general. It is a matter of instituting, preserving, and extending those practices which contribute to making life within human communities not only possible but pleasant, enjoyable, and rewarding. The crux of the moral enterprise is to make for conditions of action and interaction that are more civilized, humane, and life-enhancing. The effective production and distribution of the requisites for facilitating enjoyable and rewarding lives is a salient part of the enterprise, and so is the consolidation and diffusion of those civic virtues which—like decency, civility, courtesy, kindness, helpfulness, and the like—serve to make human interactions more pleasant and fruitful. Morality is therefore something in which all of us have a substantial stake, seeing that it is by definition geared to furthering the interests of people even as refrigeration is by definition geared to cooling.

The circumstance that morality (like medicine or communication or transportation) is a purposive enterprise possessed of an overarching characterizing aim or function makes for objectivity in questions of appropriateness. And appropriateness does not lie in the eye of the beholder. The functional nature of morality—its gearing to fostering the interests of people—thus makes for a "moral realism" of moral facts.[1] The claim that a rule or practice is morally appropriate—that in the conditions prevailing in a society it is

1. A comprehensive bibliography of the subject is given in Geoffrey Sayre-McCord, "Moral Realism Bibliography," *The Southern Journal of Philosophy* 24 (1986): Supplement, pp. 143–159.

effective in serving and enhancing the real interests of people-in-general—is thoroughly objective and "factual." Being *thought* to be morally appropriate no more makes a certain action so than being *thought* to be medically effective or communicatively efficient would render a certain practice so. And this means that morality is not something merely subjective—not a matter of people's feelings or tastes or wants, since it reflects the pursuit—albeit through variable and context-relative means—of invariant and objectively implementable ends that root in a commitment to the best interests of people-in-general. This functional aspect of morality as an inherently appropriate end-oriented project provides an obvious yardstick for the assessment of efficacy, and blocks the prospect of any relativistically indifferent view of moral behavior as a mere matter of individual inclination or of communal custom.

The purposive nature of morality therefore has far-reaching implications. For the fact that our acts have a certain causal aftermath—have effects or tendencies—is something altogether objective, something that does not turn on the wishes, desires, tastes, or opinions of particular people. That you unwarrantedly did injury to another's interests is as objective a fact as that you absent-mindedly forgot another's instructions. The moral quality of an act is thus emphatically not a matter of personal inclination, but one of rational evaluation. Once one recognizes the *functional* aspect of morality—as inculcating and fostering actions conducive to the real interests of people—then moral issues become as objective matters open to rational deliberation.[2] On this basis, the precept and procedure of a sensible pragmatism is to approach morality in the same terms which it approaches science—as a

2. It is to the credit of the utilitarian tradition that it has stressed this gearing of morality to the benefit of people, for clearly establishes issues as subject to rational deliberation. But it is to its discredit that it has construed these benefits narrowly—and crassly—in terms of plea sure and mere personal wants and preferences alone, so that here the veneer of rationality is very thin indeed.

sphere of action whose particular processes are to be validated with reference to practice, and whose practices are in turn to be assessed by their efficacy in conducing to a realization of the inherent aims of the enterprise.

As such a line of deliberation indicates, there need not be, and indeed is not, any conflict or incompatibility between morality and a sensibly developed pragmatism.

## 2. Is Rational Controversy About Morality Possible?

Morality's functional aspect means that it is not—and by its very nature cannot be—a matter of arbitrary, ungrounded choice, or of people's contingent customs and practices. Moral values (honesty, kindness, common courtesy, and so on) do—and must—rest on a ruling principle: the value of the person and the (moral) requirement to take due account of the interest of others in our own actions. That a purported moral evaluation actually qualifies as such is thereby capable of rational explanation and justification. We do not *choose* or *make* moral values, but *learn* about them by thinking through what it is that is required for safeguarding the best interest of people.[3] If morality were a

3. Jean Paul Sartre, *Being and Nothingness*, tr. H. E. Barnes (New York: Philosophical Library, 1956), p. 46. Only by turning his back upon morality altogether can an existentialist maintain, with Jean Paul Sartre, "that freedom is the unique foundation of values and that *nothing*, absolutely nothing, justifies one in adopting this or that particular value, this or that particular scale of values." For morality is, as we have seen, inextricably bound up with rationality since moral validity calls for a justification of a certain sort (in terms of protecting the interests of people). A "value" whose adoption one cannot justify with reference to cogent principles is no real *value* at all but merely an arbitrary preference. the interests of people). A "value" whose adoption one cannot justify with reference to cogent principles is no real *value* at all but merely an arbitrary preference.

mere matter of taste or of custom or of arbitrary choice, then harming helpless people needlessly, for example, or inflicting pointless cruelty on them, might, in some society's scheme of things, be seen as *morally* preferable to helping them, and this perverted "morality" would have claims to appropriateness just as good as those of practices based on kindness and considerateness. But this is patently absurd. The capacity of certain modes of personal conduct to meet, or fail to meet, the requirements of morality—to safeguard the best (real) interests of people-in-general—is clearly not a matter of "decision" or "perspective," but one of impersonal fact, so that the appropriateness of moral judgments can and should be supported in rationally sensible, intersubjectively cogent way.

And in this context we cannot divorce rationality from a concern for people's best (i.e., "real" or "true") interests. After all, reason can and should deliberate not only about what it is ill-advised to believe (because it is at odds with the truth), but also about what it is ill-advised to esteem (because it is at odds with peoples interests). Only a perversely over-narrow conception of reason that blocks it off from any concern with purposively evaluative matters can open the way to an erroneously rationality-negating moral subjectivism.

From generation to generation, skeptically minded philosophers have maintained that the moral convictions of people are no more than to a jumble of distinct and generally incompatible opinions held by different individuals or societies, with the result that rational discussion of and adjudication among them become impossible. One group's right is another's wrong. Claims that murder, torture, vandalism, or anything similar, is wrong, wicked, evil, are "merely subjective sentiments" that have no basis in objective fact. We see such things as wished but others can in theory see them as praiseworthy—and do this with equal justification. Contentions about matters of morality are neither true nor false, and any idea of obtaining knowledge or establishing facts in moral matters is simply a delusion.

The flaw of this argumentation lies in the deeply problematic nature of its initial premiss that moral contentions stand outside that realm of fact. For moral contentions are indeed about matters of fact, although, to be sure, about *evaluative* rather than merely *descriptive* facts. They too can be correct or incorrect, well-founded or inappropriate.

There indeed are logically cogent arguments leading from factual premisses to morally evaluative conclusions, but the "facts" at issue in those premisses obviously have to be "morally laden" facts. The inference from "*X* did *A* deliberately and solely to inflict pain (harm, anguish) on *Y*" to "*X* acted wrongly" involves a perfectly valid move from matters of descriptive fact to a moral evaluation. (To be sure, an enthymematic premiss regarding how the negativity of pain, lies in the background here.) That certain arrangements in regard to human action impede and others foster the satisfaction of people's interests is *also* a matter of empirically determinable fact—though, to be sure, those facts again involve an element of evaluation. That the interests of a creature such as we humans are or claim to be are advantaged (or disadvantaged) by doing *A* rather than *B* follows straightforwardly from the reason-establishable fact that *A* is more (or less) consonant than *B* is with the nature of beings that are at once rational and embodied. (In all but the most exotic of circumstances, treating people's wounds serves their interests better than inflicting injuries.) Once one acknowledges the existence of evaluative facts, the moral enterprise too emerges as objective and fact-oriented. Of course, the verification of morally evaluative facts—which ultimately turns on safeguarding the interests of people-in-general—is often complex; there may well be no quick and easy way of settling the matter of how the interests of people are affected by various actions.

But this difficulty and complexity, of course, does *not* mean that there is no fact-of-the-matter at issue here—any more than it does so in scientific matters, which are often also very complicated.

"But moral objectivity is surely counterindicated by the circumstance that one cannot validly criticize the moral code of a society by any larger 'external' criteria." Rubbish! Established practice does not make a wrong into a right. However well entrenched it may be, the social code of a society that encourages infanticide for unwanted children or enjoins suttee for widows is simply wrong from a moral point of view. *Whether* a certain operational code is intended within the ambit of its social context to operate as a moral code may well be a proper subject of discussion and controversy. But once it is settled that it is indeed a *moral* code that is at issue, then one can certainly bring principles of critical evaluation to bear. For, at this point, the question becomes paramount whether—and how effectively—this code accomplishes for its society those functions for which moral codes are instituted among men—to constrain their interactions into lines that effectively safeguard their real and best interests.

The pragmatic dimension comes to the foreground here. And when evaluating a moral code in this way, we are *not* simply exercising a cultural imperialism by judging it by the prevailing moral standards of our environing group. We are judging it, rather, by those universal and "*absolute*" standards *in* whose terms the adequacy of any code, our own included, must be appraised. For what makes an action right or wrong (as the case may be) is just exactly the issue of whether doing the sort of thing at issue injures or protects the best interests of all those in any way concerned. (To reemphasize: morality is by definition geared to the benefit of rational agents even as refrigeration is by definition geared to the cooling of material objects.)[4] This is part and parcel of the very meaning of "morally right" and "morally wrong." And it renders judgment in these matters factual, objective, and rationally validatable, seeing that morality is a purposive enterprise whose claims can, in consequence, be evaluated on a pragmatic basis.

## 3. The Ethics of Collaboration and Communication in Science as an Instance

The ethics of science and communication affords a good example of the capacity of pragmatic considerations to substantiate moral principles.

Since information is power, there is a constant temptation to monopolize it. But information monopolies, however advantageous for some few favorably circumstanced beneficiaries, exact an awful price from the community as a whole. In particular, the open scientific literature can be seen as an effective and productive system for the authentication and protection of the stake of the creative scientist in the "intellectual property" created by his innovative efforts.[5]

To be sure, the risk of deception and error is present throughout our inquiries: our cognitive instruments, like all other instruments, are never failproof. Nevertheless, a gen-

4. Does this way of viewing the matter put subrational salient actions outside the pale of moral concern? By no means. For it matters deeply to rational agents how other rational agents treat animals—or for that matter any other sorts of beings that have interests capable of being injured. We have a substantial interest in how others comport themselves who also belong to the type to which we see ourselves as those belonging.
5. The founding of the Royal Society in London, chartered in 1666, was a small but significant step toward openess. For an interesting analysis of the historicl situation, see Jerome R. Ravetz, *Scientific Knoweldge and Its Social Problems* (Oxford: Clarendon Press, 1971). Ravetz's presentation makes it clear that a consideerable transforma-

eral policy of judicious trust in eminently cost effective. In inquiring, we cannot investigate everything; we have to start somewhere and invest credence in something. But, of course, our trust need not be blind. Initially bestowed on a basis of mere hunch or inclination, it can eventually be tested, and can come to be justified with the wisdom of hindsight. And this process of testing can in due course put the comforting reassurance of retrospective validation at our disposal.

Even people who do not much care to cooperate and collaborate with others are well advised in terms of their own interests to suppress this inclination. This point is brought home by considering the matter from the angle presented in display 8.1. By hypothesis, each of the parties involved prioritized the situation where they are trusted by the other while they themselves need not reciprocate. And each sees as the worst case a situation where they themselves trust without being trusted. Each, however, is willing to trust to avert being mistrusted themselves. Relative to these suppositions, we arrive at the overall situation of the interaction matrix exhibited in display 8.2. (Here the entry 2/2—for ex-

**Display 8.1**
**A Preferential Overview of Trust Situations**

| *I Trust You* | *You Trust Me* | *My Preference Ranking* | *Your Preference Ranking* |
|---|---|---|---|
| + | + | 2 | 2 |
| + | – | 4 | 1 |
| – | + | 1 | 4 |
| – | – | 3 | 3 |

---

was involved because "a significant proportion of the great 'scientists' of that age [sixteenth to seventeenth century] were even more concerned for the protection of their intellectual property, than for an immediate realization of its value through the prestige resulting from publication" (p. 249) ample—indicates that in the particular case at issue the outcome ranks 2 for me and 2 for you, respectively.) In this condition of affairs, mutual trust is the best available option—the only plausible way to avert the communally unhappy result 3/3.[6] In this sort of situation, cooperative behavior is obviously the best policy. (We are, after all, going to end up acting alike since, owing to the symmetry of the situation, whatever constitutes a good reason for your to act in a certain way does so for me as well.)

**Display 8.2**
**An Interaction Matrix for Trust Situations**

| | *You Trust Me* | *You Do Not Trust Me* |
|---|---|---|
| I trust you | 2/2 | 4/1 |
| I do not trust you | 1/4 | 3/3 |

It is easily seen that a sceptical presumption—one which rejects trust and maintains a distrustful stance toward the declarations of others—would confront us with an enormously complex (and economically infeasible) task for the project of interpersonal communication. For suppose that, instead of treating others on the basis of *innocent until proven guilty*, one were to treat them on lines of *not trustworthy until proven otherwise*. It is clear that such a procedure would be vastly lass economic. For we would now have to go to all sorts of lengths in independent verifications. The problems here are so formidable that we would obtain little if any informative benefits from the communicative contri-

6. The situation is one of the sort called "prisoner's dilemma" by game theorists. For a good account, see Morton D. David, *Game Theory* (New York: Basic Books, 1970), pp. 92–103. See also A. Rappaport and A. M. Chammah, *Prisoner's Dilemma: A Study in Conflict and Cooperation* (Ann Arbor: University of Michigan Press, 1965); and Anatol Rapoport, "Escape from Paradox," *American Scientist* 217 (1967): 50–56.

butions of others. When others tend to respond in kind to one's present cooperativeness or uncooperativeness, then no matter how small on deems the chances of their cooperation in the present case, one it nevertheless well advised to act cooperatively. As long as interagents react to cooperations with some tendency to reciprocation in future situations, cooperative behavior will yield long-run benefits.

From a pragmatic approach there are, therefore, substantial advantages to collaboration in inquiry, particularly in scientific contexts. For the individual inquirer, it decreases the chances of coming up completely empty-handed (though at the price of having to share the credit of discovery). For the community, it augurs a more rational division of labor through greater efficiency by reducing the duplication of effort.

The process through which mutual trust in matters of information development and management is built up among people cries out for explanation by means of an economic analogy that trades on the dual meaning of the idea of credit. For we proceed in cognitive matters in much the same way that banks proceed in financial matters. We extend credit to others, doing so at first to only a relatively modest extent. When and if they comport themselves in a manner that shows that this credit was well deserved and warranted, we proceed to give them more credit and extend their credit limit, as it were. By responding to trust in a responsible way, one improves one's credit rating in cognitive contexts much as in financial contexts. The same sort of mechanism is at work in both cases: recognition of credit worthiness engenders a reputation on which further credit can be based; earned credit is like money in the bank, well worth the measure needed for its maintenance and for preserving the good name that is now at stake.

And this situation obtains not just in the management of information in science but in many other settings as well, preeminently including the information we use in everyday life situations. For example, we constantly rely upon experts in a plethora of situations, continually placing reliance on doctors, lawyers, architects, and other professionals. They, too, must so perform as to establish credit, not just as individuals but, even more crucially, for their profession as a whole.[7]

We know that various highly convenient principles of knowledge production are simply false:

- What seems to be, is.
- What people say is true.
- The simplest patterns that fit the data are actually correct.
- The most adequate currently available theory will work out.

We realize full well that such generalizations do not hold, however nice it would be if they did. Nevertheless we accept the theses at issue as principles of presumption. We follow the metarule: In the absence of concrete indications to the contrary, proceed as though such principles were true. Our standard cognitive practices incorporate a host of fundamental presumptions of initial credibility, in the absence of concrete evidence to the contrary.

Such principles of presumption characterize the way in which rational agents transact their cognitive business. Yet we adopt such practices not because we can somehow establish their validity, but because the cost-benefit advantage of adopting them is so substantial. The justification of trust in our senses, in our fellow inquirers, and in our cognitive mechanisms ultimately rests on considerations of economic rationality. And this sort of situation prevails in many other contexts. For example, the rationale of reputa-

7. Cf. H. M. Vollmer and D. L. Mills, eds., *Professionalization* (Englewood Cliffs: Prentice Hall, 1966). This credit, once earned, is generally safeguarded and maintained by institutional means: licensing procedures, training qualifications, professional societies, codes of professional practice, and the like.

tions for ability, as well as those for reliability, lies in the cost effectiveness of this resource in contexts of hiring, allocating one's reading time, and so on.[8]

The pursuit of knowledge in science can play a role akin to that of a pursuit of wealth in business transactions. The financial markets in stocks or commodities futures would self-destruct if the principle, *my word is my bond*, were abrogated, since no one would know whether a trade had actually been made. In just this way, too, the market in information would self-destruct if people's truthfulness could not be relied upon. Thus, in both cases, unreliable people have to be frozen out and exiled from the community. In cognitive and economic contexts alike, the relevant community uses incentives and sanctions (artificially imposed costs and benefits) to put into place a system where people generally act in a trusting and trustworthy way. Such a system is based on processes of reciprocity that advantage virtually everyone.

Such considerations militate for a universally advantageous modus operandi, under whose aegis people can trust their fellows in a setting of communal cooperation. And the harsh measures used to uphold the integrity of science—the destruction of careers through ostracism from the community—are thus not devoid of rational justification. Cheating is worth eliminating at great cost, because its toleration endangers and undermines the fabric of mutual trust, in whose absence the whole enterprise of collaborative inquiry becomes infeasible. Establishing and maintaining a community of inquirers united in common collaboration by suitable rewards and sanctions is a mode of operation that is highly cost effective. Individual probity and mutual helpfulness are virtues whose cultivation pays ample dividends for the community of inquirers. In these

---

8. On this matter, see Thomas Sowell, *Knowledge and Decisions* (New York: Basic Books, 1980), especially the discussion of "Informal Relationships," on pp. 23–30.

matters, the cold iron hand of individual and communal interest lies behind the velvet glove of etiquette and ethics. The commodity of information illustrates rather than contravenes the division of labor that results from Adam Smith's putative innate human "propensity to truck, barter, and exchange." The market in knowledge has pretty much the same nature and the same motivation as any other sort of market—it is a general-interest arrangement. Cooperation evolves because what is in the interests of most is, in most cases, in the interests of each. It is thus clear that all such cognitive practices have a fundamentally pragmatic rationale. They are all cost effective within the setting of the project of inquiry to which we stand committed by our place in the world's scheme of things. We here have to do with what is at bottom a pragmatic-methodological justification. In proceeding in this way, one will efficiently foster the interests of the cognitive enterprise; the gains and benefits will, on the whole, outweigh the losses and costs.

Only through cooperation based on mutual trust can we address issues whose effective resolution makes demands that are too great for any one of us alone. In the development and management of information, people are constantly impelled toward a system of collaborative social practices—an operational code of incentives and sanctions that consolidates and supports collective solidarity and mutual support. In this division of labor, trust results from what is, to all intents and purposes, a custom consolidated compact to conduct their affairs in friendly collaboration.

If its cognitive needs and wants are strong enough, any group of mutually communicating, rational, dedicated inquirers is fated in the end to become a *community* of sorts, bound together by a shared practice of trust and cooperation, simply under the pressure of its economic advantage in the quest for knowledge.

However, this cooperative upshot need not ensue from a purely moral dedication to the good of others and care for their interests. It can emerge for reasons of prudential self-interest alone because the relevant modes of mutually helpful behavior—sharing, candor, and trustworthiness—are all strongly in everyone' interest, enabling all members to draw benefit for their own purposes—the agent himself specifically included. Cooperation emerges in such a case not from morality but from self-interested considerations of economic advantage. In science, in particular, the advantages of epistemic values like candor, reliability, accuracy, and the like, are such that everyone's interests as well-served by fostering adherence to the practices at issue.

As these deliberations indicate, our cognitive practices of trust and presumption are undergirded by a justificatory rationale whose nature is fundamentally pragmatic. For what is at issue throughout is a system of procedure that assures for each participant the prospect of realizing the greatest benefit for the least cost. Our standard cognitive policies and procedures are sustained by a basis of economic rationality.

The entire process of communication—of deriving substantive information from the declarations of theirs—involves trust. But what validates this? To answer this question it is best to look at the issue in economic perspective.

A communicating community is a sort of marketplace with offerers and takes, sellers and buyers. In accepting the declarations of others at the informative face values, we extend them credit, as it were. The prospect of informative communication is predicated on such principles as (*a*) concede a presumption of veracity to the assertions of others, at any rate until such time as they prove themselves unworthy of credit; and (*b*) in communicative contexts, regard others as candid truthful, accurate, and the like, until proven otherwise. The rationale of such principles of epistemic procedure is largely or wholly economic. For here, as elsewhere, it is ultimately on the basis of considerations of cost effectiveness that we decide how much credit to extend.

After all, why do we credit people with communicative capacity—with the power to provide information? Note that the purported fact, *When he utters "the cat is on the mat," he is engaged in asserting that the cat is on the mat*, represents a belief of ours, or at any rate a supposition on our part. We make this supposition initially in desperation, as it were, because it provides the only feasible way for us to derive any benefit from the content of someone's assertions, but ultimately because we eventually accumulate evidence that indicates (with the wisdom of hindsight) that this supposition was well advised (warranted).

In extracting information from the declarations of others we rely on a whole host of working assumptions: (1) people mean to say what they apparently say (what we take them to be saying); (2) people believe what they say; and (3) people have good grounds for their beliefs (i.e., there are such grounds and they have cognizance of them). And essentially the same justification obtains throughout: unless we enter into such communicative presumptions, we deprive ourselves of any chance to extract information from the declarations of others. On this basis, we are rationally well-advised, for example, to treat their declarations as epistemically innocent until proven otherwise, exactly because this is the most cost-effective thing to do. Our communicative procedures are motivated—and justified—by the essentially profit-seeking objective of extracting the maximum benefit from our information-oriented interactions. The exchange of information, too, is clearly a mutual benefit process. It is far easier, cheaper, and more convenient for people to get information by sharing than by themselves having to undertake the often laborious inquiries and researches needed to develop it *de novo*.

Communication is predicated on conceding and maintaining credibility. It, too, is a commercial system of sorts. Credit is extended, drawn upon, and enlarged. And with communicative and financial credit alike, one could not build up credit (prove oneself creditworthy) unless given some credit by somebody in the first place. For credit to be obtainable at all, there has to be an initial presumption that one is creditworthy. Clearly, such a presumption of innocent until proven guilty (i.e., fault free until shown to be otherwise) can be defeated; one can, of course, prove oneself to be unworthy of credit or credence. But initially it must be made.

The guiding principle here is once again that of cost-benefit calculation. The standard presumptions that underlie our communicative practices are emphatically not validatable as established facts. (For example, it is certainly *not* true that people say what they mean, save at the level of statistical generality.) But their justification becomes straightforward on economic grounds, as practices that represent the most efficient and economical way to get the job done. For if we do not concede some credit to the declarations of others, then we lose any and all chance to derive informative profit from them, thus denying ourselves the benefit of a potentially useful resource. For the course of experience would soon teach us that, even where strangers outside the family circle are concerned, the benefits of trust, of credibility concession, generally overbalance the risks involved.

In sum, we hold to the policy of believing what we are told in the absence of case-specific counterindications, because it is in our interest to do so by being highly cost effective vis-à-vis our informations aims and purposes. If playing safe were all that mattered, we would, of course, suspend judgment indefinitely. But it is simply not in our interest to do so, since safety is not all. We adopt the policy of credence in the first instance because it is the most promising avenue toward our goals, and then persist in it because we subsequently find, not that it is unfailingly successful, but that it is highly cost effective.[9]

Not only is the maintenance of credibility as asset in communication, but some degree of it is in fact a necessary condition for the viability of the whole project. The precept, *protect your credibility; do not play fast and loose with the ground rules, but safeguard your place in the community of communicators*, is basic to the communicative enterprise.

From the sender's viewpoint, putting forth a message costs time, effort, energy, and the like. The rational agent will incur such costs only with a view to benefits—some sort of reward (if only in the respect or gratitude of others) or reciprocity, with a view to a quid pro quo. This point is simple but of far-reaching import. Given our need for information to orient us in the world (on both pure and practical grounds), the value of creating a community of communicators is enormous. We are rationally well-advised to extend ourselves to keep the channels of communication to our fellows open, and it is well worth expending much for the realization of this end.

And the same sort of story holds for the receivers' viewpoint as well. They, too, must expend resources on taking in, processing, and storing messages. Clearly, a rational receiver would be prepared to undertake this expenditure only if there were a reasonable expectation of drawing profit from it, be it by way of a benefit in terms of information added or resources conserved—an expectation which, in general, is amply warranted.

In general, when one endeavors to convey information to someone, various sorts of unpleasant reactions can occur—as display 8.3 shows.

9. Usefully relevant discussions can be found in David Lewis, *Convention: A Philosophical Study* (Cambridge: Harvard University Press, 1969). But contrast Angus Ross, "Why do We Believe What We are Told?" *Ratio* 28 (1986): 69–88.

**Display 8.3**
**Communicative Negativities and their Causes**

| *Negativity* | *Sample Causative Etiology* |
|---|---|
| One is disbelieved. | One speaks falsely too often (out of heedlessness or out of deceptiveness). |
| One is misunderstood. | One uses careless or inadequate formulations. |
| One is tuned out. | One speaks off the point (digresses), or speaks at undue length (even if it is to the point |

Throughout, effective communication is a matter of maintaining proper cost-benefit coordination. It is governed by such principles as:

- Be sufficiently cautious in your claims to protect your credibility, but do not say so little that people dismiss you as a useless source.
- Formulate your statements fully and carefully enough so as to avoid misunderstanding but not with so much detail and precision as to weary your auditors and get tuned out.
- Make your message long (explicit, detailed, etc.) enough to convey your points but short enough to avert wasting everyone's time, effort, and patience.
- Be sufficiently redundant that an auditor who is not intensely attentive can still get the point, but not so redundant as to bore or annoy or insult your auditors.
- Keep to the point but not so narrowly that your message is impoverished by lack of context.

All of these rules are fundamentally economic principles of balance; they all turn on finding a point after which the benefit of further gain in information falls below the cost demanded for its process of acquisition. Again, pragmatism holds the key here.

## 4. On the Rationale of Moral Obligation

In a classic paper of pre-World War I vintage, the Oxford philosopher H. A. Prichard argued that it makes no real sense to ask "Why should I be moral?"[10] For once an act is recognized as being the morally appropriate thing to do, there is really no room for any *further* question about why it should be done. The question, "Why *do* the *right* thing?" is akin to the question "Why *believe* the *true* thing?" On both sides the answer is simply: "Just exactly because it is, by hypothesis, right / true." When rightness or truth have once been supposed, the matter of validation is closed. What it is my duty to do in the circumstances may be discussible, but once this matter is settled, so is the question of whether I ought to do this. To grant that it is one's duty to do something and then go on to ask why one should do it is simply to manifest one's failure to understand what the conception of "duty" involves. According to Prichard, then, the question "Why should one's duty be done?" is simply obtuse—or perverse—because moral duty as such provides a validating impetus to action, automatically, as it were, of itself and by its very nature. If true, then "Because it's the moral thing to do" is automatically, by its very nature, a definitively satisfactorily reason-presenting response to the question of why one should do it.

But, clearly, this line of reflection, though quite correct, is probatively unhelpful. Self-support has its limitations as a justificatory rationale. Even if moral reasons indeed are good reasons, the question still remains: "What is it that *makes* reasons of moral appropriateness into good reasons?" "Why should I be the sort of person who accepts moral grounds as validly compelling for his own deliberations?" And ultimately—"Why is it my duty to care for the interests

10. H. A. Prichard, "Does Moral Philosophy Rest on a Mistake?" *Mind* 21 (1912):21–37.

of other people?" If heeding morality's demands indeed is the appropriate thing to do, there must be some sort of validating reason for it—that is, there must be some line of consideration, not *wholly* internal to morality itself, that renders it reasonable for people to be moral. We must probe yet further for a fully satisfactory resolution to the question "Why be moral?"—one that improves on the true but unhelpful answer, "Because it is the (morally) right thing to do." There has to be more to it than that. But where are we to look for it?

The most promising prospect here proceeds by looking to the nature of human person had as such, and in particular to *the ontological duty of self-realization* that appertains to any rational agent whatsoever—the fundamental obligation of endeavoring to make the most of one's opportunities for realizing oneself as fully as possible as the sort of being one is. For what is at issue here is a generic duty which, insofar as one "owes" it to anyone at all, one owes as much to the world at large as to oneself. After all, any reason-endowed agent is *thereby* under an obligation to use its reason to capitalize on its potentialities for the good. The impetus of such an *ontological* obligation is predicated on the principle that someone who systematically wastes his opportunities for the realization of potential—say by having too low a self-image and too low a level of expectation for himself—is being less than he can and should be and thus fails in that most fundamental of all duties, the ontological obligation to make the most of one's opportunities for the good. The dutifulness of this sort of obligation is inextricably connected with its inherent rationality.

Such an ontological obligation is not an *ex officio* obligation that one takes on in assuming a role (like that of the sea captain or husband), but an *ex conditione* obligation that one is born into (like that of the son or sister); it inheres in what one *is* rather than in what one has undertaken. It is an obligation that roots in personhood itself.

And a sufficiently intelligent being which deliberately, though able to realize what is at issue here, nevertheless violates this ontological obligation for typological self-development as the kind of being one is, does something that is not just ill-advised but perverse and actually wicked.[11]

To be sure, morality does not inhere in the realization of human potential as such, no further questions asked. For every person has a potential for *both* good and evil—in principle, each has it in him to become a saint or a sinner. Discerning our specifically *good* potentialities requires more than a knowledge of human nature as such; it requires having a view of the good of humankind—a normative philosophical anthropology. There is nothing arcane or abstruse about what is at issue here. Clearly, other things being anything like equal, it is better to be healthy, to be happy, to understand what goes on, and the like. The pivotal question is what endows life with worth and value—what are the conditions that make for a rewarding and worthwhile life? This issue of human flourishing—of achieving not just satisfying but a satisfactory (that is, satisfaction-deserving) life—will inevitably involve such things as:

- thriving in the pursuit of happiness
- using one's intelligence as a guide
- enjoying the good things of life
- developing (some of) one's productive talents and abilities
- making some constructive contribution to the world's work
- fostering the good potential of others
- achieving and diffusing happiness
- taking heed for the interests of others.

11. Note that such an analysis is reductive but not eliminative. It does not, like utilitarianism, try to achieve the impossible fact of extracting duties from something other than duties (*viz.*, considerations of advantage). Rather, it derives duties of one sort (*viz.*, moral duties) from those of another (*viz.*, those ontological duties of self-enhancement through the realization of positive potential).

The inherently good potentialities of personhood, in sum, are exactly those readily discernible sorts of things in whose cultivation and development a rational agent can take reflective self-satisfaction—those which help us most fully to realize ourselves as the sort of being we should ideally aspire to be. The crux is simply the matter of cultivating our legitimate interests. And we cannot do this for ourselves without due care for cultivating our specifically positive potentialities—the things that are inherently worthwhile for us humans. The obligations of morality ultimately result not in its advantages—real though they are—but in our condition-inherent duty to self-realization. And the claims that these obligations have upon us are inherent in the rationality of aiming for one's real and best interest. As intelligent beings, we rational agents have no adequate excuse for avoiding the questions: "What sort of creature am I? What possibilities and opportunities does this engender? What should I do to make of myself that which I ought to be? How can I realize my highest potential?" A pragmatism that looks to the cultivation of inherent goals and benefits comes into operation here.

What we humans aspire to is, after all, an important aspect of what makes us what we are: in part we are what we are because of what we *claim* to be and what we *wish* to be. In particular, we class ourselves as members of the special category of *persons*—of rational free agents. Homo sapiens is a creature capable of at least partial self-construction—one able to make himself into the being he ought (ontologically considered) to be, given the opportunities afforded him in the course of the world's events. And in this regard, wastefulness is wicked. If we are creatures who can realize certain goods, then we ought, for that reason, to work towards their realization—when this involves foregoing even better opportunities elsewhere.[12] By its very nature as such, an intelligent

12. What is at issue here is not the "Mill's fallacy" inference from being valued to being valuable, but the unproblematic move from being ap-

being that has the capacity and opportunity for value-realization in relation to itself ought to realize it and will, if truly intelligent, strive to do so. The principle at issue is a conceptual one, implicit in the very idea of value. One could not appropriately call something a value if it were not of such a sort that a rational agent ought to opt for it whenever it is available at a reasonable cost.

It inheres in the very meaning of the morally "right" and "wrong" that issues of morality admit of appropriate and inappropriate resolutions, and can be deliberated about in sensible and foolish ways. They are matters of impersonal fact rather than individualized fancy. A morality that does not aim to be objectively valid in this sense is no morality at all. And so, rational deliberation and controversy about moral judgments are possible precisely because claims about moral matters are—and as such must be—preeminently objective in purport and thereby rational in nature. Morality's teleological dimension—the circumstance that the moral enterprise has a goal and purpose geared to the well-being and flourishing of rational agents—opens the doorway to rationality and reason. (At the cost of compromising their very validity, rational agents must, as such, prize this characteristic of theirs.)

Moral obligation accordingly roots in the inherent rationality of acknowledging an ontological obligation to the realization of the values inherent in one's own mode of life. Being a morally good person is part and parcel of a rational being's commitment to pursuing the good in a manner that links one's own good with the general good. For us rational creatures, morality (the due care for the real interests of rational beings) is an integral component of reason's commitment to the enhancement of value. The obligatoriness of morality ultimately roots in an *ontological* imperative to

---

propriately valued by a creature of a certain constitution to being something that objectively has value for this creature.

value realization with respect to self and world that is incumbent on free agents as such. On this ontological perspective, the ultimate basis of moral duty arises from the obligation we have as rational agents (towards ourselves and the world at large) to make the most and best of our opportunities for self-development.

Behind the obligation to be moral there thus stands a still more fundamental obligation: the generic obligation to be rational—that is, to realize the potential for the food that is inherent in our condition. Our human place in the world's scheme of things—our status as self-proclaimed rational creatures—imposes on us the ontologically grounded obligation to confront issues of self-definition and self-determination, to make the most of our opportunities for realizing the good. As rational agents we "owe it to ourselves"—and derivatively to "the world at large" in virtue of our place within it—to optimize what we are: to achieve our positive potential, to realize ourselves as the sort of beings we claim to be, and thereby to take our proper place in the world's scheme of things. To stint one's ontological potential for the good through one's own deliberate action or inaction is not just egocentrally counterproductive but objectively *wrong*. We have only one chance at life and to let its opportunities for the good slip is a shameful waste—regrettable alike from the standpoint of the world's interests and our own. "Be the best you can be—become what you ought!"—so runs this ontological imperative for a rational agent to make the most / best use of its opportunities in this world to cultivate its potential for the good in the widest sense of that term. And morality is part and parcel of this venture.

What is at issue here is a pragmatic approach to deontology that is geared to a teleology of value commitment that ultimately grounds the obligatoriness of moral injunctions in considerations of axiology. Such a position represents a broadly *axiological* approach to morality—one that proceeds in terms of a value theory that envisions a generalized "economy of values," and from whose standpoint the traditional economic values (the standard economic costs and benefits) are merely a rather special case. This axiological approach sees moral rationality as an integral component of that wider rationality that calls for the effective deployment of limited resources. (Observe that such a deontological approach contrasts starkly with a narrowly utilitarian morality, seeing that the latter pivots morality on *happiness* or "utility," narrowly construed whereas the former on *value-enhancement* in a larger and far more widely inclusive sense.)

## 5. Obligation and Interests

There are many things that I *have* to do. Some because of legally binding agreements, others because they are required of me by those who exercise authority or influence over me. Such obligations become incumbent on me through external demands. The government requires that I pay my taxes; my employer requires that I provide various services; my family requires that I devote various efforts to its members. All of these are obligations of *affiliation*—be it voluntary (as with my employer) or involuntary (as with the government). They inhere in this relationship into which I have—somehow or other—entered with others, be it by choice or by circumstance. They are matters of what I owe to others through contractual or quasi-contractual relationships.

But in addition to the things that I have to do because they are required of me by others, and thus externally mandated, there are also obligations of a different sort. These are the obligations that I do not really strictly speaking *have* to do but which I *ought* to do, and whose do not concern my relationship to others, but rather my relationship to myself (so to speak). Such obligations become incumbent on me simply in virtue of what I am: that is, through my place in nature's scheme of things. They include, for example, not letting my life go to waste, not failing to cultivate at least some of my capacities, making the most of at least some of my opportunities, not fouling the environmental nest in which I live, and the like. These are duties that I owe not to others, and not even necessarily to God, but simply to myself. They are incumbent upon me in virtue of what I am as a self-proclaimed rational creature, inhering in what I can, do, and should aspire to given the place which, like it or not, I in fact occupy in the world's scheme of things.

Against this background it emerges that moral imperatives will in the final analysis be *internally exigent*, rooted not in demands *to conform to externally imposed requirements* but in a circumstantially generated *mandate to seize opportunities* for the good. Their pivotal supports are not external demands but internally acknowledged values.

Consider a question regress of the following format:

Q: What should I do?

A: You should do XYZ.

Q: Why?

A: Because it is the moral thing to do in the circumstances.

Q: Why must I do the moral thing?

A: Because it is what you (morally) *should* do.

Q: Why so what I morally should do?

A: Because given what you are, it is in your best overall interest to do so.

Q: Why should I so what is in my best overall interest?

A: You should do so for that very reason—because exactly that best enables you to realize your potential for the good.

Q: But why act for the realization of my potential for the good?

At this point the exchange had best be brought to a close. At this level of value realization, we have reached the end of the line of meaningful substantiation. And this is so not because we have reached a dead end in something "self evident" regarding which nothing more can be said. After all, more can *always* be said! Rather, the fact is, simply that we cannot reasonably be asked to go further, because what remains to be said will not and cannot be something yet more evident. To press further than this—to ask for more—would be a manifestation not of critical intelligence but of absurdity.

As John Dewey emphasized to his great credit, ethics is a substantially factual enterprise.[13] For its object is to specify, clarify, and validate claims about the conditions under which a satisfying and satisfactory human existence can be realized at the personal and social levels. And this is clearly something that cannot be done without reference to the contingent empirical and factual realities of the human situation. For the crux here lies in just this issue of how we are to see our place in the world's scheme of things. What we confront is an internally imposed mandate rather than a demand of some external agency (society, God, or the like). The inherent demands of this self-envisioned status require—in simple self-consistency—that we see ourselves as beings upon whom the demands of morality have a cogent claim. The mandatoriness of morality for us thus rests on ultimately ontological foundation: the fact that we *are* the sorts of creatures *that insists on seeing themselves* in a certain light and who in view of this self-directed vision must in simple consistency, acknowledge a force of certain demands. On this basis, then, the obligation to be moral comes to be seen as an ultimately *ontological* one that is pro-

13. See in particular Dewey's acute critique of Charles L. Stevenson's *Ethics and Language* in his essay on "Ethical Subject Matters and Languages," *The Journal of Philosophy* 42 (1945):701–12. This was written when Dewey was well into his 80s.

foundly bound up with the nature of our condition and its opportunities and needs.

What goes wrong with a failure to honor this obligation? Various things, and in particular two:

- Not to see oneself as a free rational agent is to be less than human. A loss of nerve—of neglect of opportunity—a failure of rational aspiration
- To see oneself as a free rational agent but yet refuse to acknowledge the claims of morality upon oneself is to be irrational in point of inconsistency.

In the final analysis, then, the honoring of moral obligation is a matter of rationality. To fail in this regard is to fail in respect of practical rationality's demand of knowing that what being a free agent demands of us.

The obligation to morality, like the obligation to rationality, roots in such considerations of ontology—of what we are and what we aspire to in consequence thereof. If one is in a position to see oneself as a free rational one must also—for this very reason—acknowledge the obligation to do this. And if one recognizes and prizes one's status as a free rational agent then one ought for that very reason to behave morally by taking the interests of other such agents into account. For if I am (rationally) to pride myself on being a rational agent, then I must stand ready to value in other rational agents what I value in myself—that is, I must deem them *worthy* of respect, care, or the like, in virtue of their status of rational agents. In holding that something (life, liberty, opportunity) is of value—is not just something one *wants* but something one is *rationally well advised* to pursue—we rational agents must recognize its generic value and acknowledge that others too are well-advised to pursue it.

What is at issue here is not so much a matter of *reciprocity* as one of *rational coherence*. For to see myself in a certain normative light I must, if rational, stand ready to view others in the same light. If we indeed are the sort of intelligent creature whose worth in its own sight is a matter of prizing something (reflective self-respect, for example), then this item by virtue of this very fact assumes the status of something we are bound to recognize as valuable—as deserving of being valued. In seeing ourselves as *persons*—as free and responsible rational agents—we thereby stand rationally committed to care for one another's interests insofar as those others, too, are seen as having this status.[14] *Rational* agents are therefore bound by virtue of that very rationality to accepting that valuing something commits one to seeing it as valuable, as worthy or deserving of being valued—both by themselves and by anyone like them in the relevant respects. One can, quite properly, *like* things without reasons, but for a rational agent to *value* them involves seeing them as having value by generalized standards. To see value in my own status and my doings as a rational agent I must be prepared to recognize this in others as well. For rationality is inherently impersonal (objective) in this sense that what constitutes a good reason for *X* to believe or do to value something would automatically also constitute a good reason for anyone else who stands in *X*'s shoes (in the relevant regards). So if I am to be justified in valuing my rationality (in prizing my status as a rational agent) and seeing it as a basis for demanding the respect of other agents, then

14. To be sure, someone may ask: "Why think ourselves in this way—why see ourselves as free rational agents?" But, of course, to ask this is to ask for a good rational reason and is thus already to take a stance within the framework of rationality. In theory, one can, of course, "resign" from the community of rational beings, abandoning all claims to being more than "mere animals." But this is a step one cannot *justify*—there are no satisfactory rational grounds for taking it. And this is something most of us realize instinctively. The appropriateness of acknowledging others as responsible agents whenever possible holds in our own case as well.

I must also—from simple rational self-consistency—stand prepared to value and respect rationality in others.

But what of those of us who do not see themselves as rational moral agents—who see themselves as mere organic automata? What of Spinoza?

Of course "person" is just a word. But, as with other words its meaning is not up for grabs but is inherent in the cultural and intellectual contexts within which it functions—in this case one that involves the legal, religious, and social domain of activity and process within which the term has long figured. And the fact that some other culture uses different concepts has no bearing on the issue of our discussion—any more than it matters for *our* purposes in discussion of the color green that some other culture may not distinguish between green and blue.

Now that seemingly puzzling issue of "ontological obligation" stands coordinate with this ethical dimension of the matter. What qualifies certain beings as persons is clearly their *potential* of seeing themselves as free and responsible agents. And here Spinoza is definitely in. You lose the condition of personhood by failing to think of yourself as such any more than you would so lose the condition of being ambidextrous. (To be sure, discernibly incurable madmen and idiots have lost their personhood on such a construction of the matter.)

The notable thing about capacities like intelligence and rationality and personhood is that—unlike capacities for singing or eating—one automatically incurs through their mere possession alone not so much the *inclination* as the *obligation* to exercise these capacities, to function at a level where their resources become operative. And persons ipso facto also incur the obligation to value this aspect of their nature (obligations which, like any others, one can, of course, manage to neglect). At this point self-understanding acquires an ethical aspect that it lacks elsewhere. It is incongruous for a rational being (or a person or a moral being) to fail to value this capacity in a way that it is not automatically incongruous for a secular or an amphibious being to value these capabilities.

When someone acts immorally towards me—cheats me or deceives me or the like—then I am not merely angry and upset because my personal interests have been impaired, but am also "righteously indignant." Not only has the offender failed to acknowledge me as a person (a fellow rational being with rights and interests of his own), but he has, by his very act, marked himself as someone who, though (to my mind) a congener of mine as a rational agent, nevertheless does not give us rational agents their proper due, thereby degrading the entire group to which I, too, belong. He has added insult to injury. And this holds more generally. One is also indignant at witnessing someone act immorally towards a third party—being disturbed in a way akin to the annoyance one feels when some gaffe is committed by a member of one's own family. For one's own sense of self and self-worth is mediated by membership in such a group and can this become compromised by *their* behavior. As rational agents, we are entitled and committed to be indignant at the wicked actions of our fellows who do not act as rational agents ought because our own self-respect is inextricably bound up with their behavior. They have "let down the side."

The upshot of such considerations is that to fail to be moral is to defeat our own proper purposes and to shortchange ourselves by losing out on our ontological opportunities. It is only by acknowledging the worth of others—and thereby also the appropriateness of a due heed of *their* interests—that we ourselves can maintain our own claims to self-respect and self-worth. And so, we realize that we *should* act morally in each and every case, even where deviations are otherwise advantageous, because insofar as we do not, we can no longer look upon ourselves in a certain sort of light—one that is crucial to our own self-respect in the most fundamental way. Moral agency is an essential requisite for the proper self-esteem of a rational being. To fail in this regard is to injure oneself where it can and should hurt the most—in one's own sight.

But why should one acknowledge these ontological obligations of personhood. "What's in it for me?" if I honor them. Why is it in my interest to honor such an obligation? The answer is straightforward: What's in it for me is that I am a better person for so doing—not necessarily a happier person but a better person, and not necessarily one whose life is more pleasant but on whose life affords a better basis for rational contentment. In neglecting our opportunities for the good we not only fail to make external conditions better we effectively diminish ourselves. The violation of moral principles thus stands coordinate with the sanctions attaching to wanton wastefulness of any sort. It thus reflects a pragmatic feature—a feature of ineffectiveness in relation to an aim or end that is—or should be—part of one's purposive manifold. The crux is not so much self-realization as self-optimization.

This consideration clearly makes it *prudent* (in the truest sense of the term) for me to honor the obligations of personhood. But the question remains: What makes it *obligatory* for me to do so? For it is not that I *have* to do it in the sense that there is no *possible* alternative for me but that I *ought to do it* in the sense that there is no better *alternative* that is available to me.

The answer here lies in the consideration that the ontological obligation in view is in the final analysis an axiological one. With the sort of obligation now at issue, this "better" is one not just of "better for me" but "better for the world at large." With such an ontological obligation—as with all others—something goes wrong when the obligation is dishonored. But what goes wrong is in this case something that impacts negatively both upon my condition and upon that of the world at large. In violating such obligations we diminish both ourselves and the world we live in. And so, in the final analysis, my duty to others roots in my duty to myself—that is, to make the most and the best of myself. One ought to be moral for the same sort of reason for which one ought to make use of life's opportunities in general—one's intelligence, for example, or one's other constructive talents. For in failing to do this we throw away chances to make something of ourselves by way of contributing to the world's good, thereby failing to realize our potential. And what is at issue with failure is throughout not merely a loss but a violation of duty as well.

To be sure, the obligation to morality—to conduct our interpersonal affairs appropriately by heeding the interests of others—is by no means our only ontological obligation. The epistemic obligation to conduct our cognitive affairs appropriately—to inquire, to broaden our knowledge, to pursue the truth by believing only those things which *ought* (epistemically deserve) to be believed in the circumstances—is yet another instance and the Kantian duty to develop (at least some of) one's talents yet another. The scope of ontological obligation is thus substantially broader than that of morality alone. But the fact remains that the morality of care for others is—for us—at once a matter of interest and one of obligation. Morality is *advantageous* because it contributes positively to our individual and social condition as *persons*—that is, beings that see themselves as rational free agents. But it is *obligatory* because of its essential contributory role in the self-developmental process of making us into what we can and should be. And on this basis a pragmatic validation of morality in terms of effective goal-attainment is not only compatible with but inherently congenial to the nature of the moral enterprise.[15]

15. For further aspects of this theme see also the author's *Moral Absolutes* (New York and Bern: Peter Lang, 1989), and *The Validity of Values* (Princeton: Princeton University Press, 1991).

## 6. The Pragmatic Dimension

The deontological tenor of the preceding deliberations may at first sight make it appear that the discussion has moved away from the pragmatic dimension of the issue. But this impression would be quite wrong. For the pragmatism presently at issue is a broad program geared to efficacy at goal attainment. And being able to see oneself in a favorable light—to take rational contentment in ourselves—is a cardinal good for intelligent free agents. The sort of self-optimization that underlies morality is thus very much bound up with the pursuit of wholly appropriate goals. On this basis, a straightforward line of reasoning has been at issue in these deliberations regarding morality's rationale:

- Morality is a purposive project whose constituting teleology lies in the safeguarding of the real interests of people in general.
- The obligatoriness of morality means that the purpose in question must somehow be mandatory for us. Commitment to such a purpose will therefore have to be inherent in the human condition as such.
- And this condition-inherent, ontologically mandated purpose inheres in the requisite of acknowledging in ourselves the value of that which we in our own sight are, namely, free rational agents. Moral obligation thus ultimately rests on the duty to self-development grounded in our self-image as *persons*.

As these considerations indicate, moral deliberation (much like the preceding chapter's treatment of evaluative deliberations) can be treated on pragmatic principles. It, too, is a matter of procedural efficacy in the context of an efficacious commitment to appropriate values—in the present case those which regard to one's personal self-image as a free agent. A commitment to morality thus comes to be seen as part of a purposive venture—the achievement, maintenance, and development of a mode of living that makes it possible for a rational creature to have a valid sense of self-worth. On this basis, moral pragmatism becomes a viable proposition because the utilities (personal and social) that are at issue in the moral enterprise bear upon us humans because of our very mode of emplacement in the world's scheme of things.

The thrust of the functionalistic argumentation that is at work here is clearly purposive and pragmatic. Nevertheless, the ruling purpose that is operative here—namely, safeguarding the interests of people in general because rational consistency requires us to value in others, too, those features (like the potential for intelligent choice and action) in whose possession we locate our own claims to worth—is nowise low and ignoble. A sensible pragmatism will be one whose functionalism can and should be oriented in some significant measure towards decidedly higher, more "idealistic" values.

Critics often portray pragmatism as commitment to "success in practice" in the most crass and materialistic sense of the expression, concerned efficacy and effectiveness in securing the goods of Mammon and the flesh. In particular, noting that pragmatic philosophy has been especially influential in the U.S.A., some of its European critics have depreciated it as a typical manifestation of a supposed American dedication to wealth and worldly success. But in actual fact nothing could be further from the truth. Both in its historical origins and its theoretical rationale, pragmatism embodies a broad-brush instrumentalism that measures "success" in terms of the general teleology of goal attainment—where the goals at issue can and indeed should include the "noble," "spiritual," and "idealistic." Pragmatism can thus achieve an elevation that shields it from those facile charges of crass materialism by harking back to the old Greek distinction between crass affective pleasure (*euphoria*) and rationally reflective contentment (*eudaimonia*) so as to focus specifically upon that which serves not just our mere wants but our real and best interests as the sort of creatures we do—or, rather, should—see ourselves as being. Here functional efficacy is indeed once more the pivot point. But it is a matter of proving efficient and effective in the pursuit of inherently worthy ends. And it is in the light of this perspective that a duly enlightened pragmatism also has a direct and significant bearing upon the matters of morality.

And so pragmatic / functional aspect of morality, while indeed geared to the factor of what is advantageous for us, will certainly not root is people's crass and materialistic desires. The "success" at issue is a matter of realizing a life that one can view with reflective approbation—with rational contentment. And this is something whose bearing is larger and deeper than mere decision-satisfaction, something that looks to the possibilities for the good that are inherent in the human condition. A sensibly constructed moral pragmatism—namely, one whose teleology encompasses effectiveness in the systemic realization of morality's defining goal of caring for the interests of persons-in-general—is thus entirely untouched by those traditional changes of crass wordliness. An idealistic pragmatism is emphatically not a contradiction in terms.

# CHAPTER NINE

## *Pragmatism and Philosophy*

*Synopsis*

*(1) Philosophizing too is a teleological enterprise endowed with its own characteristic practical / purposive impetus in relation to problem solving. The need for information, for cognitive orientation in the world—at every level of cognitive scale, small and large—is one of humankind's most urgent requirements. (2) But philosophy is not a matter of idle speculation; its crux lies in the realm of cognitively responsible truth-estimation. (3) Yet it differs from ordinary inquiry in its commitment to holism, for its mission consists not just in giving answers to its questions, but in providing answers that fit into a systematic whole so as to achieve an organic unity of understanding. (4) This purposive mission opens philosophizing up to a pragmatic standard of evaluation. And by this standard pragmatism itself fares well, so that philosophical pragmatism enjoys the rational virtue of self-substantiation. (5) While pragmatism can take many forms and develop its practicalistic approach in various directions, the focus of concern here has been upon a particular version of the doctrine—one that is rationalistic, realistic, and objectivistic. And the reason for this concentration*

*lies in the merits that such a version of pragmatism has over its rivals. For it is in a demonstrably better position to evade or rebut all of the sorts of objections that have traditionally been launched against pragmatism by its critics and opponents.*

---

## 1. Against Philosophical Scepticism

How can pragmatic philosophy possibly be maintained on its own principles? After all, is not its own standard that of usefulness and practical efficacy, and is not philosophy the very quintessence of the impractical? Can pragmatism manage to deal effectively with the critic who complains: "Philosophy bakes no bread. The sort of abstract theorizing at issue here serves no *practical* purpose. Hence the entire enterprise is useless, pointless, illegitimate."

In the course of the long and checkered history of the subject, philosophers have articulated and espoused a varied spectrum of antiphilosophical positions. A brief survey of them runs as follows:

—*Logophobia*. The flight from assertion. All assertion in philosophical matters is falsification: discourse cannot capture reality. Think here of some ancient cynics and sceptics, or again of the early Wittgenstein of the dictum "Where of one cannot speak . . ."

—*Irrationalism*. All reason is sophistry: reasoning just cannot reach the truth in philosophical matters. The world is incoherent, rational thought cannot do it justice. Philosopher's projects of providing a coherent account pointless.

—*Scepticism*. The human mind inadequate to the resolution of its questions, it cannot reach a stable result. What we encounter in philosophy—and are bound to have there—is a strife of systems. These clashing doctrines manifest inability to reach a decisive result. No viable conclusions can be rendered in philosophy. Think here of the exponents of sceptics in ancient (Sextus Empiricus) and medieval (Sanchez) times.

—*Positivism*. Knowledge extends only to experience. (1) Experience here is *observational* experience, and therefore *science* is all (Hume, Logical positivism, Ayer); (2) experience here is *affective* experience, and therefore *humanities* are all (Heidegger, Rorty).

—*Relativism*. You have your view and we have ours. William James. No objective validation is feasible in philosophical matters. We are inextricably caught up in the web of our own language. (Think of the dictum of the late Wittgenstein of "The Limits of our language are the limits of our world.")

As this brief survey strikingly indicates, a surprising number of twentieth-century philosophers are agreed—not withstanding their extensive discord on other matters—that philosophy ought to be abandoned, at any rate in anything like its traditional mode. Wittgenstein and Heidegger, William James and Richard Rorty, the logical positivists (Carnap, Ayer) and postmodern deconstructionist (Derrida) agree on little else but unite in insisting that philosophy as traditionally practiced is a futile enterprise.

Interestingly, however, these positions all pose the same difficulty of fitting one's own declarations into the framework of one's doctrine. Because these views—seen as articulated positions—are themselves *philosophical* doctrines, it transpires that they automatically verge on the edge of self-destruction.

In each case what is required to avert actual self-refutation is a saving *distinction* between the range of discourse one is engaging in and the range of discourse that one is talking about, between philosophy as one is condemning it, and metaphilosophy as one in practicing it. In short, making sense of these antiphilosophical positions presupposes that availability of a clear and valid distinction between philosophy and metaphilosophy.[1]

Whenever people have a position that they propose set over against other possibilities in point of claims to truth in plausibility they must—seeing that negation is also determination—set out to establish and implement a distinction between the philosophizing they propose to reject as futile twaddle and the metaphilosophical deliberations through which this position of theirs is articulated and substantiated.

And exactly here is where they cannot avoid running into difficulty. For it is clear that such a distinction will not in the end prove to be viable. The case for a "revolt against dualism" is simply too strong. Philosophy cannot be sensibly distinguished and separated from metaphilosophy, seeing that metaphilosophy is simply a part of philosophy itself.

## 2. Philosophizing as Truth-Estimative Conjecture

As the preceding deliberations have clearly indicated, philosophy, too, is a purposive endeavor. For it is part and parcel of the cognitive enterprise, seeing that philosophers

---

1. To be sure, a possible exception to this stricture might be the position of latter-day cynics who, in the manner of their ancient Greek predecessors, maintain a rigorous silence on the subject so as to betoken their conviction that there is nothing whatever to be said here. For, of course, where nothing is said there can, ipso facto, be no between the substance of one's declarations and one's articulation of them. Yet someone who formulates his position as an explicit doctrine could be guilty of an inconsistency between practice and preaching. And perhaps the extreme relativist can also seek refuge in a comparable vacuity. Where people never say "*X* is how it is" but only "*X* is how it seems to me," so that their statements are entirely autobiographical and self-referential, there will also be nothing to disagree—let alone to reason—about since no substantive claim is beings made.

generally seek to pursue their mission of addressing those traditional "big questions" regarding ourselves, the world, and our place within its scheme of things. And they do this by means of what is perhaps best characterized as *rational estimation or conjecture*, seeing that those questions arise most pressingly where the available information is not altogether sufficient—where they are not straightforwardly answerable in terms of what has already been established. What is needed here is an *ampliative* methodology of inquiry—one that is so in C. S. Peirce's sense of underwriting contentions whose assertoric content reaches beyond the evidence in hand.[2] We need to do the very best we can to resolve questions that transcend accreted experience and outrun the reach of the information already put at our disposal by scientific research and humanistic speculation. It thus becomes necessary to have a way for obtaining the best available, the "rationally optimal," answers to our information-in-hand-transcending questions about how matters stand in the world. And experience-based conjecture—theorizing if you will—is the most promising available instrument for question-resolution in the face of imperfect information. It is a tool for use by finite intelligences, providing them not with the best *possible* answer (in some rarified sense of this term), but with the best *available* answer, the putative best that one can manage to secure in the actually existing conditions in which we do and must conduct our epistemic labors.

Despite those guarding qualifications, the "best available" answer at issue here is intended in a rather strong sense. We want not just an "answer" of some sort, but a vi-

---

2. For Charles Sanders Peirce, "ampliative" reasoning is synthetic in that its conclusion goes beyond ("transcends") the information stipulated in the given premises (i.e., cannot be derived from them by logical processes of deduction alone), so that it "follows" from them only inconclusively. Cf. *Collected Papers*, vol. II: sects. 2.680 *et passim*.

able and acceptable answer—one to whose tenability we are willing to commit ourselves. The rational conjecture at issue is not to be a matter of *mere guesswork,* but one of *responsible estimation* in a strict sense of the term. It is not *just* an estimate of the true answer that we want, but an estimate that is sensible and defensible: *tenable*, in short. We may need to resort to more information than is actually given, but we do not want to make it up "out of thin air." The provision of reasonable warrant for rational assurance is the object of the enterprise.

The need for such an estimative approach in philosophy is easy to see. After all, we humans live in a world not of our making where we have to do the best we can with the limited means at our disposal. We must recognize that there is no prospect of assessing the truth—or presumptive truth—of claims (be they philosophical or scientific) independently of the use of our imperfect mechanisms of inquiry and systematization. And here it is *estimation* that affords the best means for doing the job. We are not—and presumably will never be—in a position to stake a totally secure claim to the definitive truth regarding those great issues of philosophical interest. But we certainly can—and indeed must—do the best we can to achieve a reasonable *estimate* of the truth.

We can and do *aim* at the truth in our inquiries even in circumstances where we cannot make failproof pretentions to its attainment, and where we have no alternative but to settle for the *best available estimate* of the truth of the matter—that estimate for which the best case can be made out according to the appropriate standards of rational cogency. And *systematization* in the context of the available background information is nothing other than the process for making out this rationally best case. It is thus rational conjecture based on systematic considerations that is the key method of philosophical inquiry, affording our best hope for obtaining promising answers to the questions that confront us. C. S. Peirce observed this network aspect of philosophical systematization when he wrote:

> Philosophy ought to imitate the successful sciences in its methods, so far as to proceed only from tangible premisses which can be subjected to careful scrutiny, and to trust rather to the multitude and variety of its arguments than to the conclusiveness of any one. Its reasoning should not form a chain which is no stronger than its weakest link, but a cable whose fibers may be ever so slender, provided they are sufficiently numerous and intimately connected.[3]

The object of such an epistemic exercise is to use consideration of coherence as a guide to determine how smoothly and harmoniously a thesis can be enmeshed in the overall fabric of diverse and potentially discordant and competing contentions. We seek for the best candidates among competing alternatives—for that resolution for which, on balance, the strongest overall case can be made out. Therefore, it is here not "the uniquely correct answer" but "the least problematic, most defensible position" that we seek. And the crux of our standard of acceptance lies, as we have seen, not with the issue of secure premisses but with the issue of sensible conclusions—results that fit most smoothly and harmoniously within our overall commitment to the manifold "data" at stake in philosophical matters.

One further important point should also be stressed in this connection. To someone accustomed to thinking in terms of a sharp contrast between organizing the information already in hand and an active inquiry aimed at extending it, the idea of a *systematization of conjecture with experience* may sound like a very conservative process. This impression would be quite incorrect. Inquiry—and philosophical inquiry above all—must not be construed to slight the dynamical and ampliative aspect. And systematization itself is an in-

3. Peirce, *Collected Papers*, vol. V: sect. 5.265.

strument of inquiry—a tool for aligning question-resolving conjecture with the (of itself inadequate) data at hand. The factors of completeness, comprehensiveness, inclusiveness, unity, and so forth, are all crucial aspects of system, and the ampler the information-base, the ampler is the prospect for our systematization to attain them. The drive to system embodies an imperative to broaden the range of our experience, to extend and expand the data base from which our theoretical triangulations proceed. In the course of this process, it may well eventuate that our existing systematizations—however adequate they may seem at the time—are untenable and must be overthrown in the pursuit of philosophy's goal of devising an amply comprehensively systematic framework of answers to our questions.

## 3. Pragmatism as a Via Media

The project of philosophizing in its traditional form of information seeking and problem solving has been under heavy attack throughout the twentieth century. Marxists, positivists, existentialists, science-is-all-theorists, and adherents of may other doctrines have all sought to secure its abandonment. Historically, issues of meaning have been at the center of attention, with the target of assault constituted by what might be called the "traditional"—often called "modernist"—view of philosophy that takes essentially the following stand:

> Philosophy deals in well-defined concepts that have well-defined meaning. Such philosophically central concepts as truth, fact, knowledge, reality, or the like, have a definite, essential, and characteristic core meaning and the issues involving them have a correspondingly definite and characteristic make-up. The philosopher's job is to present and

> articulate a coherent, unified theory (of meaning, knowledge, existence, etc.) that definitively explicates and elucidates these matters.

Categorically opposed to this "modernist" position is the so-called post-modernist position favored among the more recent theorists of the present century:

> Philosophical terms have no definite "conceptual core" of meaning that manage to structure the issues into objectively meaningful way. All that there is is a fortuitous jumble of more or less useful ways of talking. The work of the philosopher is thus not a venture in objectively cogent issue-resolution but is a therapeutic task of curing people of harboring after something nonexistent, of freeing them from yearning after an unrealizable delusion. Philosophical theses and theories need to be dissolved or deconstructed.

The evident problem with the "modernist" view is that the fixity and definitiveness it demands of philosophizing is something which this endeavor's history strongly indicates to be unachievable. On the other hand, the "post-modernist" has an unhappily negativistic and utilitarian mien.

It deserves to be noted—and indeed stressed—that pragmatism offers a promising and workable *via media* between these two extremes:

> Traditionalistic absolutism must indeed be rejected. But while philosophical concepts do not have a crystallinely fixed meaning structure, the realities of usage and practice are such that there is nevertheless a "conceptual geography" of meaning mappable into different regions, some of them more central and others more peripheral. And underlying this structure is a rationale—an essentially functional (i.e., purpose-oriented) account that makes it possible to explain why matters stand as they do on a purposive instrumentalistic basis.

Such a meditative position offers concessions to both sides. In contrast to "modernistic" dogmatism it abandons the idea of an absolutistic meaning-core—though not in favor of a formless jumble, but in a qualified way that leaves a foothold for objectivity. In contrast to "postmodern" deconstructionism it rejects conceptual nihilism—though not in favor of an absolutism that rejects the realities of human practice, but the basis of an instrumental view of our conceptual machinery.

A pragmatic approach thus enjoys significant advantage in its reliance on the objective realities of the human situation. Its recourse to effective practice opens the door to objectivity without absolutism, thus combining the most promising features of the traditional absolutism and present-day relativism in respect of knowledge. And the crucial fact is that such a meditative position allows a safe passage between the Scylla and Charybdis of problematic extremes.

## 4. Is Circularity a Problem?

Pragmatism takes the traditionalistic line of seeing the purposive character of the philosophical enterprise to lie in its very nature as a venture in seeking to answer our larger questions in a systematic way. But this purposive mission opens philosophizing up to the pragmatic standard of evaluation in terms of its efficacy and efficiency in realizing the purposes at issue. Because pragmatism sees question-resolving inquiry as a mode of praxis, it is able to take a fundamentally pragmatic view of the process of philosophy itself.

And this consideration brings into view one of pragmatism's important assets, namely, its self-substantiation. For the sort of philosophizing at issue with pragmatism is, of course, itself a purposive enterprise—a venture in problem solving. And so it will be exactly to the extent to which the methodological pragmatism at issue here is able to provide a satisfactory mechanism for addressing the issues of epistemology, morality, and so forth, that is the crucial consideration for its own pragmatic validation.

Yet how does pragmatism itself fare by this pragmatic standard? The deliberations of the preceding discussion go to indicate, in some considerable detail, that it actually fares very well indeed. And so pragmatism is self-sustaining. In faring well by the standards that it itself endorses and enjoins, philosophical pragmatism enjoys the rational virtue of self-substantiation on this basis. It is a position willing and able to see its own status in the light of its own teachings, thereby practicing what it preaches in a way that scepticism, say, or relativism or scientism simply do not achieve. William James is quite right when he tells us that: "I propose it [i.e., pragmatism] to my readers as something to be verified *ambulando*, or by the way its consequences may confirm it."[4] For pragmatism readily opens itself to be judged by the standard it applies elsewhere and that it can thus be seen as self-postulating—as meeting that minimal requirement of a good philosophy of emerging as proper by its own standards.

But is this sort of self-validation not vitiated through circularity? Is it not useless for position or doctrine to be meritorious *on its own telling*? By no means.

In view of philosophy's commitment to systemic coherence, it is a crucial condition for adequacy that a philosophical position be self-sustaining: that its claims can be substantiated on its own telling. A philosophical position must practice what it preaches—unlike a radical, all-dismissive scepticism, for example, it must take a stance that is appropriate on its own telling. We would hardly be

4. James, *Pragmatism*, p. 281.

prepared to accept a philosophical position that was not able to qualify as well-substantiated even on its own principles. And as the deliberations of the present chapter indicate, pragmatism can stake a rightful claim to the possession of this indispensable merit. Since it fares well by its own standard, philosophical pragmatism enjoys the key rational virtue of self-substantiation. The sort of "circularity" at issue in self-substantiation is not something vicious and vitiating, but must, on the contrary, be adjudged altogether positive and beneficial. A position that is not appropriate on its own telling cannot sensibly be accepted as adequate.

It is, all too clearly, a decidedly positive feature of any philosophical theory that it be self-substantiating and sustaining—that it be tenable on its own telling by way of meeting the standards of cogency and appreciativeness that it itself advocates. The articulation of methodological pragmatism is designed to achieve this very end. This important fact that it is not only self-consistent but also ultimately proves to be self-supportive represents one of methodological pragmatism's most significant assets.

## 5. Is Fragmentation a Problem?

It is clear that where pragmatism is concerned in the broad, schematic way that we have contemplated here—that is, in the fundamentalistic terms of purposive efficacy—then pragmatism acquires a programmatic thrust that can be developed in various ways. Indeed it can, in principle, become oriented in as many directions as there are human purposes.

Since different people have different purposes, does this not fragment pragmatism into a relativistic plausibility of discordant doctrines?

By no means. But to see that this is so, we must distinguish between practicalistic justification in general and pragmatic justification in particular. Practicalistic justifications can indeed be carried on with respect to any purpose whatever and is thus potentially person-relativized. However, with pragmatic justification proper we must construe "human purposes" not as a matter of the purposes of particular people, but rather as those of people-in-general, those inherent in the human condition as such, that is to say as those purposes at issue with human *needs*. And what is at issue here is a matter not of *mere* aims, desires, and purposes, but of rational aim, desires, and purposes.

We cannot divorce pragmatic rationality from a concern for people's best (i.e. "real" or "true") interests. Reason can and should deliberate not only about what it is ill-advised to believe (because it is probably at odds with the truth), but also about what it is ill-advised to esteem (because it is probably at odds with our interests). Rationality is not just a matter of helping our beliefs consistent among themselves and comparable with what we recognize as being as true, but also one of helping our evaluative judgments consistent among themselves and capable with what we recognize as being in our best interest.

The lesson of the deliberation is clear. A sensible pragmatism is geared to efficiency in the implementation not of aims and progress in general, but to those aims and purposes that can be legitimated as valid, that is to say those which can be validated with reference to determinable needs.[5] And it is this fact of subordination of valid purpose under the aegis of the "holistic teleology of human flourishing" (as Aristotle called it)—its gearing to the controlling power of those fictions that are at issue with the well-being of people-in-general—that prevents

5. On these matters see also the author's *The Validity of Values* (Princeton: Princeton University Press, 1993).

pragmatism from disintegrating into a chaotically relativized fragmentation of discordant doctrines.

To be sure it must be granted that there are areas of human purpose outside the realm of need satisfaction. Cognitive and especially scientific deliberations, for example, or social-interaction issues are objective issues very different from those of aesthetics or of diversion. In the former an objectionistic pragmatism of need satisfaction can work, in the latter the field must instead be left to a fragmented diversity of individualized goals. But a sensible pragmatism will suffer no damage from its own characteristic recognition that pragmatic validation—like any instrumentality—has its own characteristic and limited domain of appropriate utilization. A sensible pragmatism can be satisfied with the large and important job of philosophical validation that it can reasonably accomplish. Its appropriateness in philosophy in its proper domain does not suffer from a recognition that it is not an all-purpose instrument for addressing issues that belong on the agenda of other domains of deliberation.

## 6. The Advantages of Realistic over Relativistic Pragmatism

While pragmatism is not a single, monolithic doctrinal position in philosophy, it does take a general line of approach that manifests a definite and characteristic stance. For despite its different versions, pragmatism retains throughout a common commitment to the primacy of practice. In all of its various forms, it remains uniform in its insistence that the pivotal factor regarding a philosophical resource—be it a concept, conception, or position—lies in its effectiveness for the sort of work that it is intended to accomplish. Functional efficacy in goal attainment is pragmatism's watchword throughout.

However, pragmatism's diversity means that any sort of sensible defense or critique of the position must from the outset settle the question of exactly which version of the doctrine it proposes to address. In this regard, our discussion has focused on two areas in particular—the cognitive domain of information (and, in particular, scientific knowledge about how things work in the world) and the normative domain of evaluation (and, in particular, evaluative assessments in the moral domain). Therefore, the cognitive and the evaluative enterprises have here both been viewed in a teleological perspective that highlights how the pragmatic issue of purposive efficacy has a natural bearing upon them, providing in each case alike a teleological basis for considerations of functional rationality.

On this basis, the sort of realistic and objectivistic pragmatism advocated here is characterized by four features. It takes:

- *A functional or teleological* approach geared to a certain purposive enterprise, specifically:

  —the cognitive enterprise: explanation, prediction, and control over nature.
  —the evaluative enterprise: the guidance of human behavior for the effective satisfaction of our needs and interests.
  —the moral enterprise: the direction of human interaction in a generally fruitful and productive way, thus encompassing due care for the interests of others.

- A *procedural* method-oriented, large-scale approach that looks to the question of pragmatic efficacy not as it relates to particular steps of actions but to general methods, processes, principles.
- A *universalistic* approach that is not *personalistic* (addressed to *my* or your wants or preferences) or relativistic (addressed to the value orientation of particular groups)

but rather looks synoptically to the needs and interests that characterize the satisfaction of people in general—always and everywhere.

- An *objectivistic* approach that looks to success in goal realization not from my or your idiosyncratic angle, but in ways discernible by anyone.

It is these four commitments—functionalism, methodism, universalism, and objectivism—that endow the pragmatism articulated here with its "hard" edge as a doctrine deeply committed to the principles of (practical) rationality.

In conclusion it is appropriate to pass in review the shape of contrast that exists between a pragmatism of the left and the harder, decidedly objectivistic pragmatism espoused in these pages:

| *Pragmatism of the Left* | *Pragmatism of the Right* |
|---|---|
| 1. What we call "truth" is entirely a human construct. | 1. The truth is in substantial measure determined by the thought-independent nature of things. |
| 2. What we view as "truth" is not discovered but a human artifact produced in the process we call inquiry." | 2. Inquiry does not produce but seeks to discover the truth. What we obtain in rational inquiry is our best-achievable *estimate* of the truth. |
| 3. Our proceedings in all affairs, inquiry included, are a matter of human convention, subject only to the constraint of social consensus. | 3. Our proceedings in a well-concluded inquiry are subject to norms of impersonal rationality. |

| | |
|---|---|
| 4. The changes of scientific opinion are matters of fashion and social pressure, independent of the operation of any impersonally valid "standards." | 4. Our science, though fallible, is subject to ongoing improvements whose status as such can be determined by objective standards. |
| 5. Any and all "standards" lack any validation by the objective facts. Whatever standing they have is a matter of human convention and social pressure. | 5. Standards can be tested and validated with reference to considerations of effectiveness relative to the teleology of the enterprise at issue. |
| 6. This hold not only for our epistemic but also for our normative / evaluative standards. | 6. This hold not only for our epistemic but also for our normative / evaluative standards. |
| 7. Therefore, morality has no basis or standing apart from pure social convention. There is no difference between morals and moves. | 7. Therefore, morality has a basis and standing that goes beyond pure social convention alone. There is a crucial difference between morals and moves. |
| 8. It follows that pragmatism is committed to a sociocultural relativism that rejects any idea of impersonal appropriateness. | 8. It follows that prgamatism is committed to a cognitive and social realism that accepts objection standards as determiners of impersonal appropriateness. |

Against the background of this distinction, the present discussion has endeavored to exhibit the merits of a specifically methodological pragmatism that has demonstrable advantages over its rivals through a capacity to avoid or circumvent the range of objectives traditionally cast against traditional versions of the theory. Throughout, the aim has been to rescue pragmatism from the hands of its false friends who have been concerned to convert the doctrine into a relativistic version of philosophical nihilism. For although pragmatism can take many forms and develop its practicalistic approach in various directions, the focus of concern here has been a particular version of the doctrine—one that is rationalistic, realistic, and objectivistic. And the reason for this concentration lies in the merits that such a version of pragmatism has over its rivals. For, as these deliberations have tried to show in detail, it is in a demonstrably better position to avoid or rebut all of the sorts of objections that have traditionally been launched against pragmatism by its critics and opponents.

All in all, then, what the present discussion has tried to accomplish is to offer a version of pragmatism that achieves the dual aim of (1) being true the inaugurating ideas and insights of pragmatism's founder C. S. Peirce insofar as possible, while at the same time; (2) providing a version of the doctrine that meets or removes the sorts of objections which, almost from the start, have been launched against this philosophical position. The book has sought to show that this dual objective can indeed be accomplished through the formulation of a methodologically oriented pragmatism that can accomplish useful work throughout a wide spectrum of philosophical issues, ranging from the theory of logic and language and the theory of knowledge to enhance also such philosophical areas as metaphysics, value theory, and moral philosophy. On this basis a realistically geared methodological pragmatism emerges as a philosophical approach which fares well by its own standard of utility.

What a sensibly construed pragmatism opposes ideologically is not objective standards (quite to the contrary!), but metaphysical absolutes. Such a pragmatism stands committed to a thoroughly experimental and experiential methodology. Its line of approach is one of try-and-see, of letting the actual course of experience itself rule on the acceptability-merits of our ways of proceeding. This version pragmatism has a profoundly objectivistic and realistic mien. For its reliance on pragmatic efficacy provides for an iron-clad reality-check furnishing a truly objective control over our cognitive and practical proceedings. In such matters, we ourselves may propose but it is reality that disposes. The efficiency of a process in the realization of given objectives is not something that is responsive to our wishes and desires, not something we can make up as we go along or that lies in the eyes of the beholder. It is inextricably inherent in the objective nature of things. The theoretician has little choice here but to accept things as they are, much as with Thomas Carlyle's classic remark regarding the lady reported as having at last "learned to accept the world": "By gad, sir, she'd better." For what we have been concerned to expound and defend here is a more rigorous and meaningful version of pragmatism that capitalizes on the potential of a practice-oriented approach for equipping a theoretical position with a rationale of altogether extra-theoretical support.

## 7. The Complexity of Pragmatism

A salient feature of the methodological pragmatism that has been defended here lies in its flexibility. It deals at a very general level with how to assess the appropriateness of standards via their efficacy in relation to the inherent teleology or goal structure of whatever enterprise may be at hand. And, of course, different human enterprises have different sorts of goals and the teleology of whatever epistemic enterprise is one sort of thing while that of the moral enterprise is another. Methodological pragmatism can in principle be deployed in different directions.

Pragmatic theorists have tended to highlight and emphasize one particular dimension of the approach: the cognitive-scientific in the case of Peirce; the psychological-affective in the case of James; the societal-communal in the case of Dewey. But a just appreciation of the realities demands recognition that pragmatism is a mansion of many rooms. Its fundamental approach to rational assessment—quality-control via purposive efficacy—is a many-sided instrument whose bearing and utility spreads across a wide range.

But is pragmatism in its broader aspirations not at odds with science? By no means! Philosophy's job is to give a coherent account of experience, and in this regard it is like science. But science addresses specifically observational experience, and in this regard an enlightened pragmatism must go further in taking a broader view of our experiential reperetoire. For evaluative and affective experience also come to play a crucial role in the validation of teleologically appropriate positions. To be sure, philosophy cannot ignore observational experience—and so can neither contest nor improve upon science where scientific matters are concerned. But because its range of experiential concern is larger it can take a broader range of experiential issues into account—not because philosophy somehow supplants science, but because it supplements it in ways that carry it deeper into the realm of human values.

And so, when James yearned for a broader pragmatism, he was right. Pragmatism should care for more than matters of knowledge and inquiry. But its venture into mattes of value or morality do not abrogate but only extend our scientifically warranted convictions. For where cognitive issues confront us cognitive values are naturally decisive.

Homo sapiens is a complex creature, equipped with needs and wants that involve us in various different ranges of purpose. Some of these projects are geared to our very survival (food, shelter, collaborative companionship), other to the smoother satisfaction of such needs (knowledge, sociability), still others to a range of inclinations and desires that serve to make life pleasant rather than merely possible. And each range of purpose carries its own correlative natural teleology in its wake, each of which engenders its own department of pragmatism—its own dimension of purposive efficacy. There is effective prediction and control over nature in the case of science; harmonious and communally productive coexistence with our fellows in the case or morality; a positive and psychologically fruitful affective attainment to the larger forces of nature in the case of spirituality; and so on. And in each case a pragmatic approach in terms of purposive efficacy can be implemented. The great mistake here is that of narrowness and exclusivity—of taking one such purposive realm to be totally sufficient and all-controlling. A complex creature is clearly committed to a rationally balanced mixture of purpose and the local predominance of one dimension of purpose within its range does not entitle this factor to stake claims to global priority. And so, while a pragmatism of limited objective (be it cognitive or psychological or social) make perfect sense in its own domain, but that nowise entitles it to claims of predominance—let alone sufficiency or exclusivity—across the board.

And the complexity of pragmatism has another aspect as well. For notwithstanding currently widespread opinion, pragmatism of the left, popular though it has become, is far from being the whole story. Its postmodern relativism emphatically does *not* have the field to itself. Pragmatism is a broad church that can in principle accommodate some very diverse doctrinal tendencies. But as the present book has tried to show, an objectivistic pragmatism of the right is not only a possible but—to all plausible appearances—the most defensible and the philosophically most satisfying version of the overall position whenever issues of objective cognition and evaluation are at issue.

# *Name Index*

# Composing Useful Pasts